Getting Married in Korea

Getting Married in Korea

Of Gender, Morality, and Modernity

LAUREL KENDALL

University of California Press

BERKELEY   LOS ANGELES   LONDON

University of California Press
Berkeley and Los Angeles, California

University of California Press, Ltd.
London, England

© 1996 by
The Regents of the University of California

Library of Congress Cataloging-in-Publication Data

Kendall, Laurel.
    Getting married in Korea : of gender, morality, and modernity /
Laurel Kendall.
        p.   cm.
    Includes bibliographical references and index.
    ISBN 0-520-20198-1 (alk. paper).—ISBN 0-520-20200-7 (pbk. : alk. paper)
    1. Marriage customs and rites—Korea.   2. Wedding etiquette—Korea.
3. Sex role—Korea.   4. Gender identity—Korea.   5. Social classes—
Korea.   6. Ceremonial exchange—Korea.   7. Korea—Social conditions.
I. Title.
GT2786.K6K46   1996
392'.5'09519—dc20   95-37353

Printed in the United States of America
9 8 7 6 5 4 3 2 1

The paper used in this publication meets the minimum requirements of
American National Standard for Information Sciences—Permanence of
Paper for Printed Library Materials, ANSI Z39.48-1984.

The epigraph to Part 2 from *Small World: An Academic Romance*, © 1984 David
Lodge, is used by permission of Viking Penguin, a division of Penguin Books USA
Inc.

For Homer and Henry,
who have their own ties to Korea

Contents

Preface

This book is and is not about Korean weddings. It explores the meaning and importance of getting married in late-twentieth-century Korea, but it is also concerned with weddings as flash points of argument about the past and the present, about the desirability of women and men, and about what it means to be Korean in a shifting and intensely commodified milieu. At its core, this work witnesses the weddings of a particular group of people, those who inhabit the newest and lowest rungs of Korea's new urban middle class. These brides and grooms grew up in, or are but one generation removed from, places like "Enduring Pine Village," the community on the periphery of Seoul where I did my first fieldwork in the 1970s and to which I often return as a reference point on my own Korean journeys.

In 1983, I began a project on weddings that would consume me well into the next decade. I encountered brides and grooms in the commercial wedding halls of "Righteous Town," a market town turned satellite city where the village daughters I knew held their weddings and where many of them lived after their marriages. Their experiences are the core of this study. Most intimately, I tell the story of my fictive sister "Sukcha" and the choices she and her family made when she got married in 1991. Many years ago, when Sukcha was still in middle school, I lived with her family in Enduring Pine Village. They, like so many others, have since moved to town. I have marked their progress even as I have learned to record a "Korea" that is constantly in motion. To better appreciate the weddings of these late-twentieth-century Koreans as emergent phenomena, I have also found it useful to cast one eye back beyond my own horizon of twenty-odd years of acquaintance with Korea toward older ethnographies, folkloric records of custom, and early missionary and travellers' observations.

It would be presumptuous or, at the very least, essentialist, to present this study as a comprehensive account of "Korean weddings." It would also be a distortion to present the women and men I encountered in the wedding halls of Righteous Town as inhabiting a self-contained universe in the sense that "ethnography" in Korea was once synonymous with "village study." My subjects, the products of a mobile, class-conscious, and media-savvy culture, imbibe images of other kinds of Korean lives, of both the very rich and the very poor, and these images inform how they see themselves and their society. How one marries becomes a measure of both self and status. Weddings matter. They are the subjects of government policy, moralistic diatribes, and florid advertisement copy. To do justice to this wide-ranging enterprise, I have drawn in a number of other voices from beyond the wedding halls of Righteous Town: scholarly authorities, friends and acquaintances across the Korean social spectrum, journalists, reformers, and purveyors of wedding services. If the brides and grooms of Righteous Town do not speak for all Korean weddings, they are a part of a larger Korean conversation.

In writing this study from several voices, I found myself making an arbitrary and (to my mind) uncomfortable distinction between scholars, journalists, and other producers of texts, who appear under their own names as a way of crediting their insights, and informants, who appear under pseudonyms as a way of protecting their confidentiality while sustaining their consistent identity as "characters." Given the near ubiquitousness of and constant preoccupation with matrimony in Korea, nearly everyone with whom I spoke was a potential informant and a potential authority. The experience of "doing fieldwork" could not be restricted to any physically determined field site, and my sources could not be sorted in commonsensical ways. A casual conversation might cause a scholar to slip into confidential informant mode and emerge in the text under cover of vagueness ("a friend," "a professor long resident in the United States"). Kim Eun-Shil generously allowed me to write her into my description of a Korean wedding (in Chapter 2) under her own name, bearing her multiple identities as anthropologist, woman of marriageable age, and feminist, blurring the boundaries between field site and metropolis, data and observation. There is far less justification for the anonymity with which I have credited the insights of brides, grooms, parents, and matchmakers, except that, having promised confidentiality, I could not do anything else.

"Korea" in this writing is an admittedly inaccurate shorthand for the

Republic of Korea, the southern half of a country divided since 1945. Because I see marriage practices as unfolding within a particular history, a particular political and economic milieu, I have not included any discussion of marriage practices in the Democratic People's Republic of Korea (north Korea). This would be an interesting and valuable work with roots in a common Korean past, but at this moment in time it would be a different story.

LANGUAGE NOTE

I have followed the McCune-Reischauer system of romanization for Korean, but with two exceptions. I use a few alternative romanizations that commonly appear in English-language writing on Korea ("Seoul"). In rendering authors' names, I use their own preferred romanizations ("Lee Kwang-Kyu" instead of "Yi Kwanggyu"). McCune-Reischauer and other alternative romanizations are provided in the bibliography ("Lee Hyo-jae [Lee Hyo-chae, Yi Hyojae]"). Names appear in Korean order, surname first, unless the referent uses an "Anglo" given name ("Peter Lee"). As in my other work, I follow local practice in identifying some of my informants with the teknonymous terms used in direct address ("Yongsu's Mother").

ACKNOWLEDGEMENTS

Many people have provided encouragement and intellectual and emotional sustenance for this study. I am grateful to all of the women and men who agreed to talk with me and to numerous old friends who, knowing my research interests, shared old stories and fresh gossip with great relish. I owe special thanks to "Sukcha," "Ŏmŏni," and the other members of the family who welcomed me into their midst on lunar New Year's Eve in 1977 and have never really let me go. "Yongsu's Mother," whose instruction was so critical to my early work on Korean shaman practices, did not remain silent during this project. As always, I am grateful for her sharp-tongued wit and for the hospitality she extended to me and to my family during several visits to Korea. Professors Cho Haejoang, Lee Kwang-Kyu, and Yim Dawnhee maintained a long anthropological conversation with me during my research, leading me to important sources (including their own writing), helping me to find willing research assistants, offering all manner of advice and wisdom, and critiquing my efforts. Professor Lee Mun-Woong also had many interesting things to say on the subject of weddings. My research assistants over three different field trips—Han Jeong-woo, Han Sangsuk, Im Hŭija, Kim Chinsuk, Kim Eun-Shil, Pak Hyŏn-suk, and Park Heh-Rahn—made the topic of weddings come alive for me. Mrs. Byun Kyung Sook and Mrs. No Young Hee helped me in many ways. Members of the Confucian Academy, Korea House, the Korea Legal Center for Family Relations, the Korean Institute for Women and Development, the Korean YWCA, the Mothers' Club of Korea, the U.S. Army Library, Yongsan Branch, and the Wedding Hall Professional Association opened their doors to me. Diana Lee provided the video clips of Sukcha's wedding. Changsu Houchins, Department of Anthropology, National Museum of Natural History, introduced me to Kisan's paintings.

My research in Korea was supported by the Joint Committee on Korean Studies of the Social Science Research Council and the American Council of Learned Societies, the Richard Lounsbery Fund, and the Belo-Tanenbaum Fund of the American Museum of Natural History. The Department of Anthropology, American Museum of Natural History, has provided me with the space, time, and resources for research and writing. I am grateful for Tom Miller's editorial assistance, William Weinstein's computer expertise, and the Museum Library's help in tracking critical sources. Diana M. Salles prepared the diagram (fig. 9) that appears in Chapter 6. Vivian Park helped me to wade through a sea of women's magazines.

The opportunity to work with Charles F. Keyes and Helen Hardacre on a conference, then volume—*Asian Visions of Authority, Religion and the Modern Nation State in East and Southeast Asia* (1994)—sponsored by the Social Science Research Council and the American Council of Learned Societies helped me to crystallize my thinking about weddings and nationalism.

Martina Deuchler, Roger Janelli, Eun-Shil Kim, and Homer Williams provided detailed critiques of a near-final version of my manuscript. Although this is not the book that any one of them would have written (and that would have been four very different books indeed), it is far better than it might have been without their close readings and commentary. Rubie Watson and Heh-Rahn Park gave me some very useful comments on individual chapters.

I first discussed this book with Sheila Levine of the University of California Press in 1988. I have appreciated Sheila's advice and, above all, her patience and faith in me over the long years it took to produce a completed manuscript. Sylvia Stein Wright meticulously edited the final manuscript for the press.

My husband, Homer Williams, accompanied me to Korea in 1983, where he took many of the photographs that illustrate this work. He dragged me, kicking and screaming, into the computer world, shared his knowledge of Korean demography, provided a relentlessly argumentative reading of the manuscript, and challenged me to impose a more rigorous sense of history upon my ethnographic present. I am indebted to him in more ways than I can ever express in writing.

An early draft of Chapter 3 appeared as "A Rite of Modernization and Its Post Modern Discontents" in *Asian Visions of Authority: Religion and the Modern Nation State in East and Southeast Asia*, edited by Charles F. Keyes, Laurel Kendall, and Helen Hardacre, published by the University of Hawaii Press, © 1994 University of Hawaii Press. Portions of the discussion of the *p'yebaek* ritual in Chapter 2 and the practice of sending ritual silk, described in Chapter 6, first appeared in "Ritual Silks and Kowtow Money: The Bride as Daughter-in-law in Korean Wedding Rituals," *Ethnology* 24 (4), October 1985. Portions of the discussion of the gift box delivery in Chapter 7 appeared as "A Noisy and Bothersome New Custom: Delivering a Gift Box to a Korean Bride," *Journal of Ritual Studies* 3 (2), Summer 1989. I am grateful to the publishers of these works for allowing me to reprint this material here.

The quotation from Sally Falk Moore's "Explaining the Present: Theoretical Dilemmas in Processual Ethnography" is reproduced by permission of the American Anthropological Association from *American Ethnologist* 14 (4), November 1987. The quotation from Raymond Williams's *Marxism and Literature*, published by Oxford University Press, 1977, is reprinted by permission of Oxford University Press. The quotation from David Lodge's *Small World* © 1984 is used by permission of Viking Penguin, a division of Penguin Books USA Inc. The quotation from Edith Wharton's *The Age of Innocence* is reprinted with permission of Scribner, an imprint of Simon and Schuster, © 1920, D. Appleton and Co., © renewed 1948, William R. Tyler. The quotation from John D. Kelley and Martha Kaplan's "History, Structure, and Ritual" is used with permission of the *Annual Review of Anthropology* 19, © 1990, by Annual Reviews, Inc.

Figure 1. A Korean wedding party in Righteous Town, early 1980s. Photograph by Homer Williams.

1

Why Study Weddings?
A Confessional Introduction

> If one perceives an event—a performance or ritual—as a
> traditional survival, one may "naturally" exclude from one's data
> the modern, commercial, or evangelical forces that are everywhere
> in the culture but "peripheral" to the event. If, however, one sees
> the performance or ritual as emergent, predominantly located
> not in a past, but in a possible future, modern things become
> interesting and will be much more prominent in one's corpus of
> inscriptions.
>
> James Clifford (1990:56)

I attended my first Korean wedding in 1970 as a recently arrived Peace
Corps volunteer. At the time, it was a depressing experience. The public
wedding hall, grey and drafty, with its loudspeakers directing guests to
simultaneous ceremonies in the several different rented chambers, reminded me of an intercity bus terminal. I was sufficiently unacculturated
to be jarred by the custom of relinquishing an envelope of money at the
door, where it would be torn open and the amount of my wedding gift
matter-of-factly recorded in a ledger. A stranger handed me a small
wrapped package while executing a slight, stiff bow, a ritual that seemed
merely to enhance the commercial flavor of our transaction. On this occasion the package would yield a small plastic container in bright orange,
suitable for use as a sugar bowl.

The ceremony seemed rushed and pro forma, from the pianist's bang-
ing out of "Here comes the bride" to a final scrambling of family and
friends for commemorative photographs. My sense of alienation was com-
pounded by knowledge of the groom's courtship, a hasty selection between two candidates proposed by matchmakers on the eve of his departure for foreign study. The ceremony in the wedding hall underscored for
me the seeming acquiescence of the Korean women I knew as they prepared for their inevitable march down the aisle and into domesticity,

dramatizing the differences between their dreams and my own. Obviously, I had a lot to learn.

Most disturbing of all was the utter familiarity of it, the cliché of a bride in a white dress and veil marching down the aisle on her father's arm to meet a groom in a dark dress suit (see fig. 1). In 1970, I was still seeking "the real Korea" amid the grim high rises and urban grime of the capital city. I had seen photographs in travel brochures and one reenactment for tourists of the old wedding rite, a sequence of arcane procedures performed in colorful and distinctive costume. Like the graceful old Korean roofs of tile or thatch, this too was being discarded for what then seemed but shabby imitations of Western forms. Korean friends who shared a romantic image of the Korean past assured me that the old wedding was still performed "in the countryside," a mythical place where they as well as I still believed the real Korea existed.[1]

A decade later, with some irony and a more seasoned perspective, I designed a research project on contemporary weddings, a project requiring hours of avid attendance in commercial wedding halls and long conversations with newlyweds. The initial design was simple, a study of first-generation working women in and around my old field site of "Enduring Pine Village" to learn how their earnings translated into marriage payments (Kendall 1985b). The modest ambitions of my initial research plan were soon overwhelmed by the realization that to write about weddings is to confront some of the vast complexities of Korean life at the end of the twentieth century.

BRIDES, GROOMS, AND BEYOND

As with many new projects, the seeds of this one had been planted in a previous field trip. In 1977 and 1978, while conducting research on women's rituals for my dissertation, I had witnessed firsthand the preparations and attendant gossip over the weddings of Kkach'i and Oksuk, daughters of the two village households with whom I was most closely tied. My landlady's daughter Kkach'i, while working in a factory in Seoul, had found a man and, when her parents disapproved of the match, had baldly cohabited with him until she became pregnant and her family acquiesced

---

1. Such perceptions are by no means unique to Korea. Walter Edwards describes how, during his research on modern Japanese weddings, an informant suggested that he find some remote rural village "where they still have the *real* wedding" (Edwards 1989:143).

to a humble and hasty wedding. Oksuk had also worked in a factory until, upon claiming her severance pay, she had delivered her savings to her stepmother, the shaman Yongsu's Mother,[2] and announced that she was ready to have Yongsu's Mother find her a suitable husband and arrange her wedding. Oksuk's savings financed the most lavish dowry yet seen in the village. Kkach'i's Mother was necessarily envious of the good show orchestrated by Oksuk's stepmother, who, in turn, grumbled that Kkach'i's Mother had gotten off easy, without the stress of matchmaking and elaborate ceremonial exchanges of gifts.

By their inevitable comparisons, they introduced me to some of the pragmatics of "love" (*yŏnae*) versus "matchmade" (*chungmae*) weddings. More striking yet was the contrast between generations; the initiative and pluck shown by both Kkach'i and Oksuk in their two very different marriage strategies would have had no place in the world where their mothers' marriages were made. Kkach'i's Mother was barely seventeen years old when she became the wife of a man whose face she had not seen until her wedding day. Oksuk's stepmother, after an early indiscretion, was married to an impoverished widower several years her senior; she wept tears of protest all the way to her husband's house.[3] Radical juxtapositions of past and present, of recent and precipitous transformations, thread their way through nearly every discussion about Korean weddings, even as questions of "how" and "whom" one marries have been critical components of Korean discourses on modernity for nearly a century. As I would come to understand them, Korean weddings are about the past and the future, about morality, about identity, and about the lives of women and men as they have moved through Korea's twentieth century.

"BUT WHY WEDDINGS?"

When I went to Korea in the early 1970s as a Peace Corps volunteer and when I returned in 1976 to research my dissertation, I was unmarried. A recent college graduate when I joined the Peace Corps, my first years in Korea coincided with a season in life when Korean women were expected to marry, would do so with the help of a matchmaker if no suitable

---

2. Addressing women by the names of their children or grandchildren is standard Korean practice. "Yongsu's Mother" is more than a description of a relationship ("Yongsu's mother"); it is a term of address.

3. The story of her marriage is told in *The Life and Hard Times of a Korean Shaman* (Kendall 1988).

"groom material" (*sillanggam*) was otherwise forthcoming. By the end of my first fieldwork, I was thirty years old and solidly in the category of "old maid" (*noch'ŏnyŏ*). During the fieldwork years, I had been asked at least once a day (usually several times a day) the inevitable question of a first-met stranger, the one that followed "How old are you?": "WHY AREN'T YOU MARRIED? YOU OUGHT TO BE MARRIED!" Then followed the intimations that I must have set my sights too high, the suggestions from well-intentioned village women that they would help me so I could complete my research, go home, and assume a more normal life. Marriage seemed to be on everyone's mind.

A scan of travellers' accounts and of ethnography suggests that marriage has been an abiding Korean preoccupation. Cornelius Osgood offers the wry comment that "Marriage under the old Korean system was almost as certain as death" (Osgood 1951:103). Moose, an early missionary, followed an observation on the scarcity of spinsters in his community with a touch of hyperbole: "In fact, so far as I have been able to learn, there is not one in the entire kingdom" (1911:77).[4] Korea remains a marrying country. In 1990, one out of twenty-five women in their thirties was single, a statistic greeted in some quarters as an indication of an alarming rise in spinsterdom since 1980, when eighty-four out of every eighty-five women in their thirties would have been married (*Korea Herald* [Yeoun-sun Khang], 5 June 1992:Weekend 1). Kim Eun-Shil, conducting fieldwork in Korea as a native anthropologist and unmarried woman, notes, "When I asked women why they got married, they laughed at my absurd question and said that they wanted to live a 'normal life' " (1993:59).

Those who cannot afford to marry engender pity. By the mid-1980s, the plight of rural bachelors, unable to lure migrant brides back to the countryside, had become a national issue, brought to public consciousness by the media and in some instances by the protest suicides of unmarried men.[5] I recall one interview on the breezy veranda of a farmhouse where

---

4. Early accounts also comment on the scarcity of brides as evidenced by numbers of reluctant bachelors (Miln 1895:81; Savage-Landor 1895:68). Foreign observers attributed this lack to concubinage.

5. A spate of articles appeared in the popular press in the mid-1980s (*Han'guk Ilbo* 21 April 1984; *Yŏng Reidi* March 1985:114–119; *Newsreview* 30 July 1988:26; *Newsreview* 30 June 1990:33; *Newsreview* 7 July 1990:34). As an indication of the vehemence of the rural bachelors' desperation, the slogan "Women! Marry rural men!" was spray painted on the wall of at least one rural bus terminal (Abelmann 1990:Ch.5, 11).

a crusty old farmer explained to me how "Nowadays, the women want to live clean, and the men in the countryside cannot find wives. There are thirty- and even forty-year-old bachelors." I asked if there were any such men in his own village. "No, but I saw it on television."

In 1987, the Seoul YWCA responded to the rural bachelors' plight with a program that brought groups of prospective rural grooms and urban brides together for social afternoons in the hope that matches would be struck (*Chosŏn Ilbo*, 22 September 1987:10).[6] In 1988, the Federation of Agricultural Cooperatives set itself the target of arranging 1,900 marriages, but succeeded in seeing only 777 couples wed (*Newsreview*, 4 March 1989:30). By 1990, several social organizations, churches, companies, and even a television program were all attempting matchmaking for rural bachelors (*Newsreview* 30 June 1990). At the time of this writing, a National Agricultural Cooperative Federation program has sent rural men to Sakhalin in the Russian Far East to seek brides of Korean ethnicity, and other brides have come from the Korean autonomous region in China, replicating a pattern of decades past when farmers in relatively prosperous Kyŏnggi Province sought brides from the impoverished southwest of the country (*Newsreview*, 29 February 1991:8–9; Lee Man-gap 1960:97–98). From a feminist perspective, these events play as one more chilling instance of a global "traffic in women," and yet within Korea, those who aid and abet such marriages have been described as performing a "good work" in helping the unwed to marry.

All well-intentioned matchmaking is potentially a good work, and many an amateur matchmaker would remind me, "They say that if you make three marriages, you'll go to Heaven." Helping to bring about the marriages of others, in any way, is generally considered a good work. As we shall see, extended kin frequently and generously contribute to the weddings of siblings, nieces, and nephews. Because everyone ought to have a wedding, various social welfare agencies facilitate the weddings of impoverished couples who lack both material and social resources. Every Saturday, the Korea Legal Aid Center for Family Relations (*Han'guk Kajŏngbŏmnyul Sangdamso*) sponsors a wedding, fitting the bride and

---

6. The YWCA officer who explained this program to me described the very rigorous screening the prospective grooms must pass, but indicated that the YWCA would accept nearly any woman who showed an interest in participating in the program. As early as 1982, more than a hundred rural men and urban women participated in group matchmaking events, one at the Women's Welfare Building (*Chosŏn Ilbo*, 3 September 1986:69) and another sponsored by a professional marriage bureau (*Chosŏn Ilbo*, 13 July 1982:8).

Figure 2. Forty-seven-year-old boy and eleven-year-old man. Photographed by Roy Chapman Andrews, 1912, AMNH Neg. No. 219080. Courtesy of the Department of Library Services, American Museum of Natural History.

groom in a borrowed wedding gown and dress suit, giving the bride a beauty treatment, and providing a master of ceremonies, music, flowers, simple gifts, and photographs. This model has been adopted by the Korean Mothers' Club *(Taehan Ŏmŏni Hoe)*. The YWCA and the Seoul city ward offices offer biannual group weddings *(haptong kyŏrhonsik)* where up to a dozen couples are wed by a single master of ceremonies, and group weddings have also been sponsored by the military. So pervasive is the notion that making weddings constitutes a positive social act that even counselors in professional marriage bureaus, proprietors of commercial wedding halls, and purveyors of dowry goods claim the moral high ground in asserting the benevolent intentions of their enterprises.

The wedding ceremony initiates Korean men and women into adulthood. References to the day one "puts up the hair and becomes an adult," a commonplace of wedding hall speeches and congratulations, evoke the old practice whereby the groom's childhood pigtail was once bound up into a topknot and a bride's hair pinned into a chignon at the nape of her neck as obvious visual indications of their new standing in a delicate hierarchy of status and deference. The explorer-naturalist Roy Chapman Andrews described a 1911 encounter with "a little fellow wearing a hat, with his hair knotted on the top of his head. He was only a child, and I said to the cook, 'Is that little boy really married?' 'Whom do you mean,' he asked, 'that man?' pointing to the child" (Andrews 1919:33). Andrews photographed the "eleven-year-old man" standing next to a pigtailed forty-seven-year-old "boy" whose unfortunate bachelor condition was probably related to his servile status (fig. 2).[7] Even without the visual marker of a married man's or woman's coiffure, marriage still implies membership in an adult universe. Writing of an urban neighborhood in the 1970s, Chung Cha-Whan observed that "an unmarried man, even though he is not a boy, is socially not a man. He is treated like a boy. He is teased and often addressed as: 'You, unmarried man, what do you presume to know?' " (Chung 1977:94).

Because the wedding is an initiation, one need only experience it once, unless one's new partner has never experienced the rite. When I asked naively about the "ceremony" *(yesik)* of an elderly couple in Enduring Pine Village who had begun to live together and intended to register their marriage, I was told with a chuckle that "a widow and a widower don't need a ceremony." Further inquiries confirmed a general notion that more than one wedding ceremony in a lifetime is an awkward idea. Yet I did not comprehend the weightiness of a wedding ceremony until Hangil got married in the summer of 1983.

7. Older Koreans to whom I have shown this photograph remark not only upon the contrasting coiffures of "boy" and "man" but also upon the differences in probable status implied by their grooming: the young married man immaculate in a gentleman's long overcoat; the middle-aged bachelor without coat, bareheaded, and of a generally scruffy appearance. Some have suggested that the latter might even have been the youth's servant. This would account for the evident discomfort of the two subjects of this photograph, posed side by side.

HANGIL'S STORY

Hangil's Mother was my neighbor during my first fieldwork, an amiable widow with a limited store of social and economic capital. In 1977, Hangil worked as a laborer in Righteous Town and lived with a woman in his mother's home. I remember the cold winter day when Hangil's son was born. In 1983, the child was in grammar school, the wife had "run away," and a successor, by some reports two successors, had also fled. The sympathetic neighbor who brought me up to date explained that Hangil was not a bad person; "he just drinks a little too much." He needed to settle down. In the eyes of the village, Hangil was still a bachelor. Although he had lived with more than one "wife" *(saeksi)* and fathered a son, Hangil had never celebrated his wedding.

A bride was found through family connections, a once-married woman who, village gossips immediately and correctly assumed, had been divorced because she was childless; but then Hangil already had a son. Hangil's uncle, head of one of the most prosperous houses in the village, agreed to finance the wedding, providing for the bride's gifts of jewelry and clothing and the cost of the feast. It reflected well upon Hangil's uncle that he had sponsored Hangil's ceremony, even as wagging tongues might have already begun to reproach the wealthy (by village standards) uncle for Hangil's extended bachelorhood. Still, it was an economical ceremony, held in the village hall to circumvent the cost of a commercial wedding hall. A feast of noodles was served up outside in the manner of an old country wedding.

My former landlady and fictive mother, so addressed as "Ŏmŏni," pointed out to me that the bride, having been married once before, did not need a wedding ceremony, that the festivities were for Hangil's benefit. Ŏmŏni and her neighbors held the hope that by having a wedding and "becoming an adult" *(ŏrŭni toeda)* Hangil would gain self-control. In one such conversation, perhaps in response to a flicker of skepticism on my face, the shaman Yongsu's Mother pointed out to me that another neighbor's son, married three months previously, had been transformed from a reckless youth into a responsible husband.

As I went about my fieldwork that summer, I retained my doubts about the auspicious prospects of Hangil's marriage, but I was hearing other affirmations of the wedding ceremony's transformative power. Arnold van Gennep (1960) and Victor Turner (1967, 1968) would have been pleased to hear Yongsu's Mother advise the beleaguered wife of a drunken husband, "Next year, if you can possibly afford it, have a wedding ceremony so that your husband will feel like an adult, like the father of his child." Spokespersons at the Korea Legal Aid Center for Family Relations and at the YWCA described their charity wedding programs as benefitting vulnerable women insofar as the ceremony, over and above the separate legal registration, enhances the stability of a marriage.[8] In the course of my own interviews, I was meeting couples who, years after they had legally registered their marriages, used their savings to hold a proper wedding ceremony because it was something they felt they ought to do. While the simple act of registering a marriage is both necessary and sufficient to constitute a *legal* marriage in the eyes of the Korean state, legal registration is distinct from and utterly insufficient to the *social* recognition of matrimony conferred in the performance of a wedding ceremony.[9]

When I returned to Enduring Pine Village nearly two years later, I asked about Hangil. All was well, the neighbors claimed. He was working more and drinking less. His wife was a gem of industry and tact, and Hangil's Mother now waddled around the village with an air of contentment. Improvements in the fortunes of Hangil's household were justly attributed to the daughter-in-law's character; but these developments also validated prior assertions that Hangil had needed a wedding in order to settle down. From other women in another place, I heard the dark side of such hope in the story of an innocent country woman married to an urban ne'er-do-well through the machinations of his desperate mother. The bride became a battered wife who, at the time of our interview, was on the verge of filing for divorce. The mother-in-law's ill-placed hopes were comprehensible, even to the pitiful bride.

I was no stranger to anthropological notions of "passage rites." In my earlier work on shaman ritual, I had borrowed upon Victor Turner's

8. Participants in a recent study of marriage practices among the urban poor expressed similar sentiments: that a marriage ceremony gives the couple social acknowledgement as adults and makes a cohabiting male partner feel more responsible for his family (Pak Sukcha 1991:107). Some of Kim Eun-Shil's informants in a working-class neighborhood expressed worry and doubt about a man's leaving them if their relationship was not acknowledged with a wedding ceremony (Kim Eun-Shil 1993:203). An Chŏngnam (1991:178) relates how participants in group charity weddings speak of the event as having rid them of abiding resentment and frustration (*han*).

9. In no sense is the legal registration of a marriage necessarily simultaneous with the performance of a wedding ceremony establishing the marriage as a social condition. Legal registration usually takes place weeks or even months after the wedding. Couples attempting to expedite a visa application for residence abroad might find it expedient to register their marriage before the ceremony, and members of the working poor may postpone the ceremony for several years after a registration undertaken to legitimize the birth of a child.

(1967, 1968) explications of the transformative power of curing rituals in rendering the afflicted as healed (Kendall 1977, 1985a: Ch. 1). I understood, almost as doctrine, that weddings moved people from one social category to another, a mechanism propelling social actors through a structure from "unmarried" to "husband" or "wife," much as the moving sidewalk in an airport transports the traveller from the domestic terminal to the international. A mix of ritual studies and common sense, however, had not prepared me to appreciate Korean weddings as events of far greater consequence than their American counterparts, as rites that might transform not only the "status" but more fundamentally the character, the social and moral integrity, of those who celebrate them. The urgent and righteous tone in Korean discourse about the proper conduct of weddings stems from this perception. Journalists opine, for example, that the superficiality of the modern Korean wedding ceremony, in contrast to the solemn old Confucian rite, contributes to a rising divorce rate (*Reidi Kyŏnghyang*, 23 October 1985:261) even as the prototypical Western-style wedding is seen to correlate with an even higher divorce rate in the United States (*Chosŏn Ilbo* [Yi Kyut'ae], 4 May 1983). The notion that good rituals make better people stems from Korea's Confucian heritage wherein all demonstrations of propriety (*ye*, Chinese *li*), including the correct performance of critical passage rites, are seen as fostering harmonious human relationships and a well-run social order. I invoke "Confucianism" gingerly here, for in so much popular writing on Korea the word becomes a reductionist black box that "explains" all things from economic success to failed democracy.

In suggesting that most Koreans vest ritual with greater moral import than do most North Americans and that the roots of this attitude lie in a body of ideology and practice we call, for verbal economy's sake, "Confucianism," my aim is not to foreclose discussion, but rather to open it and let in recent history. Given that ritual is taken seriously as an instrument and symptom of the social condition, my intention is to show how changes in the performance of wedding rites, and perceptions and discourses about the performance of rites, have been set at play in the shifting social milieu of recent and contemporary Korea.

TIME AND THE FIELD

Johannes Fabian (1983) illuminates a pernicious tradition of the discipline whereby anthropologists describe the "non-Western other" as removed from history, of timelessness as a function of social and geographic distance from the metropole. Fabian's tidy dichotomy of a "Western" anthropology that casts its gaze upon distant "non-Western" subjects founders on the complex circumstances of contemporary nation-states and the flowering of non-Western anthropologies. Even so, his basic insight that anthropology often renders its subjects in the past tense and so exoticizes them is sustained in many different circumstances of anthropological practice, including those that define an *internal* other. Rosaldo writes of how, in the Philippines, ethnographers lavish attention upon cultural minorities who are seen as having "cultures" amenable to study, while Landinos and lowlanders are seen as "civilized" and consequently "so much like 'us' that 'our' common sense categories apparently suffice for making sense of their lives" (Rosaldo 1989:199). Similar internal dichotomies characterize the ethnographic enterprises of China and Vietnam, both primarily concerned with the study of minority peoples and, to a more limited degree, with "peasants" (Schein 1993 for China). Within the West, Mediterranean societies are inscribed as the "aborigines" of Europe, as an Other still inhabiting a past (Herzfeld cited in Sant Cassia 1992:3).

Until very recently, anthropologists working in Korea—Korean, Western, and Japanese—have shared in the unstated assumption that a "more genuine" Korea could be observed in rural villages, untainted by modern conveniences and urban life-styles. One went to "the field" by leaving Seoul, boarding a bus or a train, and going to the countryside. Granted, the village where I resided in the mid-1970s was little more than an hour and a half from downtown Seoul, but even this journey, involving a single transfer from an intercity bus to a country bus, was sufficient to mark my transformation into anthropological mode and lend authenticity to the things I described.

" 'Country' and 'city,' are very powerful words," Raymond Williams tells us, because they have come to stand for vast bundles of association in the human experience (1973:1). Although Korean city and country carry their own specific history of a people moving through time, there are Korean resonances in Williams's characterization of a countryside which represents simple virtue and innocence, but is also a place of ignorance and limitation, and a city which is a center of achievement, learning, and light, but also a place of worldliness and ambition (Williams 1973:1). City and country give space to a polarity of "tradition" and "modernity." These dichotomies are invested with commonsensical but ambivalent and fluid meanings, as in the story of shifting reactions to styles of wedding ritual from rejection to nostalgia, from celebration to denigration.

The initial mapping of intellectual journeys from town to countryside may be found in the advent of modern Korean folklore studies *(minsok-hak)* in the late 1920s, an intellectual response to Korea's situation as a colony of the Japanese Empire (between 1910 and 1945) (I. H. Choi 1987; Janelli 1986; Robinson 1988).[10] For cultural nationalists, folk traditions would provide symbols of Korean identity and national pride, while an understanding of Korea's "old culture" was seen as essential to the construction of a reformed and strengthened society (Janelli 1986:30–31; Robinson 1988:32).[11] The object of the folklorists' project was thus the reconstruction of an uncolonized, uncorrupted Korean past; and like their colleagues in Europe (Linke 1990), China (Linke 1990; Hung 1985), and Japan (Yanagita 1970), they sought the vestiges of this past in the countryside, an equation which probably first came to seem commonsensical in the emergent urban culture of colonial Seoul in the 1920s.[12]

By 1975, when as a graduate student preparing for fieldwork I was immersed in readings about "peasant societies," a majority of the (south) Korean population already lived in cities. During my first residence in Korea, I had already encountered urban shamans. Still, there was no question on either side of the Pacific that as an anthropologist studying folk religion I would live in a village. Even in the 1980s, my interlocutors sometimes expressed surprise that I would spend my time observing new-style rather than traditional weddings, and I further confused the issue by

10. A case can also be made for an older indigenous tradition of folklore scholarship. Some Korean scholars find the indigenous roots of Korean ethnology and folklore studies in the seventeenth- and eighteenth-century writings of those scholars of the Practical Learning School who conducted empirical investigations of local conditions and practices (Janelli 1986:25).

11. Richard Bauman has argued that "From the invention of the concept in the late eighteenth century, folklore has always been about the politics of culture. Whether motivated by a romantic vision of traditional, preindustrial ways of life, or as a critical corrective to the discontents of modernity, or by a rationalist impulse to expose the irrational, supernaturalist foundations of folklore as impediments to progress, students of folklore have valorized certain ways of life over others in the service of larger political agendas" (Bauman 1989, cited in Bauman and Sawin 1990:288). See also Linke (1990).

12. As a measure of what it meant to live in the city of Seoul in those years, a group of historians notes that, in order to appreciate the transformation of urban life in the colonial period, "one need only compare photographs of Seoul in the late Chosŏn period with similar photographs taken in the mid-1930s. The former show a city that seems distant and alien to the modern eye—less a city, in fact, than an overgrown village of thatched-roof cottages that the famous nineteenth-century explorer Isabella Bird Bishop likened to an 'expanse of overripe mushrooms.' By contrast, pictures of Seoul in the 1930s show a city that is distinctly modern and familiar" (Eckert et al. 1990:390).

continuing to live in Enduring Pine Village while spending time in the tinseled urban wedding halls where village children got married. Meanwhile a vital and socially conscious anthropology had emerged within Korea, making a radical break with older folklore studies. It was thus to the dismay of my brilliant field assistant that I bothered to ask people about old customs at all when I had promised her a project that would focus upon the weddings of young working women.

Today, the sites for a possible anthropology of Korea proliferate. Some anthropologists, both Korean and foreign, still conduct fieldwork in rural villages, but few believe the rural village is a privileged site from which to apprehend an essential Korean culture. Recent studies have been set in large corporations (Janelli with Yim 1993; Kim Choong Soon 1992), in factories (Kim Seung-Kyung 1990; Spencer 1988), urban squatter communities (Thomas 1993), middle-class high-rise apartments (Kim Myunghye 1993; Moon 1990; Yi Eunhee Kim 1993), ob/gyn clinics (Kim Eun-Shil 1993), and amidst the fray of social movements (Abelmann 1990), presenting in sum a patchwork of the contemporary Korean moment. This moment is most often refracted not through a nineteenth-century history of rural gentry and peasants, but through a twentieth-century story of colonization, foreign domination, and authoritarian government.

KOREA IN RECENT TIMES

Liberated from colonialism with the fall of the Japanese Empire in 1945, Korea was literally sundered in two by the occupying armies of the United States and the Soviet Union, then devastated in the fratricidal Korean War (1950–1953). For the next two decades, south Korea (hereafter "Korea") remained an essentially rural society, impoverished in the aftermath of war. In the 1960s, the promise of industrial employment began to draw great numbers of migrants from the countryside to provide the cheap, relatively educated, and initially docile labor force which would give Korean products their competitive edge. In 1962, the Park Chung-hee (Pak Chŏnghŭi) regime initiated its ambitious series of five-year plans that would ultimately result in Korea's phenomenal success as an industrial tiger.[13]

13. The story of an interventionist Korean state favoring large corporations and stifling labor unrest among an educated and highly motivated new proletariat has been told and debated, as has the relative weight of development initiatives that preceded the 1960s. See Amsden (1989), Eckert (1991), Eckert et al. (1990:Ch. 20), Haggard, Kim, and Moon (1991), Koo and Kim (1992), and Moskowitz (1982), among many other sources.

Austerity was the order of the day and "development" the slogan. America, as the most significant Other in the Korean gaze, was seen not only as the primary source of military support and foreign aid, but as a bearer of all manner of cultural influences, at once enticing and danger-ous. Those of us who left American campuses in the late 1960s to serve as Peace Corps volunteers in Korea found ourselves implicated in a most contradictory cross-cultural encounter. Many of us would be stunned by the extreme conservatism, pro-American postures, and avid anticommun-ism espoused by many of our students (this was supposed to be the Third World), even as they were understandably wary of our seeming lack of patriotism, our overt criticism of our country's war in Vietnam (Were we not in the employ of that same government? Might we not be spies?). In the 1980s, everything would change.

The Chun regime's brutal and bloody suppression of demonstrations in the city of Kwangju in May of 1980 marked a critical juncture.[14] "Kwangju!" as event, memory, and slogan compromised all claims of the government's legitimacy and ushered in an era of increasingly vehement protest, reaching a crescendo in the massive public demonstrations that brought down the Chun government in 1987.[15] It was a time when all manner of social phenomena, from workers' rights to women's status to the once taboo subject of national reunification, were thrown open to pub-lic discussion. Kwangju also marked a critical turning in Korean percep-tions of the American Other, now implicated in the massacre insofar as the troops sent to Kwangju were nominally under the authority of the United Nations command, but more significantly in the recognition that the United States had supported authoritarian regimes in Korea since cast-ing its lot with Syngman Rhee in 1945.[16] But even without Kwangju, the magnitude of Korea's economic success would have precipitated a critical reorientation of nation, self, and other. When I returned to Korea in 1983, it was to a "newly industrialized country" where Korea's rising stature in the world was already confirmed by the choice of Seoul as the site for the 1988 Summer Olympics. American pressure to open Korean markets,

14. For a discussion of the Kwangju incident and its broader implications, see Clark (1988).

15. The events of 1987 are an important backdrop to ethnographies by Roger Janelli with Yim (1993) and Kim Choong Soon (1992). Public protests are graphi-cally described in work by anthropologists Nancy Abelmann (1990) and Kim Kwang-ok (1994).

16. See Clark (1991) for a discussion of multiple and shifting Korean percep-tions of the American relationship.

another source of tension, prompted comments that "lazy" Americans were seeking an unfair advantage over "hard-working" Koreans.

The 1980s was a decade of prosperity that saw the emergence of a full-blown consumer culture, at once celebrated, mocked, and criticized. It was a time of intense national pride, but also of uneasy wondering whether, in pursuit of economic stability and a comfortable standard of living, too much of Korea's own heritage had been surrendered or corrupted by Western influences. Other voices, new voices, began to question the costs industrialization had exacted from the lives of workers and farmers and the justice with which the fruits of economic success had been distributed. Some spoke of the social problems associated with weddings as further evidence of profound social inequities. I have mentioned the widespread concern over the plight of rural bachelors unable to find wives, but there was also consternation at the high cost of dowries exacted from working women, the extortionate fees charged by professional matchmakers who pander to the very rich, the superficiality, expense, and excessively "Western" flavor of contemporary ceremonies, and the deeply rooted patriarchal premises of all Korean marriage custom.

The observations expressed in the following pages, my own and others', are very much a product of shifting moods in Korea during the 1980s and on into the 1990s. In these years, conversations about weddings often became conversations about feminism, social justice, consumerism, or national identity. Gathering information during several short field trips, a consequence of personal and professional circumstance, I learned, through the sheer impossibility of establishing a fixed ethnographic present, to confront the emergent quality of marriage practices and the shifting locus of argument about what constitutes a good and proper wedding. The meandering process of this study, in and out of wedding halls, homes, government offices, and social welfare agencies, through the pages of women's magazines, back in time through old books, and on into heated conversations with Korean friends, colleagues, and field assistants, stretched and finally sundered my tidy notions of "fieldwork" in Korea.

In 1983, I returned to Enduring Pine Village to pursue the topic of working women and their weddings. I conducted long semistructured interviews with brides and grooms and members of their families during several visits over the next few years. Numerous casual village conversations also yielded much valuable information on the topic of matrimony. Because I despaired of gaining a full sample of weddings from Enduring Pine Village, I interviewed strangers first encountered in the commercial wedding halls of "Righteous Town," where Kkach'i, Oksuk, and other village newlyweds had celebrated their weddings. These were brides and grooms whose experiences replicated the stories of Kkach'i and Oksuk, village children inventing new lives, or the children of parents who had themselves made the transition from village to town. The sum of these interviews, twenty-nine couples interviewed in 1983 and 1985, constitute the core experiences of this study, the weddings of working-class Koreans and those who have made a tentative reach into the lower rungs of middle-class respectability.

The brides and grooms whom I met in the wedding halls of Righteous Town represent a spectrum, but by no means the full spectrum, of Korean life. A few were poor, laborers or precarious entrepreneurs at the margins of the Korean economic miracle, some so poor as to have postponed their weddings for years after the births of their children. Most of the couples I met, however, would think of themselves as inhabiting that broad, diffuse social space wherein a majority of Koreans rank themselves as "middle class" (Kim Seung-Kuk 1987). The husbands were either low-ranking civil servants or were involved in relatively stable enterprises, both large and small. Nearly all of the women had worked before marriage, some in factories, some in service industries, and some at clean and honorable "pink-collar" work. They do not conform to a Korean middle-class ideal of college-educated couples, of husbands employed as white-collar workers in large corporations or as professionals and wives who have made a swift and smooth transition from coed to housewife. Rather, the ideal exists as a measure of all the things they cannot be in this generation but might hope to accomplish in the next. Still, the Righteous Town couples are representative of the vast numbers of Koreans who have forged unprecedented life-styles in the wake of the urban transformation and in the heady rush of a new consumer culture.

Because these lives are informed by a larger world of Korean experience, I also interviewed the friends and relations of my research assistants for a comparative universe of families that were not only more affluent but also more confident of their urban and middle-class identities, families that have defined themselves as "modern" and celebrated "new-style" weddings for at least a generation. For a broad appreciation of weddings, I interviewed amateur and professional matchmakers, purveyors of dowry goods, proprietors of wedding halls, and organizers of charity weddings; read women's magazines and etiquette books; and benefitted immeasurably from the shared experiences and insight of Korean friends and colleagues through numerous conversations over many long years.

I suppose that I chose to study the weddings of first-generation working women like Kkach'i and Oksuk because the topic was unambiguously contemporary. In my earlier work, I had described shaman rituals as a vital contemporary phenomenon and was amused, then exasperated, when the very existence of shamans was denied by many urban and middle-class Koreans.[17] In 1983, I felt a certain smugness in proclaiming that I was "working on weddings," a topic for which nearly every Korean of a certain age was a potential informant and even the unwed were situated subjects bearing their own opinions and trenchant observations. And this is precisely why I was swiftly pulled beyond the narrow focus of my original intention to determine how women's own wages translated into marriage payments (Kendall 1985b).

I received the initial shove from my field assistants, Korean graduate students in anthropology who were, at the same time, women of marriageable age and thoroughly involved in the topic at hand. A story of so important a personal event as a meeting with a potential marriage partner would be shared with me as "data" subject to our mutual analysis. When I visited professional marriage bureaus, an advance telephone call from a well-spoken female student enhanced the likelihood of my being granted an interview, and my assistants usually left these places with multiple copies of brochures and business cards "to give your friends." One assistant expressed great ambivalence on the subject of marriage bureaus. Although a friend of hers had paid a large sum for a slim return on potential matches, my assistant would consider this route if she were still unwed in her late twenties. She was doing more than accompanying me on an interview with a professional matchmaker; she was conducting her own reconnaissance. Another woman found her highly developed social consciousness affronted by the posturing of a wedding hall proprietor who presented his expensive enterprise to us as a philanthropic endeavor. She embellished her field notes with parenthetical expressions of rage at the debt one family had incurred to finance a wedding and denounced the proprietor's comments as "ABSURD!" in big block letters, the English word inserted for emphasis. Meanwhile, my friends in Enduring Pine Village offered their opinions on the young women from Seoul who, like the

17. These attitudes have been less prevalent since the 1980s, when shaman rituals gained popular appeal and media attention as celebrations of national culture.

anthropologist years before, studied overmuch when they should be getting on with the important business of marriage and children.

I began to see the question of weddings as a wide-ranging roundtable discussion that extended the length and breadth of Korea, a quality I have attempted to preserve in the writing, with an echo of Frederick Barth's observation that "Recent reflexive anthropological writing, while stressing the contingent and positioned nature of accounts, has focused too egocentrically on the native's dialogue with ourselves and too little on their dialogue with one another" (Barth 1989:134).

As ethnography, this work addresses some classic anthropological concerns: it describes how matches are made; how brides, grooms, and their respective families proceed through the rites; and how they finance ceremonies and elaborate exchanges of ritual goods. I shall be particularly concerned with the way these processes serve to construct an image of "bride" and "wife" and how this image has shifted through the twentieth century. At its core, this study is about change and perceptions of the consequences of change. My interest in Korean weddings was broadened by the work of those who have found in the self-conscious invocation, reconstruction, and invention of "tradition" the critical responses of a people to the history and politics of their time.[18] In Korea, as elsewhere, local knowledge and rural experiences have been selectively discarded, adapted, transformed, and elaborated in the weddings of a rapidly urbanized population, sometimes as a matter of public policy, sometimes as a measure of distinction. "Tradition" must be understood here in Raymond Williams's (1977:115) sense of "an intentionally selective version of a shaping past and a pre-shaped present, which is then powerfully operative in the process of social and cultural definition." Ultimately, a discussion of Korean weddings becomes a discussion of Korean identity as Koreans in many different circumstances attempt to define themselves through their own history and against changing perceptions of the West, most specifically against an American Other. Chapter 3, in particular, illustrates how the "new-style" *(sinsik)* Korean wedding came to represent a "modern" *(hyŏndaejŏk)* institution of matrimony and why this seemingly Western ritual has been criticized in an era marked by rising national pride and anti-American sentiment.

18. From somewhat different angles, this theme appears in the work of Bauman (1986), Clifford (1988), Comaroff (1985), Hall (1981), and Hobsbawm and Ranger (1983).

An interest in the changing circumstances of Korean women led me to the wedding halls. New approaches to the study of gender as a mobile construct, invested with shifting definitions of what is material, necessary, and desirable (Foucault 1980:152), helped me to interpret what I saw there.[19] Statements about Korean women are made not only through the structure and symbolic content of marriage practices, but also through a critical discourse about Korean weddings. Women, for their part, participate in both the construction of Korean matrimony and its unfolding critique as matchmakers, brides, kinswomen, and social commentators. Changing gender relations are implicated in every phase of the marriage process, from matchmaking and courtship, through the exchanges of ritual goods from the bride's side and from the groom's side, to the wedding ceremony. Although the sum of these events details a profound transformation in Korean gender relations, Korean women have not marched steadily in the direction of greater "equality," much less "liberation." Among the multiple voices heard in this ethnography are those that cry out in advocacy of women.

If Korean weddings yield commentary on gender, status, national identity, and the social good, these things are not social "givens," but objects of contestation. Their realization in ritual is a subject of public policy, family argument, and the often self-conscious manipulation of ritual forms. I do not present an authoritative description of "custom" so much as Korean arguments about what constitutes "good custom" in a changing social field. The study thus owes much to Bourdieu's lesson that marriage strategies are best regarded not as rules of structure, but as "something people *make*, and with which they *do* something," for stakes that may be both material and symbolic (Bourdieu 1977:35–36, 186–187). But I am also in sympathy with those who, while they value Bourdieu's basic insight, find his work limiting in its reduction of complex human motivations and feelings to self-interested political strategies.[20] Many of those who spoke with me and the Korean authors of much of the commentary I read would probably find Bourdieu's perspective congenial with a local cynicism that regards contemporary Korean marriage negotiations as

19. See, for example, studies by Abu-Lughod (1990), Bailey (1988), Bernstein (1991), Kondo (1990), and Ong (1987, 1990). Studies by Abu-Lughod (1990), Boddy (1989), and Ong (1987) make specific reference to wedding procedures, styles of dress, and ritual as symptomatic of new readings of gender.

20. See, for example, Abu-Lughod (1991:140–141), Trawick (1990:139), and Yanagisako (1985:13).

schemes to advance wealth and status.[21] Such concerns are evident in the discussions of courtship and exchanges of ritual goods described in subsequent chapters and in the jokes and other folklore of modern urban Korean life that accrue around the subject of matrimony.

It would be both intellectually tempting and an honest reflection of these discourses to present Korean weddings strictly in Bourdieu's terms, a kind of truth but not the immediate experiential truth of women like Kkach'i and Oksuk. This is not a study of the macropolitics of Korean matrimony, although such a study would be both valuable and interesting. It does give an occasional nod to such concerns when they appear in the media, in jokes, and in the shared perceptions that inform experiences and conversations as ordinary women and men measure their own lives and as they live out the consequences of both choice and circumstance (Williams 1977:37). Some of their stories, the personal accounts presented here, are intended to provide a fine-grained and intimate perspective on getting married in Korea, a style of anthropological practice Lila Abu-Lughod characterizes as "an ethnography of the particular" that resists the authoritative generalizations of an older ethnography to present its subjects as "people going through life agonizing over decisions, making mistakes, trying to make themselves look good, enduring tragedies and personal losses, enjoying others, and finding moments of happiness" (Abu-Lughod 1991:158). The following chapters describe the concerns of those who marry, their families, bureaucrats, feminists, matchmakers, purveyors of commercial wedding services, and the media. These heterogloss voices offer accounts of romance, pragmatic assessments of matrimony, tales of exploitation, discourses on Korean custom and Confucian morality, commercial hard sells, and the hyperbolic humor of cynical residents of Seoul.

Like those of whom I write, I am also attempting to make sense of Korean weddings against an unfolding history. While I vastly prefer to read and to write ethnographies that privilege the local voice, I have found it necessary to combine informant narratives with my own (sometimes lengthy) speculations and to present my subjects' voices against a range of other material, including the writings of other scholars, journalists, and amateur observers. To do less than utilize a full tool kit would be a disser-

---

21. See, for example, anthropologist and feminist Cho Haejoang's (1988) citation of Bourdieu in her study of Korean gender relations, *Han'gugŭi yŏsŏnggwa namsŏng*.

vice not only to the reader, but to those Korean women and men who so generously shared their time with me in the construction of this work.

The weddings I describe are not generalizable practices garnered from fieldwork in a village or other tightly circumscribed setting so much as the subject of a series of conversations carried on in the Korea of the 1980s and early 1990s. The dilemma of the foreign anthropologist is thus exposed. In contrast to my early and continuing interest in shaman rituals, I write here of many things that are self-evident to most Koreans and recognize that, for Korean readers, the primary interest of this work may be in the odd slant I give to familiar subjects. In a mirror image of my position, Kim Eun-Shil (1993:12) writes in her dissertation of how fellow anthropology students in Korea scorned her research interest in Korean women.

> Everyday life, it was assumed, might be a subject for foreign scholars who are not familiar with Korean culture, so that they could write about everyday life with curiosity. Many Koreans seemed to think that writing about everyday life by a Korean for Koreans was pointless because they thought that they knew what it looked like and what was normal and natural. However, they might think it possible if I wrote for foreigners who did not know about Korean culture.

As ethnographers, Kim Eun-Shil and I are engaged in the same project: to find insight through the destabilization of the familiar (Marcus and Fischer 1986). Necessarily, our paths to that end are different. Kim Eun-Shil must collapse the comfortable commonsense assumptions of a middle-class Korean position.[22] For my part, I have tried to "write against" the notion of Korea as an exotic place as Lila Abu-Lughod (1991) would have us "write against culture." I began this work in the manner of many ethnographies, with a trope of alienation (Pratt 1986), but my alienation in that drafty wedding hall was a function of things known and already shopworn, rather than of things strange. If, as Pratt (1986) suggests, the ethnographic trope is borrowed from "the tropology of travel writing," then my introduction to Korean weddings might find affinity in the jaded travel writing of our own era, where it is always *Video Night in Kathmandu* (Iyer 1988). The Korea of this work is part and parcel of late-twentieth-century time (Fabian 1983), a place where translations of Edward Said's *Orientalism* are heaped upon bookstore tables and where any

22. See Kirin Narayan's (1993) recent and insightful discussion of the "native" anthropologist whose positioning may be neither self-evident nor easily generalized.

meaningful discussion of weddings must be cognizant of the mythologies generated by women's magazines and television soap operas. This is not a story of sociological certainties in an evolutionary process from "tradition" to "modernity," as so justly criticized by Jean Comaroff (1994), but it does concern the fluidity of discourse and practice over time. Rather, it is a story about how people invest and reinvest the categories of "tradition" and "modernity," and how these investments so often obscure the gendered consequences of change. It is a story in which the Korean familiar might destabilize some tidy assumptions that are closer to home.

But while I might appropriately compare my ethnographic intentions to those of Kim Eun-Shil, I do not and cannot share her positioning as a Korean feminist, however sympathetic I might be to that project.[23] As an outsider, my own participation in the wide-ranging discussion of Korean weddings that I describe is necessarily qualified. While my attitudes concerning the position of women in contemporary Korean society should be transparent to any reader, I am not directly engaged in the process of transformation, as bride or mother or reformer. Kim Eun-Shil writes of her field experience as "a Korean woman who was regarded by [her] informants as having emotional experiences similar to theirs or at least a cultural understanding of their experiences." As a consequence, some women regarded her as a spokesperson for their problems and complaints about health care policy and hospital administration. Other women, however, saw her unmarried state as a critique of their own lives (Kim Eun-Shil: 22). In no sense would the women she interviewed permit her to regard herself as a neutral observer, and in no sense was she neutral.

My own stance was far more ambiguous. Korean colleagues did challenge me to regard my material as something more than "data," and these encounters inevitably plunged me into the depths of relativist liberal immobility and guilt. When I presented to a Korean scholarly forum an interpretation of the custom of delivering wedding gifts to the home of the bride on the eve of the wedding, I was soundly taken to task by my discussant for failing to denounce this practice as rowdy and wasteful (I had simply mentioned that such opposition exists). On another occasion, I necessarily disappointed a generous and much-respected friend by refusing to appear on Korean television to discuss my research concerning "the

---

23. See also Cho Oakla's (1992) discussion of her situation as a feminist activist "Doing a Fieldwork as a Native Anthropologist" in Korea.

dowry problem."[24] In both instances, I did not believe that the practices I had been observing merited the vehemence of criticism directed against them; these points of view seemed often to patronize the intelligence and managerial abilities of working-class Koreans. At the same time, I did not want to serve as a scholarly apologist for practices that give much solace to the knowledge that I shall never marry off a daughter in Korea. Even had I the courage of my convictions, in the heated anti-imperialist climate of the late 1980s, American critiques of Korean social practice would have served no positive purpose.

But if the anthropologist is not a part of the struggle, her reticence evokes the larger issue of whether a Western woman ought to be writing of non-Western women at all. Chandra Mohanty (1988) speaks of the "discursive colonization" whereby the diverse experiences of women in the Third World have become generalized "objects" of Western scholarship and Trinh T. Minh-ha (1989), of the appropriation and distortion of women's voices as other women's "data." Those of us who would write an anthropology of women have come to recognize the uncomfortable politics of our "ethnographic authority" (Clifford 1983), of describing those who are seldom empowered to contradict us.[25] Women anthropologists have responded both by finding new ways of writing about women's lives[26] and by frank, constructive soul searching.

Feminist anthropologists Margery Wolf (1992) and Lila Abu-Lughod (1991) have responded to critiques of the ethnographic enterprise with an uneasy acknowledgement of the politics of ethnographic writing, of a privileged outsider "speaking for" muted subjects; yet both affirm that there is value in describing the humanity of otherwise unknown lives and the conditions of class, gender, and global and national politics that inform the living of those lives. There are more and less responsible, respectful, and effective ways of writing about women's lives. Wolf's remarks are both a caution and a challenge: "no matter what format the anthropologist/reporter/writer uses, she eventually takes the responsibility for put-

---

24. See Louisa Schein's thoughtful discussion of the multiple and contradictory circumstances in which an anthropologist might find herself as an unintentional agent of cultural production (Schein 1993).

25. See, for example, essays by Abu-Lughod (1990, 1991), Spivak (1988), Visweswaran (1988), and M. Wolf (1992).

26. Some representative recent works might include Abu-Lughod (1993), Behar (1993), and Kendall (1988); but note also a dawning recognition of a longer tradition of innovative, but long marginalized, ethnographies written by women about women (Abu-Lughod 1990; Visweswaran 1988).

ting down the words, for converting their possibly fleeting opinions into a text. I see no way to avoid this exercise of power and at least some of the stylistic requirements used to legitimate that text if the practice of ethnography is to continue" (M. Wolf 1992:11).

I found my own ironic vision of the late-twentieth-century anthropologist while considering the late-twentieth-century Korean matchmakers whose work is described in Chapter 5, women who provide an essential service to those who lack a more direct means of getting together. The matchmaker's work is appreciated, but her words are also prudently taken with a grain of salt. Sometimes her efforts engender lifelong gratitude and sometimes curses for a gross misrepresentation of fact and circumstance. Anyone who would undertake the matchmaker's task must learn to live with this ambivalent regard, and any anthropologist might profit by learning to live with suspicion; it helps to keep us honest. In setting out to write a work of ethnography, the anthropologist would benefit by remembering the Korean matchmaker's proverb, "Do well, then three cups of wine; if you fail, then three slaps on the face" *(chal hamyŏn suli sŏkchan, mot hamyŏn ppyami sŏktae)*.

1  CEREMONY

The issue of the day is how to address the fieldwork
enterprise in a poststructuralist period, how to
understand the fieldwork time as a moment in a
sequence, how to understand the place of the small-
scale event in the large-scale historical process, how to
look at part-structures being built and torn down.

Sally Falk Moore (1987:730)

2

A Wedding in Righteous Town

In cultural production (and all consciousness is in this sense
produced) the true range is from information and description,
or naming and indication, to embodiment and *performance*.

Raymond Williams (1977:139)

Chapter 1 began with a naive visit to a wedding hall. Chapter 2 also begins
in a wedding hall, more than ten years later. The homesick Peace Corps
volunteer has become an anthropologist whose recent research proposal
includes a promise to "provide a description of the Korean 'new-style'
(sinsik) wedding, filling a lacuna in the ethnographic literature on Korea."
By the summer of 1983, Korea has also changed, entered the ranks of the
"newly industrialized countries" (NIC) and been selected as the site of the
1988 Olympics. The drabness of 1970s Seoul is giving way to genuine
glitz, and the traffic on the road to Righteous Town is jammed due to
massive subway construction. But already this ethnographic present is
more than ten years past. As a measure of the distance between that moment and the present one, Kim Eun-Shil, the scholar whose dissertation I
have cited in the previous chapter is, in 1983, my field assistant. A decade
later, she will generously permit my inscription of her younger self into
an ethnographic text for a more honest portrayal of how that text was
constructed.

I recorded Pak Yŏnghŭi and Yi Chongil's wedding and many others in
my field notes, intending then to homogenize them into a description of
"the ceremony," "the groom," and "the bride," one wedding as every
wedding. Writing now, I am mindful of the critics who see generalized
accounts as removed from time and thus severed from the social, economic, and political forces which constitute a history.[1] This story of a
wedding deals playfully with the ethnographic present of 1983, juggling
time and space. Its reference point shifts to other weddings and back again,

---

1. See, for example, Clifford (1988), Fabian (1983), McKnight (1990), and Sanjek (1991).

moves between what actually happened and an etiquette book's account of what ought to have happened, and slides between 1983 and years of subsequent fieldwork and between the new-style wedding ceremony and the old Confucian rite of matrimony that it replaced. I make allusions to the presence of the state within the wedding hall and to the general commodification of the wedding enterprise, foreshadowing themes which will thread their way through subsequent chapters.

JULY 9, 1983

On a hot July Saturday in 1983, I find myself in the Rose Wedding Hall in Righteous Town, about to crash the wedding of Pak Yŏnghŭi and Yi Chongil. The affable young manager of the Rose, amused and seemingly flattered by my research efforts, has given me the schedule of this and other weddings. The Rose Wedding Hall, a modest operation, sits at the end of an unimposing row of two-story concrete structures just outside the Righteous Town market and conveniently close to the country bus terminal. Like other commercial wedding halls, this "ceremonious space" (yesikchang) offers a package deal that includes the use of the hall, pianist, photographer, a rented dress and veil, gloves and flowers for the bridal party, and a beauty parlor session for the bride. A list of the government's "prohibitions against empty ceremonies and vulgar ostentation" (hŏrye hŏsik haengwi kŭmji) hangs in the front office next to a display of wedding portraits.

The Rose's two large ceremonial halls, carpeted and upholstered in fading red, and its rabbit warren of dank hallways linking office, halls, beauty parlor, and auxiliary chambers, suggest that the Rose is neither the newest nor the best wedding hall in Righteous Town. By 1985, the Rose and its local rivals will be overshadowed by the "Seoul-style" Hollywood Wedding Hall, its many pastel chambers hung with crystal chandeliers and lit with soft, colored lights. The Hollywood will, in turn, yield its popularity to the Mammoth Wedding Hall, boasting spacious parking facilities for the family cars that will be clogging Righteous Town streets by the late 1980s. But on this Saturday afternoon in 1983, the Rose retains its solid reputation for good service and is a perfectly respectable place to get married.

The wedding of Pak Yŏnghŭi and Yi Chongil begins with a flurry of greetings and congratulations that extend from the stairwell along the corridor and into the wedding chamber. Some of the matrons wear Korean dresses with long, full skirts and short, crescent-sleeved jackets. The mother of the bride and the mother of the groom, each the center of a gaggle of well-wishers, are conspicuous in Korean costumes of pink and aqua blue, respectively. I have been told that these pastel dresses are a new custom, already rationalized by an aphorism: that the groom is as lofty as the heavens and the pride of his mother, who wears the color of the sky, while pink suggests the bashful bride. Friends of the bride and groom, suited and skirted in their best clothes, maintain their own knots of conviviality. A few carry wedding presents in auspicious red wrapping paper decorated with the logos of Seoul department stores. (In one recent wedding season, the subways sported posters of a bride in a white lace veil and the legend "M. Department Store—for joyous shopping!")

A representative of each family, seated at a functional metal desk, accepts the guests' white envelopes and enters the amount of their cash contributions into a businesslike ledger. Today, most of the envelopes will contain 3,000 to 5,000 *wŏn* ($3.75 to $6.25 U.S.). Five years later, 10,000 *wŏn* ($14.50 U.S.) will be standard, and by the early 1990s, the figure will double to 20,000 *wŏn* ($25 U.S.). Inflation, coupled with a rising standard of living, is a commonplace of contemporary Korean life; the overall cost of getting married will nearly double between 1985 and 1990.[2]

Although the names of the bride and groom are posted, the limited number of Korean surnames and the generational popularity of certain given names have inspired a bit of urban folklore in the claim that, on a busy Saturday or Sunday in a large wedding hall, the unwary guest can deliver an envelope of cash to the wrong wedding. That will not happen at Pak Yŏnghŭi and Yi Chongil's wedding. The hall is small, and this is its only wedding on a slow summer Saturday between the peak spring and autumn marriage seasons. With luck, the money in the envelopes will enable both families to recoup the costs of the wedding hall and the restaurant feast that follows the wedding. Some weeks after their wedding, Pak Yŏnghŭi and Yi Chongil will assume that this was the case, but

2. A survey of urban couples conducted in 1985 by the Central Committee for the Promotion of Thrift (Chŏch'uk Ch'unjin Chungang Wiwŏn Hoe) estimated the average total cost of wedding expenses at 8,230,000 *wŏn* ($10,291 U.S. at 1985 rates) (CCCWH 1985:9). A similar study by the Consumer Protection Board in December 1989 estimated average total costs at 18,330, 000 *wŏn* ($26,186 U.S. at 1989 rates) (*Newsreview* 3 March 1990). Even allowing for inconsistent sampling between the two surveys, the figures are striking.

they will be vague because these ceremonial expenses are handled by their parents.[3]

I take a deep breath before plunging into this crowd of strangers. Here we go again, invading someone's wedding to snap photographs, explaining that I am "studying the marriage customs of Korea," making polite conversation, and above all, trying desperately to garner information. I will offer to deliver the photographs "after the honeymoon, at some convenient time" in exchange for a conversation with the bride and groom about their wedding. Someone will scribble an address, with luck even a telephone number, into my notebook. In 1983, telephones are not yet ubiquitous in Righteous Town households, much less in the surrounding countryside. Ten years later I will be embarrassed by my ineptness at manipulating the buttons on Yongsu's Mother's cordless telephone.

At one recent wedding the groom's cronies playfully suggested that I was from the *New York Times*, rural youths grinning at their own cosmopolitan knowledge. Although no one has turned me down, I am uneasy with this process of soliciting interviews, knowing that I will be asking near strangers a great many delicate questions about money. There are uncomfortable parallels between my chosen profession and that of a door-to-door salesman or itinerating proselytizer. I take comfort in the presence of my field assistant. Kim Eun-Shil combines a young intellectual's confident assertiveness with a well-bred Korean woman's sense of etiquette. She is much better at this sort of thing than I am.

Women have crowded into the beauty shop to inspect Pak Yŏnghŭi's makeup and coiffure. The aunts proclaim that she is a beautiful bride. The friends hover close, offering moral support as they escort her from the beauty shop to "the bride's waiting room," a tiny chamber at the back of the wedding hall. Two or three of them manage to cluster inside with giggles, and I recall American college lore about crowded telephone booths. Someone produces a camera and snaps a series of sentimental photographs as friends pose for the last time with the still-maiden Yŏnghŭi.

---

3. Roger Janelli reports that, in the large corporation where he conducted fieldwork in 1986 and 1987, cash wedding gifts were collected by section, and each section's envelopes were given to another worker from the groom's section, who later gave it to the groom so that the couple might benefit directly from the gift. It was thought that if the cash gift were given over to the groom's parents in the conventional manner, the parents would keep it all, claiming it had been used to cover wedding expenses. In such arrangements, one discerns a conflict of interest between the social and ceremonial obligations of parents and the needs of a couple endowing a new household (Roger Janelli, personal communication).

The groom also has a waiting room, but Yi Chongil does not retire until the last possible moment. Instead, he paces at the back of the hall, surrounded by his well-wishers, offering a grin, a handshake, or a bow to passing guests as appropriate to their respective status and relationship. Unlike many grooms who are undone by the stress of anticipation, he does not puff compulsively upon a series of cigarettes.

In the throng around the groom, we strike up a conversation with the friendly young man who will serve as announcer *(sahoe)*. He works in a photography shop and, noting our equipment, gives us his card. He assures us that he has served as the announcer in many weddings and seems ever so slightly vain of his verbal skills. Later in the day, when teased by the bride's friends, he will ask me for a defense of his performance style *(somssi)*. In our later interview, Yi Chongil will tell us that he was grateful to have a college-educated friend who could serve as his poised and well-spoken announcer.

The bride's grandparents, a frail old couple in Korean dress, have slowly navigated the length of the aisle and taken their seats at the head of the hall, next to the seats reserved for the bride's parents at the right-hand side of the low stage. I will learn that concern for the grandparents' precarious health prompted this midsummer wedding. A death in the family and a period of mourning would occasion a long (and for a matchmade marriage, awkward) delay. The groom's father, for his part, wanted to see his middle son wed before his own retirement in August.

Friends of the bride and groom have begun to claim the several rows of seats at the front of the hall, the groom's party on the left, bride's party on the right. Women and children form a more-or-less cohesive cluster of guests behind the friends, and Kim Eun-Shil and I find our seats among them. Eun-Shil is fairly bursting with something to report. The groom's friends extracted a very large fee from the bride's family when they delivered the box containing her gifts from the groom's family *(ham)*. The bride's friends think that the men may have received as much as 150,000 *wŏn* (more than $200 U.S.), well above the local standard, and intend to bargain for a fair share of the take when they "sell" the bride's flowers to the bachelors after the wedding. Eun-Shil has made preliminary inquiries and yes, we can attend the bargaining session, scheduled for an hour after the wedding in a local bakery. For now, we are content to simply observe.

Older men, who have lingered over conversations in the foyer, drift in and sit toward the back. The guests continue to chat among themselves as they will throughout the ritual. The Rose's manager, anxious to begin, extricates the groom's mother from her crowd of well-wishers and, gently but firmly tugging on her arm, escorts her down the aisle to her seat at the front of the hall. With booming voice he announces "Will the bride's side please sit down." The bride's mother hastens to her seat beside the grandparents. A final cluster of friends leaves the bride's waiting room, and the well-groomed young women slide into their seats with a flutter of nods and smiles. The pianist, a perky young woman who moonlights from an office job, assumes her position at the piano. The moderator strides to the microphone at the left-hand side of the hall and makes his first announcement.

"*The wedding of Master* Yi Chongil *and Miss* Pak Yŏnghŭi *will now commence. The honorable Mr.* Sŏng Ŭijol *will preside as Master of Ceremonies.*" The *churye* (master of ceremonies), solemn and dignified as befits a ceremonial elder, takes his place behind the podium. A few lingering guests now finally settle into their seats.

The announcer declaims the steps of the new wedding, following the outline on a crib sheet provided by the wedding hall. Outlined in the Family Ritual Code and explained in etiquette books, this sequence of procedures is presented here in italic. From the perspectives of the wedding hall manager, the etiquette book, and most participants, this *is* the new-style wedding, with its shifting personnel of "groom____," "bride ____," and "churye ____," a structure with neither a past nor a future, a structure without a story.

[While Kendall the hesitant fieldworker sits and watches, Kendall the older and possibly wiser writer of ethnography has slipped into the Rose Wedding Hall by way of recollection to annotate her observations with the accumulated knowledge of fieldwork, reading, and rumination. This is cheating; Kendall has by now learned things that were unclear to her on that July afternoon. Moreover, she risks breaking the stride of her story with the duller stuff of comparison and ethnographic generalization. She would restrict herself to the essentials, but is pulled in other directions by obscure bits of information and detail that betray both the "unique" and "representative" features of an afternoon at the Rose Wedding Hall. By such artifice, we may distinguish a moment in July 1983 from a "typical Korean 'new-style' wedding" that never really happened.]

"*The groom will now enter the hall. Groom, enter the hall.*" The pianist strikes up a rousing processional beat as Yi Chongil, a bespectacled young man with a soft, youthful face, walks down the aisle looking straight ahead. Those spectacles nearly cost Yi Chongil a bride. Pak Yŏnghŭi would confide in us that her first impression, at a meeting arranged by a matchmaker, was of a "bookworm" *(ch'aek pŏlle)*, but she had been more favorably impressed by his mother's warm personality. On his wedding day, Yi Chongil walks the gauntlet of spectators with more grace than the many grooms who lower their heads, square their shoulders, and move at a brisk pace. He wears a more serious expression than those grooms who march down the aisle with unabashed grins on their faces. He stops just below the dais, executes a stiff bow to the *churye*, and turns toward the guests in anticipation of the bride.

"The bride will now enter the hall. Bride, enter the hall." The pianist strikes up "The Wedding March." All eyes turn to the back of the hall to watch Pak Yŏnghŭi enter on her father's arm, eyes demurely cast down, a faint smile on her carefully painted lips. Barely a decade ago, in the early 1970s, brides were enjoined not to smile on their wedding day lest their first child be a girl. Perhaps the pervasive, irresistible media image of a radiant bride triumphed over custom. Pak Yŏnghŭi is short, plump, and pretty. We will discover, when we meet her again, that her round face is fresh and sparkling, even without the exacting professional makeup she wears today. Her long veil spills from a tiny lace hat, tilted toward the left brow, that lends a pert air to her features.

A bride's march down the aisle on her father's arm is a solemn moment, and some brides seem close to tears. As in an American wedding, many of the guests' eyes are moist. Korean patrilocal traditions enhance the pathos of "raising a daughter and giving her away." This short journey down the aisle to the waiting groom replicates folk memories of a father accompanying his daughter to her in-laws' house and leaving her there in a distant place to begin a new life. *Passage Rites Made Easy,* a popular etiquette book, urges the bride and her escort to step slowly so that the full poignancy of this moment can be savored (Ko 1982:109).

The perils of navigating a narrow aisle in a long dress and veil further induce the bride to maintain a decorous pace. Sometimes a helpful woman will lean from her chair and help the bride ease her billowing skirt through the passageway. As Pak Yŏnghŭi and her father start down the aisle, Mrs. Bae, the female attendant at the Rose, moves behind them and deftly extends the bride's long veil so that it trails behind her in a wake of gauze and lace. Mrs. Bae is the commercial wedding hall's answer to the kinswomen and maidservants who guided the bride through the complicated procedures of the old rite of matrimony. In an elegant Seoul wedding hall, each wedding party would be assigned one among a staff of attendants, all resplendent in traditional Korean costume. At the Rose, there is only Mrs. Bae, sometimes darting between two nearly simultaneous ceremonies, efficient in her artificial pearls and fashionable drip-dry clothes, and functionally invisible like the black-garbed stagehands of Japanese kabuki theater.

When the bride and her father reach the front of the hall, Mrs. Bae, who has already circled around the side of the hall, is waiting for them. She guides Pak Yŏnghŭi's hand from her father's arm to the waiting arm of her future husband. In this and many other matchmade marriages, the bride and groom are awkward about touching each other in public. Yi Chongil escorts his bride, somewhat stiffly, up to the top step of the dais, where they stand just below the *churye*'s podium. Mrs. Bae and the pianist catch the hem of the bride's veil and give it an experienced toss so that it falls in a graceful cascade over the steps. The effect is calculated, since guests and photographers will have only this view of the couple for most of the ceremony.

"The bride and groom will now bow to each other." The *churye*, with a quick pantomime, directs the bride and groom to turn and face each other and bow slightly from the waist. In the old rite of matrimony, the bride and groom would, each in turn, sink to their knees and bend forward to greet each other with a full kow-tow. The exchange was asymmetrical since the bride was expected to sink to the ground at least once more than the groom.[4] In the wedding hall, the bow is a reciprocal salutation *(matchŏl)*, like the gentle dips and bobs one makes in greeting on Korean city streets. Even so, *Passage Rites Made Easy* suggests that "it looks better if the bride bows just a bit more deeply than the groom" (Ko 1982:109). At another wedding, the bride drew chuckles when she gave a deep and solemn perpendicular bow. "That's excessive," the wedding hall manager told me with a grin. The bride explained later that she had been so overwhelmed by wedding day emotions that she had not known what she was doing. Kim Eun-Shil reminds me that most brides remember their weddings only as a blurred emotional experience, and this will be the memory of my fictive sister Sukcha after her wedding in 1992.

When Pak Yŏnghŭi and Yi Chongil have turned again to face the *churye*, Mrs. Bae promptly arranges the bride's skirt and veil. Shortly thereafter, out of the corner of my eye, I catch sight of Mrs. Bae bolting out of the chamber bearing two parcels wrapped in red cloth. I surmise that these are the meats and wine that the bride will offer to her parents-

---

4. That the bride bows once more than the groom is a sore point in attempts to revive the old wedding, as we shall see in Chapter 3.

in-law in the final rite of the wedding, performed in a small separate chamber of the wedding hall.

"The bride and groom will now say their vows." In fact, the *churye* reads them; the bride and groom merely affirm with a slight nod the words enacted in the Family Ritual Code, and repeated in every Korean wedding hall. *"The groom, Mr. Yi Chongil, and the bride, Miss Pak Yŏng-hŭi, vow to love and honor each other always, whatever the circumstances, to revere their elders, and to fulfill all the duties of a faithful husband and wife."* Then the *churye* declares: *"Now in the presence of their two families and their friends who have come together in this place, the groom, Mr. Yi Chongil, and the bride, Miss Pak Yŏnghŭi, have solemnly sworn to share the joys and sorrows of a lifetime as husband and wife. As* churye, *I solemnly swear before you that this marriage has been satisfactorily accomplished"* (Ko 1982:110).

The spatial positioning of the master of ceremonies, commanding the wedding hall from behind a podium, suggests a Christian minister, as does his oratorical style. As primary officiant, the *churye* performs the critical work of the wedding ritual. In Austin's (1962) sense, he "does things with words," proclaims the couple into being a husband and a wife. But the *churye* who accomplishes the marriage is a thoroughly secular figure, a respected elder who is invited by the groom's side to preside at their son's wedding. In this, the new wedding follows solidly upon a tradition of Confucian family rites for which there is no designated clergy. Instead, knowledgeable and virtuous elders ensure that the procedures are carried out according to the teachings of the sages.

It reflects well on one to be asked to be a *churye*, the more so to be asked many times. Some *churye* begin their remarks with an announcement of the number of weddings they have performed, sometimes in three digits, and are rewarded with applause (Mark Peterson, personal communication).[5] The Rose's manager described the *churye* to me as "someone who has a reputation for virtue and whose family is flourishing. People think that if such a person blesses and congratulates the new bride and groom, the couple will also receive blessings." His view of the *churye* projects into the contemporary wedding hall the old Sino-Korean notion

---

5. In the 1960s, writers and educators were popular candidates for the role of *churye*. One novelist, reputed to have been the most popular *churye* in Korea, is said to have presided at more than a thousand weddings (*Korea Herald*, 4 September 1966).

that when those who assist the bride and groom at their wedding are "lucky" or "blessed" *(tabokhan saram)*, the new couple will share their good fortune.[6] One gentleman, many times a *churye*, claimed that people ask him to take this role because he is a "lucky person"; not only does he hold a prominent position, but he is also the proud father of three sons and only one daughter. He claims (without wishing to brag) that 90 percent of the couples he has served as *churye* have had firstborn sons. Another respected individual refuses numerous offers to serve as *churye*, feeling that his own disharmonious marriage renders him unfit for the role.

Ideally, the *churye* is the groom's teacher and mentor, an appropriate person to congratulate and advise the groom on his wedding day. A few of the *churye* at the weddings I attended were genuine mentors: the groom's teacher, office superior, or military commander. On interviewing several couples, however, I learned that the *churye* at a Righteous Town wedding is more often a distant acquaintance of the groom's father, frequently a local politician or administrator, and often a person totally unknown to the groom, as was Yi Chongil's *churye*.

In the 1980s, members of the bloated National Assembly were frequently invited to serve as *churye*, and distinguished *churye* were compensated for their trouble with expensive gifts such as tailored suits or lengths of good fabric. On a busy Saturday or Sunday afternoon in the peak wedding season, one encounters sartorially commendable *churye* bolting from one wedding hall to another. *Passage Rites Made Easy* decries the trend "to have a socially prominent individual as *churye*, even if he is not acquainted with the bride and groom."

> While there are those [*churye*] who can bring this off with dignity, many are merely pompous. . . . The *churye* must be the sort of elder who can conduct the wedding ceremony with skill and dignity and, in addition to this, he must sustain his concern for the couple even after their marriage and be able to offer them direct and indirect guidance. In choosing a *churye*, if one importunes an elder because he has some sort of social standing, even though one does not know him at all, not only is this

6. Accounts of wedding customs often mention that the man who carried the box of gifts *(ham)* from the groom's family to the bride's house should have enjoyed a harmonious marriage and been the father of a firstborn son, and in some communities, his house should have been free from fire. The woman chosen to accept the gift box was similarly lucky, above all the mother of a firstborn son (Ko 1982:104; MCIBCPP 1977 "Chŏnnam":130, 1977 "Kyŏngnam":144, 152, 1978 "Kyŏnggi":72; Lee Kwang-Kyu 1974:71, 1984:155).

Figure 3. The *churye* addresses the bride and groom. Photograph by Homer Williams.

counter to the true meaning of a *churye* but it also imposes upon the person who is asked to preside (Ko 1982:91).

This idealized vision of a mentoring *churye* is more easily attained in economically comfortable and socially prominent families whose own social networks include respected and well-spoken individuals and whose children, as budding professionals, have had genuine mentors at school or work. Rural and newly urbanized families tend, with great humility, to look beyond their immediate circles for a *churye*. Yi Chongil's *churye* is a compromise, an educational administrator known to his schoolteacher father.

"The churye will now give us his words." The *churye*'s speech *(churyesa, churyeŭi malssŭm)* is his most significant contribution to the wedding (see fig. 3). Mr. Sŏng begins his remarks true to type, by thanking the guests and introducing the bride and groom, personalizing his introduction insofar as he is able.

The wedding candles have been lit, and now I shall offer some words of congratulation to the bride and groom. But first let me sincerely congratulate the parents who bore and raised them and the relatives of the two families. On behalf of the bride and groom I would also like to thank all of you guests who have come to offer your support to the bride and groom, showing your concern for their future happiness. I am especially delighted to preside as *churye* at this wedding since I have always respected Mr. Yi Taewŏn, the father of the groom who is marrying the daughter of Mr. Pak Sangsu.

I beg your indulgence for what I am about to say, but I would appreciate it if you would refrain from idle talk during the ceremony. [The chatter in the wedding hall subsides for a moment, then swells to full volume.]

I understand that since his graduation from high school, the groom has been an employee of the H—— Food Company, and is a youth with bright prospects. The bride also held a job after graduation and I know that she is an accomplished scholar in those arts that make a wise mother and a good wife [*hyŏnmo yangch'ŏ*].

In the *churye*'s portrayal, the bride and groom come to their wedding as children of their respective families, most explicitly of their fathers. Consistent with the ideals and expectations of the Korean middle class, the groom has bright career prospects, balanced by the bride's excellent potential as a domestic helpmate. Pak Yŏnghŭi's own brief career as a wage earner merits only passing mention since, like most brides, she has left her job. The *churye* inscribes her as a wife, but a few months ago, she was a nurse's aid. The *churye*'s remarks also affirm the bonds of kinship and friendship that have brought the guests to the wedding hall. Finally, he musters the authority of his position (in an ultimately futile effort) to curtail the otherwise ceaseless chatter in the wedding hall. Having set the proper tone, he offers the couple his capsule philosophy on how to attain a happy and successful married life. Mr. Sŏng probably recycles this section of his speech each time he serves as a *churye*. Like many *churye*, he organizes his remarks around three main points.

First, I believe that love is the most important element in the relationship between husband and wife. Without love, a man and a woman cannot be considered husband and wife. . . . A bride and groom have as their one responsibility to work in harmony for the development of the family, to foster individual growth, and to serve the nation and society. Without love they could never become an exemplary household that serves the nation, nor could they develop as individuals.

Let me say a little something about how one loves. First the bride and groom must respect each other's character. The husband should esteem and love his wife, and he should take care of her. The wife should regard her husband as a wise ruler [*hyŏn'gun*] and always render wifely assistance as an accommodating wise mother and good wife. It is the husband's responsibility to lead and guide the family while the wife follows her husband's guidance in managing the house frugally so that when the husband goes about in the world he can set his mind at ease. These days it has become common for husbands and wives to joke and banter with each other. In the past, a husband and wife would always address each other with formal speech, that was our nation's ancient custom. Nowadays, one seldom hears terms of respect between husband and wife. Instead, they greet each other as friends. In my opinion, this is wrong. Feelings of esteem, endearment, and respect emerge when you use respectful formal language. . . . When the husband comes home from work, the wife should greet him in a womanly way, acknowledging with a tender smile that he has been working hard all day, and the husband should affectionately acknowledge all of the household cares of her day. . . . Love is something that is given and something that is received.

Eun-Shil, a feminist, lets this and other *churye* texts wash over her without a grimace. She feels that the cliché-ridden speeches we have heard together are a consequence of location, appealing to the farmers, shopkeepers, and emerging professionals of Righteous Town. She wants me to appreciate that more erudite Seoul *churye* offer more elevating remarks, and indeed, I will subsequently savor some of the wit of distinguished Seoul *churye*. Nevertheless, *churye* texts from the budget wedding halls in Righteous Town offer a popular commentary on matrimonial precepts and expectations. The text of this *churye*, a professional educator, is one among many which reconfigure Confucian ideology as a conservative social philosophy for contemporary life. The old notion of the virtuous wife as the moral equivalent of the loyal subject is meshed seamlessly to an urban white-collar vision of a weary breadwinner returning to a happy homemaker. The harmonious family is portrayed in Confucian terms as the moral cornerstone of the good society, but the "wise mother, good wife" *(hyŏnmo yangch'ŏ)* who presides within is the product of "enlightened" efforts to educate women to the benefit of the modern nation-state.[7]

In the remainder of his *churye* text, Mr. Sŏng offers practical advice for living, remarks that seem intended primarily for the groom. Mr. Sŏng's pragmatic assessment of "today's society" is fused with older notions of

7. The phrase "wise mother, good wife" *(hyŏnmo yangch'ŏ)*, invoked twice in the *churye's* speech, probably entered early-twentieth-century Korea via Japan, where it was coined as an intentional substitution for the older aphorism "Man is respected and woman abased." A radical notion in its day, the enlightened wife and mother was seen as benefitting the process of national development (Sievers 1981). Cho Haejoang equates the currency of this slogan in 1920s Korea with the desires of men who wished, by acquiring educated wives, to shore up their status as members of an emerging professional elite (Cho 1988:227).

right conduct; Mr. Sŏng's Horatio Alger is also a Confucian gentleman who practices virtue and knows propriety.

The second thing I would tell you is to chart your life's course carefully. The couple standing before me has the potential for boundless growth and development, but if you do not carefully construct a life plan, you will not match the success of other people and have a happy home. Set goals for yourself, be ambitious, and make a great lifelong effort. . . . Guard against doing the many things that you will later regret. Be self-reliant, don't depend upon others. Be mindful of time, don't waste a minute in the pursuit of your goals. . . . Today's society is an economic society. Whoever exerts the most effort, whoever makes the most effective use of his time will succeed. . . .

The last thing I would like to mention is the importance of guarding your health. . . . Today, with so much environmental pollution, it is easy to injure your health, the health that was bestowed upon you through the goodness of your parents who raised you. . . . Maintain harmonious family relations . . . be frugal and accumulate wisely. Next, be mindful of human relations. Only when you strive to distinguish yourself do others recognize you: "That young man knows propriety, he is responsible in the tasks he undertakes as well as diligent and hardworking. He is an outstanding human being." Through praise such as this, one succeeds in society.

There is something more I would like to say—the bride and groom seem to be perspiring, so I will conclude these remarks. . . . [It is a hot day. One of his friends has already appeared on the dais to mop the groom's brow with a pocket handkerchief.] If you can, through your affection for each other, make a joyous and happy home, then I think you will have fulfilled this *churye*'s instructions.

Pak Yŏnghŭi, in agreement with some other brides and many men who have served as *churye*, will later describe the *churye*'s speech as the most significant element of the wedding: "He gives you direction in your unknown life ahead. Even if we can't live up to his teachings, we should at least try to live according to his model." Yi Chongil will be less enthusiastic: "The *churye*'s remarks are too formal. The real question is, 'How are the bride and groom going to live the life that's ahead of them?' "

Others are far less tolerant of long-winded speeches by self-important *churye*. Yongsu's Mother's estimation of *churye* was fresh in my mind as I sat through Mr. Sŏng's oration:

Oh the *churye*! The *churye* talk too long. When they just make some brief remarks, that's fine, but when they go on and on, it gives me a headache. Do they really think that people will remember what they say? . . . All a *churye* does is tell the couple to treat their parents well; he tells the bride to be considerate of the groom and the groom to be considerate of the bride. What is there to being a *churye?* Even you could be a *churye.* Nowadays there are women in the National Assembly. Why can't a woman be a *churye?*

A few years later, I will be privy to a heated discussion between two academics, a man and a woman, concerning their female colleague who has actually presided as a wedding *churye.* The woman will argue that the female *churye* was eminently worthy and acquitted herself well. The man will hold that this breach of propriety could have a deleterious effect upon the marriage, that weddings are too serious a matter to toy with in the name of making a feminist statement. His implication that a female *churye* constitutes a serious violation of cosmic order will be countered by the pretended innocence of my question, "Were there *churye* in by-gone days?"

Back in 1983, after the conventional speech by a conventional *churye,* two young women rise and sing a congratulatory song for Pak Yŏnghŭi and Yi Chongil. Kim Eun-Shil will learn that the singers are friends of the bride's younger sister, and I will recognise one of them, weeks later, as my dry cleaner's daughter. Most Righteous Town weddings do not include a special vocal or instrumental piece, although the practice is common at middle-class weddings in Seoul. The congratulatory song, like the bride's particularly fancy and therefore slightly more expensive lace hat, put this wedding of an aspiring white-collar couple at the high end of possible celebrations in the Rose Wedding Hall.

> *"The bride and groom will now give you their greetings."* [The *churye* instructs the couple to turn and face the guests, bow, and then proceed down the aisle.] In the past they would have sought you out at home and greeted you. We ask that you indulge them in receiving their greeting here in the wedding hall. I will be most grateful if you applaud them in a gesture of encouragement for the road ahead.

To applause and recessional music, the bride and groom descend from the dais and march down the aisle. The moderator announces that *"The wedding ceremony of Yi Chongil and Pak Yŏnghŭi is now complete."* When the couple has marched two-thirds of the way down the aisle, they are stopped by the pianist, who has dashed from her seat to turn them around and send them back to the front of the hall for photographs. She lifts the bride's veil off the floor and loops it around her own arm. With practiced steps, she kicks the long rainbow satin aisle runner into a bundle of folded cloth as she follows the couple back up the aisle. Mrs. Bae, ever brisk, has already removed the two plaques bearing the names of the bride and groom from the sides of the dais and slapped them together as a foreground for the photographs. The operation proceeds with clockwork precision; on a busy afternoon, another wedding party would already be claiming access to the hall, another bride in the waiting room, another crowd of guests swarming through the foyer to congratulate another pacing groom.

As the guests begin to mill about the hall, some to depart, the *sahoe* announces the locations of the two Chinese restaurants where, in separate parties, the guests of the bride's family and the groom's family will all be treated to noodles and drink, supplemented with rice cakes and side dishes carried in from home. In 1983, such feasts are one of the "vulgar ostentations" banned by the Family Ritual Code. This prohibition is commonly ignored in Righteous Town, where giving the guests a bowl of noodles in gratitude for their presence and cash contribution is considered an essential courtesy.[8] By 1985, the ban on wedding feasts will have been rescinded; and by the end of the decade, in an atmosphere of liberalism and prosperity, the Family Ritual Code will have been suspended.

The wedding hall photographer rolls in his equipment and begins to take the four formal portraits that are a part of the standard wedding hall package. Mrs. Bae and the pianist arrange the bride and groom one step below the *churye* on the dais. Again, the bride's veil is carefully arranged. For the next shot, the bride and groom are posed as a couple, the image most likely to be installed in a decorative frame in their innermost room (*anbang*). Now, calling through a bullhorn over the din of the departing crowd, the manager invites, then urges the members of both families to come to the front of the hall for a group portrait. He and the attendants sort relatives of all ages, including a number of lively children, into a suitably symmetrical assembly around the bride and groom.

Next, the manager calls for friends of the bride and groom to take their places around the couple, but now something unprecedented happens. A significant cluster of young women remains seated. "Friends of the bride, please come up here. Friends of the bride, we beseech you to get on up

---

8. In the early 1970s in Seoul, when I made my first acquaintance with Korean weddings, economies of time had replaced the feast with "gratitude gifts" *(tamnye p'um)*, wrapped packages of rice cake, towels, or plastic containers. These, too, were banned by the Family Ritual Code. When the code was rescinded in the late 1980s, both the giving of gratitude gifts and the hosting of wedding buffets were in full swing in the capital city. Even in 1983, a display of boxed rice cakes in a bakery window blatantly advertised this merchandise as "gratitude gifts," an indication that the practice, while still illegal, was creeping back into the wedding halls of the capital city.

here." They refuse to budge. The moderator approaches the seated women and attempts to coax them to the front of the hall. A young man with a camera adds his plea. The bride's friends are making a show of determination, informing the groom's friends that they will hold out for a generous fee when they "sell" them the bride's bouquet later that afternoon. One of the groom's friends, already posed for the photograph, calls to them, "If you don't come up, we won't give you more than 3,000 or 4,0000 *wŏn* [$2 or $3 U.S.] for the flowers." This moves them.

Once the women are in place for the portrait, the friend with the camera bolts from formation, takes his shot, and resumes position before the wedding hall photographer can click his shutter. Pak Yŏnghǔi now poses for a formal portrait with a few close friends and again with the two women who sang the congratulatory song. These portraits are "extras" not included in the basic wedding hall fee. Friends take advantage of the setup and click their cameras.

Mrs. Bae swoops in and steers the bride away in the direction of the dressing room. A knot of friends follows behind, bearing the large suitcase that holds the Korean dress Pak Yŏnghǔi will wear in the *p'yebaek* ceremony and her clothes for her honeymoon. Eun-Shil and I join the throng and follow the bride into the dressing room. The ever-efficient Mrs. Bae removes the long white wedding gown and veil. Over full pantaloons and a long slip, Pak Yŏnghǔi puts on a Korean bride's red skirt and yellow jacket, a gift from the groom's family. Mrs. Bae expertly ties the tapes and bows that make this costume hang just right, then helps the bride into a gauzy chartreuse jacket encrusted with shimmering gilt paint decoration and cut with wide, rainbow-striped sleeves. Long white sleeves, elasticized at the wrist, fall over the bride's hands and down almost to the floor. Mrs. Bae adds a little beaded crown, centered just above the bride's forehead, and places a large brass dragon-headed pin through her heavily lacquered hair. Pak Yŏnghǔi, minutes ago the beaming bride in white lace, now stands in the costume that princesses wore in the palace and ordinary women, if they were fortunate, wore for the old Confucian rite of matrimony *(hollye)*.

In the *p'yebaek* chamber, Yi Chongil is undergoing a similar but not so thorough transformation. Mother and aunt help him into an approximation of the royal blue robe worn by officials in dynastic times, the classic groom's costume. A scholar-official's black hat, with its horizontal ears, sits upon his head. Yi Chongil's dress shirt and tie are visible through the yoke of his robe. Like most grooms at Righteous Town weddings, he has not changed into Korean dress before donning his costume, although his bride is thoroughly layered in Korean clothing, down to her intimate apparel. Now, as on subsequent formal occasions, the married woman in Korean clothing *(hanbok)* will be an icon of national tradition, counterposed to her husband in a Western dress suit and tie *(yangbok)*.[9]

The *p'yebaek* is the most conservative segment of Pak Yŏnghŭi and Yi Chongil's wedding, the final and only surviving rite of the old Confucian wedding ceremony, the Rite of the Father-in-law and Mother-in-law *(kugorye, kyŏn'gurye)*.[10] The bride pays obeisance to the parents and relations of her husband's home by greeting them with a full kow-tow, then offering them wine and meat. In the mid-1980s, the government-sponsored Institute for Women and Development would recommend the inclusion of the bride's parents and close kin as recipients of *p'yebaek* bows, a thorough subversion of the patrilocal logic of a rite originally intended to mark the bride's incorporation into her husband's kin group. By the early 1990s, bride's kin were appearing in some *p'yebaek* in Seoul but not, so far as I could determine, in Righteous Town. Ŏmŏni scoffed at this practice when I described it during a discussion of plans for the wedding of her fourth daughter, Sukcha, in 1992.[11]

Unlike the public wedding, the *p'yebaek* is an intimate family ritual held among the groom's kin. The *p'yebaek* chamber, decorated with a simple folding screen, replicates intimate household space, and as on entering a Korean home, participants remove their shoes before stepping up into the chamber. The wedding hall charges a small fee for the use of the costumes and *p'yebaek* chamber, and some families hold their *p'yebaek* at home. Wedding halls began to offer special rooms for the *p'yebaek* only in the 1970s, accommodating families who found this arrangement more convenient than gathering scattered relations together again at home when the couple returned from their honeymoon (Choi Chungmoo, per-

---

9. Some grooms do receive Korean dress as part of the gift of clothing bestowed by the bride and her family, but in Righteous Town weddings, this was a low-priority, high-status addition, in contrast to the essential gift of a two-piece suit, shirt, and tie. Men who own Korean clothes usually wear them for the Mid-Autumn Festival *(ch'usŏk)* and for the lunar New Year celebration, major holidays with strong traditionalist associations.

10. The term *p'yebaek* itself does not appear in any of the ritual handbooks (Martina Deuchler, personal communication; Pak Hyein 1991).

11. Ŏmŏni was, however, looking forward to joining the mother of the groom in lighting the candles in the wedding hall at the start of the ceremony, an innovative bilateral acknowledgement of maternal ties that had not yet reached the Righteous Town wedding halls in 1983 and 1985.

sonal communication). The use of traditional costumes, with additional photographic opportunities, was probably also a draw.

The *p'yebaek* at this wedding begins with another professional photograph, this one of the couple kneeling behind a low tray on which the *p'yebaek* meat, dates, and chestnuts have been arranged, an image frequently replicated on wedding hall posters. The posed portrait in the *p'yebaek* chamber is yet another extra, and I note that the *p'yebaek* meat is beef, artistically decorated with strips of egg and red pepper, not the nearly ubiquitous and less expensive chicken. By the time of Sukcha's wedding, nearly a decade later, wedding halls will routinely cater *p'yebaek* meats in three grades of cost and elaboration.[12]

Mrs. Bae brusquely directs one of Pak Yŏnghŭi's friends to go back to the dressing room for a crucial bundle, containing the wine, that they have inadvertently left behind. The woman rushes off. Mrs. Bae shouts, "The two friends who want to help the bride bow, come up here now." The friends replace the maidservants who once accompanied well-born brides to their in-laws' home and helped them through the rite, the grooms' kinswomen in staid contemporary weddings, or wedding hall attendants in the absence of any of these. *Passage Rites Made Easy* suggests that when her own close kinswomen or friends assist the bride, it sets her mind at ease (Ko 1982:135). The desire to gracefully accomplish the great kow-tow (*k'ŭnjŏl*) in front of one's new parents-in-law can induce anxiety in young women not accustomed to floor-level etiquette in Korean dress. Both *Passage Rites Made Easy* and *Treatise on Propriety* (*Yeron*), an etiquette book for young women, include detailed diagrams to instruct brides in performing the great kow-tow (Cho et al. 1983:55; Ko 1982:137).

Mrs. Bae tells the parents to kneel behind the tray of *p'yebaek* food to receive the couple's greeting, then directs the bride and groom to bow twice and sit.[13] For this and subsequent bows, Pak Yŏnghŭi raises her covered hands to her face and, supported by a female attendant at each elbow, sinks to the floor in a slow genuflection, then bends forward at the

12. Already in 1983, chicken restaurants advertise that they cater fowl for the *p'yebaek*.

13. In a very few wedding hall *p'yebaek*, cups of wine are first poured for the ancestors, and the couple bows to pay their respects to the dead *(sadang chŏl)* before greeting the living. This, too, was a crucial segment of the old Rite of Matrimony, but I saw it performed only twice in a public wedding hall. While this procedure is consistent with propriety, insofar as the ancestors are acknowledged in advance of anyone else, it does symbolic violence to the rite of ancestor veneration by removing the ancestors from the home, as in a shaman ceremony held in a public shrine.

torso and lowers her head, long sleeves spread on the floor in front of her. She pauses, then rocks back onto her feet, rises, and bows from the waist. Yi Chongil, unassisted, bows in unison with his bride. The groom's bow is a recent innovation, and some grooms seem genuinely surprised when told that they are expected to bow in the *p'yebaek. Passage Rites Made Easy* advocates the joint bow: "In the old way of doing things, the groom stood and only the bride bowed, but it is best if he bows with the bride insofar as he is seeing his parents for the first time since his marriage" (Ko 1982: 135).

The Rose's manager described this joint bow as the couple's first salutation as man and wife to the groom's parents, and a kinsman at another wedding goaded a reluctant groom to bow and "report to the elders that today you have taken a wife and put up your hair" (become an adult). These justifications betray a subtle shift in the symbolic intention of the old rite, from the acceptance of the bride into her husband's family and household to the celebration of a new and almost invariably neolocal couple like Pak Yŏnghŭi and Yi Chongil.[14] The couple's activities after the ceremony also celebrate their conjugal bond. The bride of yesteryear would spend her first three days sequestered in the nuptial chamber in her in-laws' house, a period of initiatory liminality paralleled in the sequestering of a newborn Korean child. Contemporary Korean newlyweds go off by themselves in the most romantic of all innovative wedding customs, the honeymoon. Pak Yŏnghŭi and Yi Chongil will spend five days at Sorak Mountain.

The bows completed, Mrs. Bae fills tiny cups of wine, passes them briefly in the direction of the bride and groom, then offers them to Yi Chongil's mother and father on behalf of the bride. Yi Chongil is confused by the procedure and asks, when the cup first comes his way, "Shall I touch it?" Mrs. Bae gives him a swift negative nod. The groom's father empties his cup with an exclamation, "That's good!" "Aw, Dad!" one of his daughters is heard to titter.

Yi Chongil's mother takes great handfuls of dates and chestnuts and casts these fertility symbols at Pak Yŏnghŭi's long white sleeves, spread

---

14. Between 1966 and 1980, years spanning Korea's industrial transformation, stem households declined from 23.31 percent to 16.46 percent of all Korean households. The most precipitous decline was in the already small number of households where couples co-reside with two living parents, from 6.66 to 1.85 percent of all households (Census of Korea 1966, 1980). These figures seem to indicate that co-residence is most likely with a widowed parent in a later phase of the domestic cycle.

Figure 4.   The *p'yebaek*. Fertility fruit and nuts dot the bride's white sleeve. The groom's dress shirt and tie are visible under his robe. Photograph by Homer Williams.

out on the floor in front of her (see fig. 4). "Not so many, Mother!" shouts the groom. "I'm greedy; I want a lot of grandchildren," she chuckles as she makes her toss. Her tasks completed, Yi Chongil's mother sets an envelope of kow-tow money *(chŏlgap)* on the tray, then scans the crowd and asks, "Where's Auntie gone?" Someone suggests that the groom's paternal aunt has already gone on to the restaurant, but she emerges from the crowd in the doorway and takes her place behind the tray to receive bows and wine and to cast dates and nuts at the bride. She leaves a 5,000 *wŏn* bill (less than $7 U.S.) on the tray for the bride without having placed it discreetly in an envelope. "Why so much?" the groom's mother asks with just a touch of gentle sarcasm. Mrs. Bae, masking impatience with levity, urges other relatives in by saying, "Come on, the groom seems to want kow-tow money."

Maternal aunt is next. She makes a show of refusing the cup of wine but drinks it in the end, intruding an etiquette of womanish demurral into the *p'yebaek* where it merely causes delay. She sees me juggling my camera and calls out, "Take a pretty picture, American Auntie!"

In the end, Pak Yŏnghŭi receives more than 60,000 *wŏn* (more than $80 U.S.) from the combined contributions of her parents-in-law, the groom's paternal aunt, his maternal aunt, and his father's brother's wife. Pak Yŏnghŭi will claim that she contributed all of her kow-tow money to the cost of her honeymoon and the gifts the couple gave both families when they returned, but discrepancies in the prices the couple quote will suggest that Pak Yŏnghŭi may have set something aside as personal savings.[15]

The giving of kow-tow money is another new custom; women of Pak Yŏnghŭi's mother's generation did not receive it when they performed the *p'yebaek* bows.[16] Intended to cover honeymoon expenses, the kow-

15. For a discussion of Korean kow-tow money in contrast to a similar-seeming Chinese practice, see Kendall (1985b) in contrast to Cohen (1976:149–191).

16. Normative accounts of traditional Korean weddings do not mention kow-tow money (Ko 1982:123–125; Lee Kwang-Kyu 1974), and while two localized accounts of traditional weddings recorded in the 1970s describe gifts of cash or measures of rice, they do not indicate the historical depth of these practices (MCIBCPP 1977 "Chŏnnam":133; 1977 "Kyŏngnam":156). In the elite weddings of another age, the maidservants who accompanied the bride to her in-laws' house and assisted in the *p'yebaek* might receive small cash tips set on a waiting tray (Lay 1913:9; MCIBCPP 1977 "Kyŏnggi":76). In the past, a mother-in-law might signify her satisfaction with the bride by bestowing clothing and jewelry, usually a pair of heavy silver rings and a silver pin to bind up the married woman's hair, but the *p'yebaek* was not necessarily the occasion of gifting (Chai 1962:95; Lay 1913:9; Scranton 1898:296).

tow money is further affirmation of the conjugal bond. Kow-tow money, *chŏlgap*, is literally "the cost of the bow," not *sulgap*, the cost of the (bride's) wine. It rewards the bride's show of etiquette, just as children are rewarded with kow-tow money and good wishes when they bow to their elders on New Year's Day, and so softens the bride's act of humility in prostrating herself before her new in-laws. It is also a tacit acknowledgement, in giving the bride a little something to spend, that she has purchased to the limit of her resources in preparation for her wedding (Kendall 1985b) and that she will manage household money in her new life.

For some, this intrusion of cash into a demonstration of propriety is evidence of the increasing commodification of social life. "Today, they only do it for the money," notes a cynical Yongsu's Mother, smarting over the memory of the excruciating number of unremunerated bows she performed as a bride. And indeed, when I offered sympathy to a 1980s bride who had performed the great kow-tow to a vast number of husband's kin, she chuckled and said, "On the contrary, I received a lot of envelopes."

Back in the *p'yebaek* room, the friends gather Pak Yŏnghŭi's envelopes into her now bulging handbag and struggle to shut the clasp. Mrs. Bae provides a plastic bag for all the dates and chestnuts that the relatives have cast at Pak Yŏnghŭi's sleeves, and these are stowed in her suitcase to be consumed by the couple on their honeymoon in a wish for fertility and general auspiciousness. The friends bundle Pak Yŏnghŭi back to the dressing room, exchanging final information about the time and place of their meeting with the groom's friends to barter over the bride's bouquet. We confirm once again that yes, we are welcome to join them in the bakery and observe the bargaining. Someone invites us to the wedding lunch, but this we politely refuse, having arrived at the Rose today fresh from another wedding feast. The crowd drifts away, and with the crowd, Eun-Shil and I go out again into the bright July afternoon.

CONCLUSION:
A PARTICULAR WEDDING AND A CERTAIN KIND OF RITUAL

The wedding of Pak Yŏnghŭi and Yi Chongil, like all "new-style wedding ceremonies" (*sinsik kyŏrhonsik*), unfolds against a recognized master script for wedding rituals as packaged and marketed by the Rose and other commercial wedding halls. Although the wedding hall is its most popular venue, the new-style wedding can also be seen in churches and chapels and less often in free public space such as village meeting halls, a practice the government encourages for the sake of thrift. It would have been both logical and intellectually defensible to present the new wedding as its master script. Even the individually authored *churye*'s speech has a formulaic quality, readily susceptible to parody as when one of my assistants recorded in her notes for a wedding in 1985, "Less than ten people listened attentively to the *churye*'s speech, which took only twelve minutes from 'Thank you for having come here when you are so busy' to 'I am asking you as a personal favor to please guide and encourage this couple in future days.' "

The weddings I attended were a tepid contrast to the shaman rituals (*kut*) I had studied in my first fieldwork. Each *kut* had its own cast of living participants and particularly potent spirits who, while honoring a prescribed general sequence of appearances, stereotypical portrayals, and routine theatrical business, improvised among themselves an appropriate script to address the crisis of the moment (Kendall 1977, 1985a:Ch. 1). Possession rituals, like the Korean shaman's *kut*, are profitably studied as emergent phenomena rather than as fixed structures. As enacted realizations of personal and collective knowledge, they draw their legitimacy and power from the intimacy and immediacy of the ritual transaction.[17]

By contrast, the Korean wedding ceremony draws its legitimacy and power from the *replication* of textually ordained gestures and movement. Like the old rite of matrimony (*hollye*) that it replaced, and other Korean family rites (*karye*)—funerals, ancestor veneration, and celebrations of the sixty-first and seventy-first birthdays[18]—the wedding ceremony

17. Some works which capture this emergent quality in ethnographic writing about ritual include Atkinson (1989), Boddy (1989), Brown (1991), Choi (1989), Kapferer (1983), Laderman (1991), Schieffelin (1976), Tambiah (1977, 1979), and Vitebsky (1993).

18. The original "four rites" *(sarye)* were initiation (or "capping"), weddings, funerals, and ancestor veneration. Initiation, the putting up of the hair and assuming adult status, was usually performed as a preliminary to the wedding; the phrase "put up your hair and become an adult" is instantly recognized as a reference to weddings. The possibility of strictly hewing to the ritual manual and holding an initiation well in advance of and distinct from the wedding did exist; Landis (1898) described these rites but did not indicate whether he was recording actual observations or a reading of ritual texts. Traditionalists have attempted to "revive" the initiation; a government-sponsored association for the promotion of traditional culture offers candidates a preparatory course intended to imbue today's youth with Korean etiquette and mores (*Seoul Monthly Magazine*, June 1989). Celebrations of the sixty-first and seventy-first birthdays *(hwan'gap, hoegap)* were not included in the original four rites, but are widely recognized today as "family rites" in the family ritual code, household etiquette manuals, and popular discourse.

abides in an esteemed domain of cultural practice associated with written texts and learned transmission. In commonsense perceptions, and as portrayed in etiquette books, a Korean wedding is a fixed and formulaic process of recognizable steps from courtship, through the exchange of gifts, to the realization of a wedding ceremony. The descriptions of sequence and structure that characterized an older anthropology are thoroughly compatible with Confucian notions of ritual; indeed, the Confucian fit may be why many anthropologists of East Asia found structuralist interpretations to be particularly compelling long after they had been discarded by mainstream anthropology.

But if one acknowledges and then politely sets aside the bare bones of procedure, considers instead the changing content of the *p'yebaek* ritual, the government's injunctions to thrift, the very creation within living memory of a "new-style wedding," then Korean weddings, whatever their pedigree, may be regarded as objects of cultural production transacted upon shifting ground (Williams 1977:37). Some of these shifts and transactions are revealed in the following chapters. The *churye*'s remarks, the argument about the female *churye*, and the women's sit-down protest to demand their share of the men's reward suggest that weddings not only say things about gender; they are sites where notions of gender are both affirmed and contested.

3

A Rite of Modernization
and Its Postmodern Discontents

Selections from a Clipping File

OLD STYLE WEDDING OUT OF STYLE:
KOREA HOUSE SHOWS WHAT IT WAS LIKE

Wedding ceremonies in the traditional Korean style are as hard to
observe in today's cities as to find a knot-haired gentleman in his
horsehair hat on a Seoul street.

Korean Republic magazine, July 1962

TRADITIONAL WEDDING CEREMONY CONVENED BY RIGID RULES:
OLD STYLE FAST DISAPPEARING

Korea Herald, 11 February 1968

TRADITIONAL WEDDING ENACTED FOR TOURISTS

Korea Times, 3 June 1973

The various peoples of today's world conduct their wedding
rites in accord with their ancient customs and this is a way of
maintaining their national pride. Even though we also have a
traditional wedding ceremony replete with the spirit of our
ancestors, we shun it, calling it "old style" [*kusik*]. This decay
of national pride and tradition can only be considered a cause
for distress.

Our Traditional Wedding Rite, Ministry of the Interior, 1986

TRADITIONAL WEDDINGS ON THE RISE: YOUNG PEOPLE
HAVE NO STOMACH FOR QUICK, IMPERSONAL CEREMONIES

Tonga Ilbo, 4 May 1987

OLD WEDDING/NEW WEDDING

A style of wedding rite regarded in the 1960s and 1970s as "old style"
(*kusik*) and disappearing, a curiosity performed for tourists, was revived
in the 1980s as "our traditional wedding" (*uriŭi chŏnt'ong hollye*). The

"new style" (*sinsik*) of the 1960s and 1970s, then perceived as a mark of progress and enlightenment, is now sometimes denigrated as "the Western-style wedding" (*sŏgusik hollye*). The oppositions "old style"/"new style" and "Western"/"our tradition" reflect two distinct moments in recent Korean history. The former clothed social and economic aspirations in Western dress. The latter celebrates a uniquely Korean triumph of the will as measured by the gross national product of a newly industrialized country and acknowledged internationally in the choice of Seoul as the site of the 1988 Olympics. But Korean weddings provide more than a lens refracting the times or a measure of shifts in the popular mood (cf. Hobsbawm and Ranger 1983:12). In the eyes of the state and in popular opinion, such rituals are, in and of themselves, vehicles of morality and of personal and national identity.

This chapter explores the links among ritual, morality, national identity, and bureaucratic jurisdiction through an examination of the form and content of the two styles of wedding: the old rite whose demise I lamented during my first encounter with Korea and the new-style wedding enacted throughout the peninsula in places like the Rose Wedding Hall. Here, and in subsequent chapters, we must cast one eye backward while fixing the other on a shifting horizon for an appreciation of how the past has been selectively interpreted, and reinterpreted, to explain a present and give shape to a vision of the future.

The cartoon rendering of the old and new wedding (see fig. 5) illustrates an iconographic contrast of styles that most Koreans would immediately recognize. The panel on the left illustrates the older ritual. The groom wears the costume of an antique civil official; the bride wears the crown and embroidered jacket of a palace lady, her face painted white and decorated with *yŏnji konji*, auspicious red dots on her cheeks and forehead. The couple is positioned on either side of a ceremonial tray, about to exchange formal bows. The panel on the right recalls the wedding of Pak Yŏnghŭi and Yi Chongil. Korean ceremonial dress is replaced with "Western clothes" (*yangbok*), the groom's dark dress suit and the bride's white lace dress and veil. The couple stands before the master of ceremonies (*churye*), who addresses them from behind a pulpitlike podium in a tableau that resembles a wedding ceremony in a Christian church.

The Korean viewer assumes the larger settings for these two rituals. As a "family rite," the traditional wedding was performed on the broad courtyard (*madang*) of a Korean country home, a space used for threshing grain and drying foodstuffs but transformed on ritual occasions to accommodate a village community of celebrants. Some champions of cultural

Figure 5. Cartoonist's view of "old style" and "new style" from *Han Sŏkpong Ch'ŏnja Mun Manhwa Haksŭp Kyobon* (A cartoon textbook for the Han Sŏkpong thousand character classic, Hwang Inhwan, illus., Seoul: Samil Ch'ulp'ansa, 1981).

revival celebrate the broad, flat *madang* as "democratic space" where celebrants frolic as equals, literally all on the same level. The new wedding, on the other hand, is performed in nontraditional public space: a Christian church, public hall, or most often the minimalist multistoried block of a commercial wedding hall like the Rose, where the bride marches down the aisle, on her father's arm, to Mendelssohn's "The Wedding March." An image whose associations are old, rural, intimate, and Korean is thus replaced by an image whose associations are contemporary, commercial, urban, and to Korean eyes, "Western."

The written words in both cartoon panels reveal a further contrast in the substance of the two weddings. In the top left bar, "wedding ceremony" (*kyŏrhonsik*) is written in Chinese characters and glossed in Korean script, now used almost exclusively. Sino-Korean expressions of congratulation, with Korean alphabetic glosses, appear with the traditional image. Signboards in Korean script identify the new-style bride and groom.[1] The new wedding is vernacular, filled with the spoken language of modern Korea in the moderator's announcements of procedures and in the *churye*'s proclamations and homilies. The ritual language of

1. The cartoon comes from a comic book designed to familiarize children with the Chinese characters contained in the first textbook of a classic education, a traditionalist project.

the old wedding was classical Chinese, the language of scholarship in dynastic times; or rather, the language of the old wedding was a language of gestures and procedures performed according to the classical Chinese text of a ritual manual declaimed (with Korean pronunciation) by a knowledgeable elder as officiant (*chimnae, chipsa*). The groom pledged his fidelity by presenting a wooden goose at the home of the bride (*chŏnallye*); the couple greeted each other with formal bows (*kyobaerye*) and marked their oath of union with an exchange of cups of wine (*hapkullye*).[2] In the classic weddings of cultural memory as embodied in more recent cultural performance, the groom arrived on horseback, heralded by musicians, and the bride departed for her new home in a sedan chair.[3]

In a series of interviews with newlyweds, their families, and members of the wedding hall profession, I asked why the old ritual had been discarded in favor of the wedding hall. Again and again I was told that marriage customs had "developed" (*paltal*) with everything else since the 1960s, or that Korea is now an "enlightened culture" (*munmyŏng munhwa*) as a consequence of the last century of its history. Criticisms of the old rite usually characterize it as long, complicated, and difficult to follow because the procedures are declaimed in arcane Sino-Korean. A ceremony in the wedding hall is "better suited to modern life." "The whole society has been Westernized and marriage just follows other changes in social life." The customs changed "naturally"; "it's the way the world turns"; "this is what present-day society is like."

This vague but abiding sense of inevitability is linked to a more explicit practicality embedded in the notion that new weddings are "simpler." "You just knock it off quickly in a wedding hall," to borrow the energetic Mrs. Bae's turn of phrase. The wedding hall provides all the necessary services, from the bride's gown and flowers to appropriate piano music. Even the white dress and veil can be vested with the virtue of simplicity. A wedding hall proprietor, with just a dash of earthiness, remarked on the dress's superiority over the complications of antique ritual garb, "All the bride needs is the wedding dress and her panties."

Because the old wedding rite assumed a traditional Korean home as its

2. Today, etiquette books and household encyclopedias routinely include the rites of matrimony as important cultural information that precedes the advice, cautions, and etiquette associated with present-day marriage.

3. An early missionary observed how the bride might travel "on the back of a sturdier ox, should she be a country bride" (Jones 1896:49).

setting, the more cramped conditions of urban housing are often cited as one reason why city people hold their weddings in commercial halls. The relocation of even rural people's weddings to town and city wedding halls reflects a declining rural community—a consequence, in part, of how country children now live and marry. Wherever possible, they leave the countryside and find their spouses in the towns where they work or study. A fiancé met in the town may even hail from another province. Their weddings bring together diverse, sometimes distant communities of kin and friends for whom a town wedding hall is more readily accessible than any rural village. Public transportation is more frequent, the condition of the roads more reliable, and even casual passersby can quickly point out the location of the wedding hall as a distinctive feature of the local land-scape. Recollections of long and complicated journeys to the bride's village in days gone by occasioned some grumbling.

While romantics (like my younger self) mourn the lost conviviality of a country wedding, rural women with still-vivid recollections of hosting one recall the onerous task of feeding all the guests. A wedding meant a feast—sometimes days of feasting—for a steady stream of well-wishers, first in the home of the bride and then in the home of the groom: "Old-style weddings were a bother; you had to feed everyone who came by"; "guests arrive all day, nonstop." A single representative of the household may bring an envelope of gift money to the wedding hall and partake of the celebratory meal in a nearby restaurant, but at a village feast, "the whole family comes by to eat wedding noodles." One woman winced and grimaced as she melodramatically pantomimed her memories of dishing up an eternity of long noodles to an interminable parade of wedding guests. A meal at a short-order restaurant is universally conceded to be easier, even though the hostess supplements this repast with plates of rice cake, meat, and side dishes from her own kitchen and helpful kinswomen and neighbors labor to keep the several tables covered with heaping plat-ters.[4]

Convenience may account for the emergence of commercial wedding services among an urbanizing population, but it does not explain why Koreans found it necessary to evolve a ritual that was such a profound

4. Under the Family Ritual Code, feasts were illegal until the provision was liberalized in 1985. In my experience, the prohibition was commonly ignored in the countryside near Seoul, although I have heard of instances elsewhere in the country where guests were slipped cash for a meal to circumvent the code (Lee Mun-Woong, personal communication).

departure from the old rite. Japanese wedding halls offer a Shintō and consequently "Japanese" ritual (Edwards 1989), and recent efforts to revive the traditional Korean wedding have, for the most part, been commercial adaptations held in public space. Even the arcane ritual language of the Confucian ceremony was not an insurmountable obstacle to innovation during the recent campaign to revive the old rite. To appreciate why informants describe the new rite as "better suited to modern life," how the state found a point of intersection with those perceptions, and why the now nearly universal new wedding has fallen under criticism, we must consider the distinguishing symbolic content of both rites as well as the historic circumstances that engendered them.

ANTECEDENTS AND PRECEDENTS

As in China, the premodern Korean state was the moral arbiter of social and ritual life, defining "good, rich custom" as that which, by Confucian measure, fostered the morality and well-being of the people (Deuchler 1980:82, 1992). Like anthropologists, but for far longer, Korean Confucians have regarded ritual as both an expression and instrumental affirmation of significant relationships and values. They would have agreed with Clifford Geertz that rituals are both "of" and "for" society (Geertz 1973:114). Yet though the anthropologist is content to cast an ethnographic gaze through the lens of ritual, the Confucian bureaucrat has never been a passive voyeur. Reforming officials in the service of the newly established Chosŏn dynasty (1392–1910) used the rites outlined in Chinese-derived texts as rituals of and for a virtuous society, essentially different in its premises of kinship, gender, and decorum from the world of their ancestors.

Korean reformers of the fourteenth and fifteenth centuries participated in an intellectual tradition that Western scholars call "Neo-Confucianism." They were among the intellectual heirs of Song period (960–1279) Chinese scholars who, through a critical reading and commentary upon ancient Confucian texts, sought to restore the moral order of a lost golden age (Deuchler 1980). Patricia Ebrey describes Confucianism as a school of thought that exalts the value of ritual, and of ritualized behavior in general, as a means of effecting moral behavior and social harmony (Ebrey 1991a:xiii). In some Korean villages, this was the stuff of both articulate ideology and observable social practice among the conservative descendants of noble *yangban* families into the 1970s (Dix 1977,

1979:87).[5] In the Song period, new methods of printing books gave scholars better access to the classics and promoted the circulation of their new
commentaries within China and beyond China's borders. The Song Neo-
Confucian philosopher Chu Hsi (1130–1200) is said to have authored
Family Rituals as a manual of ritual practice that would be accessible to
both rich and poor, a compromise between the ritual forms recorded in
ancient texts and twelfth-century Chinese practice (Ebrey 1991a:xxi).

Ebrey suggests that the wide circulation of *Family Rituals*, and the
modified editions of this text which appeared in the next two centuries,
facilitated the standardized practice of Chinese weddings, funerals, and
ancestor rites across regions and classes; and through ritual, they also
inculcated key conceptions about cosmic and social order (Ebrey
1991a:xxix; Naquin 1988; Rawski 1988). In two controversial essays,
James Watson has suggested that a general consensus regarding acceptable
forms for the enactment of rites ("orthopraxy") permitted local variation
in the minutiae of actual practice while providing a common sense of
participation in a common "Chinese" culture (Watson 1988a, 1988b).
Whether Watson is correct in giving primacy to ritual form over the beliefs and values which Ebrey (1991a) and Rawski (1988) hold to be implicit
in ritual practice, the rites set broad parameters not only for Chinese identity, but for non-Chinese who saw themselves as participants in a larger
Confucian civilization. Chu Hsi's *Family Rites* came to be revered in Korea, Japan, and Vietnam (Ebrey 1991a:xiii). *Family Rites* was the ultimate
source of the old Korean rite of matrimony whose demise I lamented in
my first encounter with Korean weddings.

In Korea, between the fifteenth and eighteenth centuries key social
institutions were transformed to accord with the Confucian vision of a
harmonious and well-ordered society. A society of loosely affiliated bilateral kin groups that vested daughters as well as sons with social, ritual,
and economic rights was transformed into a society dominated by agnatic
and strictly exogamous lineages. From the eighteenth century, inheritance
was patrilineal and favored the firstborn son, marriage was patrilocal, and
daughters were disinherited and excluded from venerating the ancestors.[6]

---

5. This sentence is necessarily qualified and its frame intentionally narrow.
Rather than suggesting a ubiquitous "Confucian" culture lingering on in the
countryside, ethnographic accounts remind us that a great many villages did not
have *yangban* traditions and that many patterns of interaction observed by ethnographers could not be so described (Brandt 1971; Chun 1984; Guillemoz 1983).

6. See Deuchler (1977, 1980, 1987, 1992), Kim Tuhŏn (1969), Peterson (1983),
Wagner (1983), and Lee Kwang-Kyu (1977).

So thorough was the Confucianization of Korean society that today few besides students of history are aware of the prerogatives enjoyed by Korean women six centuries ago. Even many feminists assume a history of eternal Korean "patriarchy" (*pujujuŭi*).

The practice and kinship logic of the rites were critical to the implementation of the Confucian vision. Sons would honor fathers and ancestral elders through rites of veneration that strengthened the agnatic kin group, and the women who bore male heirs would be incorporated into the husband's family through marriage practices which severed them from their own kin. Initially the performance of family rites (*karye*) was enjoined upon members of the office-holding elite (*sadaebu*), but the process of adherence to and acceptance of the restrictive definitions of kinship implied in their practice was gradual, the subject of scholarly debate and increasingly specific legislation as the Chinese-derived rituals were reconciled with Korean practice (Deuchler 1980, 1987:54, 1992).[7] Of the four family rites—initiation (or "capping") (*kwan*), weddings (*hon*), funerals (*sang*), and ancestor veneration (*che*)—the wedding rite proved to be the most indigestible of all.

In Chinese practice, the marriage culminated in the bride's presentation to her husband's kin and ancestors, procedures signifying her incorporation into her husband's kin group and affirming principles of family organization which seem to have had ancient roots (Watson and Ebrey 1991). In late Koryŏ and early Chosŏn period Korea, by contrast, marriages among the nobility were similar to the matrimonial arrangements of tenth-century Japanese aristocrats described by Murasaki Shikibu in *The Tale of Genji* (McCullough 1967). Daughters of noble families remained in their own homes after marriage, joining their husbands' kin years later as secure matrons who might already have produced children, inherited a portion of their own family's slaves and lands, and might now supplant a

---

7. It remains to ask the most interesting question of all: why did sixteenth-and seventeenth-century Koreans find it expedient and compelling to adhere to the rites? Early in the period, the government did impose sanctions for failure to establish and maintain proper ancestral shrines (Deuchler 1987, 1992), but the pervasive acceptance and internalization of the rites suggests that there were both symbolic and material advantages to performing the rites and subscribing to the definitions of kinship and status implicit in the performance of the rites. Rituals which affirmed new, more restricted definitions of kinship and affinity perpetuated the status claims of *yangban* descendants, even as the members of this group increased in number and were distanced genealogically from office-holding ancestors. See Fujiya Kawashima's (1992) useful discussion of the emergence of gentry associations in the Andong area.

deceased or aged mother-in-law. A daughter's husband was often close blood kin to his wife's family, and familial feelings born of extended residence might even be realized in his tending his father-in-law's ancestral shade.[8] These practices appalled the reformers by confounding the Confucian notion that ancestral virtues and vitalities (*tŏk* and *ki*) are transmitted from father to son, from generation to generation, through the act of begetting and are sustained by a son's performing the rite of ancestor veneration (*che*) for his own father.

Filial piety (*hyo*), an obligation and emotion sons owe their biological fathers and genealogical elders, was diluted by indigenous Korean marriage customs. Through repeated legislation and royal example, members of the nobility were urged to induct brides into the husband's home through the performance of the Confucian marriage rite, until a compromise was struck between doctrinal purity and a pragmatic assessment of elite *yangban* custom.[9] A critical sequence of procedures in the final rite of matrimony would be performed in the courtyard of the bride's home, where the groom would present a goose (usually wooden) and the couple would exchange bows and cups of wine and then be left alone together in the nuptial chamber.[10] This done, they assumed the social identity of husband and wife (Deuchler 1977, 1992). Martina Deuchler (1992:251 and personal communication) regards the public performance of wedding rites in the courtyard of the bride's home as the critical element of a *yangban* wedding, insofar as *yangban* status was repeatedly validated by one's ability to claim daughters-in-law from other recognized *yangban* lines and to send one's own daughters out as the brides of other *yangban* households. Weddings were thus public demonstrations of a *yangban* family's local

8. See Deuchler (1977, 1980, 1987, 1992), Kim (1969), Peterson (1983), Wagner (1983), Lee Kwang-Kyu (1977).

9. By strict legal definition, *yangban* were nobles with close genealogical ties to civil and military officials and who enjoyed various prerogatives of status, including the right to sit for the civil service examination and hold public office (Deuchler 1980:82–83). In strictly social usage, the term *yangban* seems to have meant different things in different times and places until, by the twentieth century, it was loosely used to designate all of the genealogical descendants of *yangban* ancestors, or even more broadly in common speech in the sense of "gentleman" in contemporary English usage.

10. The *Book of Rites* term for these procedures, *ch'inyŏng*, refers to "the groom's induction of the bride into his own home," which was counter to Korean practice. Descriptive accounts of the "traditional Korean wedding" refer to the procedures that begin with the groom's arrival at the bride's house as *ch'inyŏng* (for example, Lee Kwang-Kyu 1974).

elite status. More generally, the wedding in the courtyard of the bride's natal home conferred legitimacy upon the children of a *yangban* union.[11] The signal rite of matrimony in Chinese practice—the bride's presentation to her husband's parents and ancestors—could, in Korean practice, be postponed for extended periods of time. Even into the twentieth century this event might take place days, months, or even years after the wedding, depending on local custom and the vicissitudes of terrain.[12] Ironically, the only survival of the Confucian wedding rite retained in new-style weddings is this most problematic element of the older reform, the *p'yebaek* ceremony, now performed in antique dress in the wedding hall and consequently removed from the once significant spatial context of the groom's family home.

As in China (Ebrey 1991a:xxvii–xxix), Korean scholars fostered the diffusion of family rituals by preparing annotated and amended manuals, the most successful of which was Yi Chae's (1680–1746) *Practical Guide to the Four Rites* (*Sarye pyŏllam*) (Deuchler 1992:113; Fang 1969:23). Confucianized family rites were gradually adopted by the hereditary nobility who enjoyed various prerogatives of status. Family rites were again gradually imitated as both virtuous and prestigious activities until customs of noble *yangban* families came to signify a "Korean" wedding, funeral, or ancestor rite, recounted today in folklore and film to evoke a ubiquitous national past, a ubiquitous cultural memory that elides the differences of class and region. I recall the response of one old country woman to my naive query, "And did your bridegroom come for you, riding on horseback?" "Don't you know that only the rich did that? An ordinary person like me went off in a sedan chair with my clothes tied up in a little bundle."

11. Note the critical difference between late traditional China and late traditional Korea, insofar as Korean lineage organizations, family rites, and matrimonial alliances functioned in part to maintain and advance the status claims of a hereditary *yangban* nobility, for which there was no late Chinese equivalent.

12. See Deuchler (1992:256–257), MCIBCPP 1977 "Kyŏngnam":150–152, 1977 "Chŏnnam":132), Ross (1891:315), Lay (1913:10), and Lee Kwang-Kyu 1974:73). Despite superficial resemblances, the Korean compromise is in marked contrast to the custom of "delayed transfer marriage" that Janice E. Stockard (1989) has described for the Canton delta. Delayed transfer marriage follows the logic of Chinese practice insofar as the bride is inducted into her husband's home and is thereafter required to visit on festival days until she takes up residence as a proper daughter-in-law. The rite in the courtyard of the Korean bride's family home rendered the couple "husband" and "wife" before the bride set foot in her husband's home.

By its very nature, the Confucian wedding rite was a *yangban* custom. It assumed the presence of at least one learned member of the community to determine an auspicious hour for critical events, declaim the Sino-Korean text, and guide the couple through the intricate procedures specified in the ritual manual. Done well, it required slaves or commoner tenants to perform customary service carrying the bridal sedan chair and transporting ceremonious goods. Turn-of-the-century accounts suggest that the daughters of commoners were sent to their husbands' households without rites or feasting in the courtyard of the bride's home.[13] Moose, an early missionary, reports how on a preaching tour he visited a village house and was disturbed by the sound of crying in the women's quarters:

> The crying continued till my heart was touched with the pitiful wailing of the child, and I asked the men that were there with me what was the trouble and why the child continued to cry so much. The answer was: "It is only a bride that is about to be taken to her husband's house." In the afternoon two men came with a chair. There was no groom on horseback attended by lantern bearers and other friends, but just these two men who were to carry the chair and in it the poor little girl, who had most likely never spent a single night away from her father's house. . . . The poor little bride was led out and placed in the chair, her little body trembling with fear and emotion, while the sobs from her little heart could not be suppressed into quietness (Moose 1911:168–170).

The most impoverished families sent their daughters out as child brides, *minmyŏnŭri*, to be raised in the households of their future mothers-in-law. Years later, the daughter-in-law's hair would be rolled up into a married woman's chignon, and she would be sent to share her husband's sleeping pallet.[14] The marriages of slaves and concubines were bereft of ceremony (Martina Deuchler, personal communication).

However thoroughly it had once been associated with class distinctions, by the eve of its disappearance, the wedding rite had come to be regarded as the proper Korean wedding, described in nearly every ethnography, whatever the social composition of the village. Folklorists conducting a regional survey in South Kyŏngsang Province in the 1960s noted that

13. See Lay (1913), Moose (1911:168–170), and Sorensen (n.d.).

14. For descriptions of *minmyŏnŭri* marriage, see Griffis (1892:255), Han (1949:50–51), Harvey (1983), Kim (1964:130), Lay (1913:14), Moose (1911:77), Saunderson (1894:305–306), and Savage-Landor (1895:159). In this same period, according to Sorensen, "Japanese researchers into Korean customary law noted that there was customarily no idea that a marriage was invalid simply because no ceremony was performed" (Sorensen 1986b:31). Clearly, numerous "marriages" took place without the benefit of a wedding ritual.

"The *Manual of the Four Rites* (*Sarye pyŏllam*) has diffused to farming and fishing villages and there are both instances where the procedures are followed precisely and instances where only the most important points are invoked" (MCIBCPP 1977 "Kyŏngnam":130). In communities lacking a local scholarly tradition, an elder might shout out the sequence of rites in remembered approximation "due to the fact that there isn't anyone who is capable of proclaiming the written procedure" (MCIBCPP 1977 "Kyŏngnam":130). Chun Kyung-soo (1984:51–52) describes a wedding on Chin Island where the ritual intentions were clear, but the rite's procedures were approximate indeed.

THE RISE OF THE NEW-STYLE WEDDING

The origins of the new-style wedding were both Western and at least mildly iconoclastic. Judging from their writings, the Christian missionaries who introduced the prototype at the turn of the last century saw Christian marriage as an instrument of family reform, "this real marriage of two kindred minds 'whom God had joined' (not bargaining parents without consent of the two parties)" (Winn 1921:21; Kim Yung-Chung 1977:211). While in diametric opposition to the premises of Confucian matrimony, some missionaries yet seem to have shared with their ideological adversaries a sense that ritual was implicated in larger social transformations. For at least one missionary writer, the Christian wedding confounded the patriarchal order with a new public affirmation of mutual respect between husband and wife:

> There was not one snicker when *he* promised to love and honor her. I liked the ring in his voice and the way he answered up. It took much coaxing on my part to induce her to speak up audibly because for centuries, it has been considered next to a crime for a *saxie* [*saeksi*, bride] to speak on her wedding day. Not only was the entire village present but many from all the surrounding villages. This was an eye opener for them as well as for the bride (Erwin 1918:74).

Missionary women, in particular, were concerned with the manner in which converts celebrated their marriages: "The objectionable features of weddings as observed by non-Christian people are discarded, that which is different but looked upon as desirable is retained by our Christians" (Scranton 1898:295). These early Christian weddings were synthetic: "The bride, with closed eyes, bowed four times. The groom bowed twice; then together these two strangers walked to the chapel where the Christian ceremony was performed" (Scranton 1898:297). Great was Cordelia Erwin's glee when a prospective groom's father told her that he wanted a "strictly Christian wedding with not the least savor of heathenism" (Erwin 1918:73–74).

The white wedding dress and veil were missionary innovations. Mrs. Scranton thought the traditionally garbed bride with her full red skirt, yellow jacket, crown, and thick makeup "too nearly resembled the bright colored pictures we so often see in the temples" (Scranton 1898:297). Cordelia Erwin, for her non-"heathen" wedding, had the women of the bride's family fashion a gauzy white veil, pleated in imitation of the hoods many women wore for public modesty (Erwin 1918:73–74).

Criticism of the Confucian family system was not a Christian monopoly. In the twilight years of the Chosŏn period, young progressives challenged the legitimacy of family authority, which they saw as grounded in precisely those conservative, wasteful, and authoritarian traditions which had led the nation down the road to humiliation at the hands of foreign powers (Robinson 1988:35). Influenced by Western notions of "enlightenment," these men would fault the conservatism and empty ritualism of the past, and Korea's historic subservience to Chinese-derived Confucian culture, for the shame of Korea's annexation into the Japanese Empire in 1910 (Robinson 1988, 1991). As part of a larger iconoclasm, marriage practices long rationalized by Confucian ideology became the subject of a passionate critique. Early Korean nationalists saw the absence of choice and consent in matrimony as an obstacle to individual development and social progress (Robinson 1988:Ch. 1). The Kabo Reforms of 1894 legislated (but could not enforce) the abolition of child marriage and granted widows the legal right to remarry (Eckert et al. 1990:227).

In the colonial period (1910–1945), participants in the tenuous new culture of an urban middle class would begin to redefine the premises that governed their lives: the role of the family, the status of women, the spatial organization and style of daily life, and the meaning of matrimony (Michael Robinson, work in progress).[15] Wedding rituals became public celebrations detached from the matrix of family life. Shintō wedding ceremonies were conducted under colonial auspices, but upon liberation in 1945, they vanished from Korea along with all other traces of Shintō practice (Lee Kwang-Kyu 1983:1282).[16] The colonial period also saw the first

---

15. Changes in courtship in this same period are discussed in Chapter 4.

16. In Japan, the performance of explicitly Shintō weddings in shrines, in lieu of simpler ceremonies in private homes, followed upon the wedding of Crown Prince Yoshihito, the future Emperor Taisho, on May 10, 1900. Like the Korean new-style wedding, the Shintō ceremony was constructed in awareness of Christian weddings (Edwards 1989:103–104; Hardacre 1989:111).

attempts to evolve a secular version of the Christian wedding as a symbolic dissociation from both a repressive familism and an arcane ritual tradition. Pak Hyein suggests that in this period, with the corrosion of Confucian values in the countryside and the influence of Christianity and Japanese-derived Western culture in the cities, the wedding rite first came to be denigrated as "old-fashioned" or "old style" (*kusik*) in contrast to a more positive "new style" (*sinsik*) (Pak 1991:49). According to the writer Cho P'ungyŏn:

> The new-style [wedding] seemed simpler and the number of persons desiring it increased. Since it was not permissible to hold a church ritual if one were not a Christian, the wedding profession [*yesigŏp*] developed. The Kumgu Yesikchang and the Minhwadang, the first of such enterprises to appear in Seoul, were not actual wedding halls but rather places that rented out wedding dresses, dress suits, and flowers. For the wedding itself, restaurants like the Myŏngwŏlgwan and the Siktowŏn were used. Once the ceremony was finished, the adjoining room could be used as a banquet hall where they served the wedding noodles. As the population increased and with it, the number of marriages, the professional wedding hall emerged (Cho 1983:35).

The secular new wedding thus borrowed upon both the Christian ceremony and Japanese attempts to evolve a style of public weddings. Proto–wedding halls and the white wedding dress became popular in the 1930s. The giving of gratitude gifts, the holding of wedding banquets in public restaurants, and possibly even the fashion for Western-style wedding dresses seem to have been borrowed from an emergent wedding culture in Japan (Pak Hyein 1991:17, 52–54).

After the liberation, elements of an evolving new-style wedding—the bride's and groom's costumes, the master of ceremonies,[17] a procession of the wedding party down the aisle (prohibited under subsequent austerity measures)—were elaborated into a form that is recognizable today (Lee Kwang-Kyu 1983:1282). The head of the Wedding Hall Professional Association considers the Chongno Yesikchang, opened around the time of the liberation, to be the first commercial wedding hall in the contemporary sense. Anthropologist Lee Kwang-Kyu characterizes the weddings of this period as lavish exhibitions by the *nouveau riche*, the "empty formal-

---

17. Not only does the *churye* merge the role of the virtuous elder who officiated at Confucian rites with the image of the Christian minister; his role also recalls that of the *tanomare nakodo* who presides at Japanese weddings, another prototype that was available to those who participated in the construction of the new wedding.

ities" which the Family Ritual Code of 1973 would aim to counter (Lee Kwang-Kyu 1983:1274–1275, 1282). Cultural ambivalence had a spatial dimension in this early period as first-generation urbanites marked their transition between two distinct social realms and identities with a new-style wedding in the city, attended by their friends and associates, and a traditional wedding at the family home in the countryside (Lee Kwang-Kyu 1983:1282).

For those who defined themselves as "modern," the old-style wedding came to represent a rural past that was quaint but also tinged with distasteful recollections of old-fashioned matrimony. The association of the Confucian wedding rite with patriarchal familism is nearly automatic in Korean writing about the traditional wedding: "When you think about it, this ritual was performed in deference to a Confucian mind-set; the parents' face and connections were of greater concern than the two people who were getting married" (*Chŏnt'ong Munhwa* 1983, 6:5). "Weddings in our country were a consequence of the extended family system. . . . The patriarch regulated all matters . . . of family conduct, and since marriage would have a profound effect upon the family's prospects, it was a major event that absolutely could not be dealt with casually" (Cho 1983:30). "The modern tide of free marriage (*chayu hon*) has been one of the causes of this change from the old ritualistic custom" (Lee Kwang-Kyu 1974:75). Even the Ministry of the Interior's pamphlet advocating the revival of traditional weddings links their near-disappearance to "the collapse of the extended family system" as Confucian ethics faded under the onslaught of modernization (Naemubu 1986:18–19).

The ritual structure of the new wedding celebrates conjugality in symbolic counterpoint to the old wedding's association with family authority. The bride and groom greet each other with a mutual bow, a reciprocal bow of common greeting (*matchŏl*), in contrast to the asymmetry of the bride's excessive prostrations in the Confucian rite (although, as we have seen, the bride may be expected to bow just a bit more deeply than the groom). During the wedding, the bride and groom are set apart as a couple, elevated on a low platform as they stand before the master of ceremonies and vow "to love and honor each other always whatever the circumstances, to revere the elders, and to fulfill all the duties of a faithful husband and wife." The master of ceremonies' remarks, although they often include exhortations to practice filial piety, advise the couple, as a couple, on the course of their new life together: "In my opinion, if a couple does not love each other, then they should not marry, but the marriage vow means love in all circumstances"; "Usually in a wedding ceremony the couple is told, 'love each other,' and 'be happy,' but I will tell you that if one lives sincerely and diligently, pursuing one's guiding star, then love and happiness will follow quite naturally"; "To use a metaphor, let's say we're boarding a boat. The husband works the oars and the wife tends the helm and if they are both diligent they can easily navigate the vast sea."[18]

The imagery is optimistic and romantic. Both women and men suggested that women want to be married in a wedding dress and veil, to participate in a romantic image of nascent womanhood purveyed through the media, as in the West. So pervasive is this image that brides who are married in antique dress in the courtyard of the Korea House restaurant have the added option of being photographed in a white dress and veil. The manager of wedding services explained, "This is how they want to see themselves; it's the one opportunity of a lifetime to wear a wedding dress." I recall my fictive sister Kkach'i's horror when her father suggested holding a traditional wedding. She sputtered in consternation at the prospect of being powdered and dotted in traditional bride's makeup and wore a maternity-cut wedding dress and lace veil in the end.

Some years ago, in a study of proletarian theater in Indonesia, James Peacock suggested that certain ritual and performance phenomena may be best understood as "rites of modernization": the symbolic content and spatial arrangements of action in these events are, to the spectators' eyes, evocative of "modernity." Participants, as both actors and spectators, are encouraged to empathize and identify with these themes and ultimately to structure their thoughts and actions in recognizably "modern" ways (Peacock 1968:6–8). This last assertion, that "rites of modernization" function as passage rites bridging the transformation from "tradition" to "modernity," is ultimately unprovable, yet thoroughly compatible with anthropological (and Confucian) notions of ritual as a force which transforms persons, time, space, and consciousness.[19] The Korean new wedding might be dubbed a "rite of modernization" insofar as it linked a vision of "modern" matrimony to more general associations with a way of life that was detached from the rural past. While it would be difficult to prove that participation in new weddings encouraged Koreans to think and act in new ways, there is clear evidence that many Koreans saw their acceptance of the new wedding as a "modern" thing to do and took the increasing ubiq-

18. These quotations were recorded in the summer of 1983 in Righteous Town on the northern periphery of Seoul.

19. See, for example, Comaroff (1985), van Gennep (1960), Turner (1967, 1968), and Kelly and Kaplan (1990).

uitousness of the rite as a measure of "progress" and "development."
With the implementation of the Family Ritual Code of 1973, the state
inscribed its own modernizing text upon the new wedding through ironically Confucian prerogatives and logic. The premise that wholesome
ritual fosters a wholesome society claimed the power of an internalized
reflex.

THE FAMILY RITUAL CODE

The beliefs and practices, the ceremonies and superstitions described
in this book are derived from ancient traditions. Literal belief in "folk
wisdom" and the lavish adherence to elaborate and wasteful customs
began to disappear rapidly with the development of modern social institutions in the second half of this century. In particular, birthdays,
weddings, memorial services and funerals have become more economical, frugal, and simple.

> *Customs and Traditions. Korea Background Series*, vol.
> 10. Seoul: Korean Overseas Information Service, 1982.

The Family Ritual Code (*Kajŏng Ŭirye Chunch'ik*), first promulgated in
1969 and significantly strengthened in 1973, was intended to curb the
unproductive use of time and resources for ritual activities, to do away
with "harmful practices [which] imply nothing more than elitism and a
fruitless waste of energy in the obsessive pursuit of face and, as a consequence, pose many obstacles to modern social life" (Kim et al. 1983:339).
Injunctions to thrift were not alien to the Confucian tradition. Deuchler
(1992:245) notes a long history of prohibitions against extravagant weddings in Korea from as early as the fourteenth century.[20] The particular
moral tenor of twentieth-century Korea may be heard in the code's equation of rationality with thrift and efficiency, in its utilitarian valuing of
the material products of labor over the symbolic capital accrued through
ceremonial display and communal feasting (cf. Bourdieu 1977:171). Weddings (*hon*), funerals (*sang*), ancestor veneration (*che*), and sixty-first
birthday celebrations (*hwan'gap*)[21] were the immediate targets of the

---

20. In his influential manual on the proper conduct of family rites, Chu Hsi
himself condemned "covetous and vulgar people [who] first ask about the value
of the dowry when selecting a bride and the amount of the wedding present when
marrying a daughter" (Ebrey 1991a:55).

21. The sixty-first birthday celebration, while not one of the classic "four
rites," is a significant celebration in Korea, performed according to procedures
approximating a Confucian rite of ancestor veneration (*che*), with significant

Family Ritual Code. As economies of both time and money, procedures were to be simplified, guests limited, and costs curtailed. The code regularized the new-style wedding and imposed a time limit on its performance, reduced the number of guests by banning printed invitations, and prohibited floral displays, feasts, and the distribution of gratitude gifts (*tamnye p'um*) like the plastic container I received on my first encounter with a Korean wedding (Kim et al. 1983).

The code was silent on the subject of traditional weddings, although by regularizing procedures for the new wedding, prohibiting feasts, and circumscribing the length of rituals, the framers of the code clearly favored the new wedding. Commercial wedding halls, as enterprises subject to licensing, were more likely than a myriad of scattered households to honor the provisions of the Family Ritual Code of 1973. A signboard enumerating the code's "prohibitions on empty formalities and vulgar ostentation" was prominently displayed in the reception room of every public wedding hall. A professional association of wedding hall proprietors served as a conduit for directives issued by the Ministry of Social Welfare. When I visited the association's Seoul office in the 1980s, the walls bore posters advocating frugal dowries and the one-child family.

The code's fundamental assumption, that time and money spent on rituals constituted an impediment to progress and enlightenment, was consistent with the developmental priorities and progressive worldview espoused by the Park regime as it embarked upon a series of ambitious five-year plans. A language of "progress and enlightenment" gained wider credence in Korea through frequent sloganeering. These became the words many Koreans used to describe and understand the world in which they lived, the vocabulary my informants used in the early 1980s to explain what was, in their eyes, the inevitable evolution of the new wedding.

As a self-conscious modernizing agenda, the code drew on older notions of ritual as a vehicle of morality; the elimination of harmful customs (*p'yesŭp*) would foster a good society. Although the intention of the code and the responsibility of the state were to foster "wholesome family rites" (*kŏnjŏnhan kajŏng ŭirye*), the code curtailed practices that had theretofore been esteemed as "propriety" (*ye*) and status-enhancing custom. The

---

transformations in the symbolic text to accommodate the presence of a living elder rather than an ancestor (Janelli 1975). Following on the success of the wedding hall profession, commercial facilities have begun to cater sixty-first and seventy-first birthday celebrations.

authors of the code adopted an intrinsically Confucian gambit: reform becomes a restoration of older, "better" custom (cf. Deuchler 1980:80 for the fifteenth century). The preamble of the Family Ritual Code states:

> From long ago, our country has been praised as the East Asian Country of Propriety. . . . However, while we have revered propriety to excess, it is also true that we have forgotten the true meaning of our rituals and have the vice of stubbornly carrying out rituals that are only contrived formalities. And so it happens that, bound to ancient ritual forms, we blindly go through the motions of holding family rituals on the authority of "family tradition" and the like, and these harmful practices block progress and enlightenment (Kim et al. 1983:339).

In appealing to "the true meaning of our ancestors," the code echoes a defense of the Confucian tradition which evolved in response to radical critiques in the early twentieth century. Apologists claimed the essential truths of the tradition could be distinguished from the reactionary attitudes and practices which had encrusted it over time (Duncan 1988; Robinson 1991). The selective preservation of custom in the name of progress and enlightenment is by no means unique to the Confucian tradition of Korea and China. Geertz's young Balinese, "better Weberians than they knew," would distill "the truly sacred" from a Hindu tradition cluttered with "human customs performed out of blind habit and tradition" (Geertz 1973:183, 184). Similarly, Indian reformers attacked what were, in their eyes, "objectionable religious customs" as being "incompatible with the 'true' spirit of religion," the "perversions and inessentials" that obscured the genuine Indian core of Hindu practice (Werblowsky 1976:86, 90–91). The particular ease with which the modern Korean state claimed prerogatives for regulating morality by purifying custom, however, may have antecedents in Confucian statecraft wherein the authority of secular bureaucrats extended to ritual matters. Post-Confucian states of both the left and the right have perpetuated this role, enforcing rationality and thrift in the name of progress while assuming an older notion of the state's role as the moral arbiter of social and ritual practice (Keyes, Hardacre, and Kendall 1994).[22]

---

22. See, for example, Anagnost's (1994) discussion of the state and popular religion in the People's Republic of China and various descriptions of Maoist period weddings (Chen 1973:72–88; Myrdal 1965) and more recent backsliding (Frolic 1980:87–99). Note also the rhetoric of the right-wing Guomindang's New Life Movement several decades earlier (White and Jacoby 1946:123–124), attempts made in the Republican period to promote group weddings for the sake of thrift (Ayscough 1937:62–76), and more general rhetorical affinities in the modernizing

Themes struck during the reform of family rites in the 1970s were sounded again during the campaign to encourage the traditional wedding in the 1980s, but in response to a new set of social and political circumstances. The 1960s and 1970s vision of "development" and "modernity" along essentially Western lines was modified, in part by its own achievement, in part by the opening of an opportunity for argument about Korea's place in the world, the significance of being Korean, the reevaluation of Korean culture—among many other issues.

WESTERN WEDDING/OUR TRADITIONAL WEDDING

By the 1960s, village weddings were rural folklore, supplanted in the cities by the commercial wedding hall. By the 1970s, the old country wedding was disappearing (MCIBCPP 1978 "Kyŏnggi":70; Sorensen 1981:122). When anthropologist Paul Dredge left the village of "Okch'olli" in 1974, he was presented with the village's communal set of costumes for the wedding rite. The villagers explained that since it was time to replace the costumes with a fresh set, these seemed an appropriate gift for the departing anthropologist. When he returned to Okch'olli a few years later, Dredge discovered that this time, the wedding costumes had not been replaced. There was no need since all village weddings now took place in a commercial hall (Paul Dredge, personal communication). The costumes are now a part of the Asian ethnographic collection in the American Museum of Natural History.

By the late 1970s, the old wedding claimed the curiosity appeal of an endangered species. In 1977, during my first fieldwork, I was bustled from my room to join the village women who were rushing to see a bride and groom in traditional wedding dress dismount from a taxi at the groom's family home. My ethnographic curiosity was thoroughly matched by my companions' enthusiasm: "You hardly ever get to see an old-style wedding anymore." I reflected on the irony that the instigator of this foray carried the distinction of being the community's first bride to have celebrated a "new-style" wedding in the early 1960s (cf. Pak and Gamble

discourses and policies of the Chinese left and right (Cohen 1991). In Vietnam, extravagant and symbolically reactionary weddings and funerals were a concern of nationalist organizers against the French and a periodic target of government policy in the Socialist Republic (Luong 1992; Malarney 1993: Ch. 7). "Wasteful ceremonial expenditures" were an issue of public concern in postwar Japan (Edwards 1989:43) and of public discourse in Korea under Japanese colonial rule (Eikemeier 1980:40–41).

1975:163 for this same region). By the 1980s, a wedding hall proprietor could note with self-satisfied cynicism that "when they hear that there's an 'old-style wedding,' everyone rushes to see, but they choose 'new style' when it's their own wedding."

At Korea House in the late 1960s, where Korean performing arts were showcased for tourists, and then in the Korean Folk Village theme park from the mid-1970s, traditional weddings were reenacted as entertainment much as bank holdups and shootouts are performed at American western theme parks. And like the theme park phenomenon, these cultural performances were "nostalgic" as Anthony Brandt (1978) and Christopher Lasch (1984) bid us understand the term. Nostalgia does not evoke a desired return to the past so much as it underscores one's separation from it; the past remains frozen in an ahistorical reconstruction, something that exists just beyond the curtain of time, an object of collective memory subject only to memory's fickleness and contradiction. Or in Nicholas B. Dirks's terms, "The modern not only invented tradition, it depends upon it. The modern has liberated us from tradition and constantly conceives itself in relation to it" (Dirks 1990:27–28).

Nostalgia, thus understood, may be an apt characterization of Korean cultural memory in the 1960s and 1970s. Both Choi Chungmoo (1987) and Kim Kwang-ok (1988) have described the contradictory cultural policies, initiated under the regime of the late President Park Chung-hee, to simultaneously efface backward practices while preserving unique Korean traditions. Agents of the New Community Movement attacked "superstitious" local rituals, but some of these same events would eventually be celebrated as "intangible cultural properties" (*muhyŏng munhwajae*) under the Cultural Properties Preservation Act established by the Park government. Key performers, including shamans who had been the targets of antisuperstition campaigns, would be vested with government stipends to encourage the perpetuation of their art (Choi 1987:65–70).[23] While the Family Ritual Code circumscribed the elaborate rites through which local elites demonstrated their own distinctiveness and superiority, those same elites were mollified through the government's lionization of important Confucian figures and the refurbishing of local shrines dedicated in their honor (Kim 1988:7–9). Both Choi and Kim see the cultural policies of the Park regime as a cynical attempt to enhance its legitimacy as protector

---

23. Choi Chungmoo (1987) has described the many delicious ironies contained within the Ministry of Culture's efforts to "preserve" Korean shaman rituals as an art form.

and defender of the national heritage, even as its policymakers initiated profound social and economic changes.

The success of these programs, despite—or perhaps because of—their contradictory agendas, reveals something about intellectual moods and perceptions in an era of rapid transformation. As elsewhere, the necessity of "preserving" ritual and custom drew a full stop on the past; "tradition" was by definition a thing to be observed and tended, not the living, breathing stuff of daily life. The precariousness of its survival and the artificiality of its enactment could be taken as one more measure of triumphant development. A member of the wedding hall profession, who described the revived celebrations of the traditional wedding as nothing more than a "good work," nevertheless insisted that I see a performance at Korea House. This advice was echoed by two other wedding hall proprietors on the assumption that a view of the old rite was essential to my education in Korean customs. Customs were, after all, a wellspring of Korean identity. The past was good to think, even good to view, but not to do.

While the new-style wedding has enjoyed phenomenal success as the nearly ubiquitous ritual form, it garners faint praise. Several of the brides and grooms I interviewed in the 1980s told me that, in order to avoid the impersonal chaos of the commercial wedding hall and the streamlined speed of the ritual, they had considered such alternatives as a traditional wedding or a wedding in a Buddhist temple. In the end, they had succumbed, with an air of resignation, to the easily accessible, omnipresent wedding hall. Despite, or perhaps because of, the nearly universal use of commercial wedding halls, their swiftly processed services now provoke unfavorable comparison with the old rite. "Compared with the present day 'new-style' ceremonies cranked out routinely and with great clamor in the wedding hall, how much better is the flavor [of the old ceremony], thick with ancient traditions and far more intimate" (Kim 1983:55). "The wedding hall is as noisy as the floor of a crowded market. The bride enters to the Wedding March from Wagner's *Lohengrin,* the master of ceremonies' remarks are 'the shorter, the better,' and it's done. . . . Young people are looking on the traditional wedding with new eyes" (*Tonga Ilbo,* 4 May 1987:5).

This embrace of a more "Korean" style of wedding coincided with a swelling of national pride in the 1980s. National economic success could be (and was frequently) compared to reports of high crime and economic downturn in the United States, the affluent Other of decades past. One often heard it stated that perhaps too much of Korean culture had been thrown away in the rush to modernize. Revival is a necessarily self-conscious process, reinscribing "traditions" by so defining them. In Korea "tradition," as embodied in a "traditional wedding," must be reclaimed from across several decades of profound social transformation where urban memories claim contending visions of a rural past and where urban life-styles impose new constraints upon its reconstruction.

The revival of traditional weddings in an urban setting began at approximately the same moment that traditional weddings disappeared from the countryside. From the early 1980s, the Ministry of Culture's Bureau of Cultural Properties Preservation has attempted to arrest the utter obliteration of the traditional wedding by encouraging and monitoring performances officiated by ritual experts at the Confucian Academy (*Sŏnggyun'-gwan*).[24] These demonstration rituals were actual weddings which also provided instruction in the correct conduct of the traditional ritual. With such guidance, the Society for the Preservation of National Treasures began to offer traditional weddings at Korea House in 1983 (where staged versions of the old wedding had once been offered to tourists). Both efforts were extremely successful. By the end of 1986, twenty-three hundred weddings had been performed at Korea House, with the number rising each year. Bookings were full well in advance of the peak spring and fall marriage seasons (*Tonga Ilbo* [Ko Misok], 4 May 1987:5). By 1986, when the Ministry of the Interior initiated its own campaign to revive "our traditional wedding," traditional weddings were also offered on the rooftop of the Bando-Chosun Arcade, and it was possible to rent space for their enactment in the Children's Park or at the Seoul Open-air Theater (*Seoul Nori Madang*) (*Chosŏn Ilbo*, 25 May 1987:6).

Like the wedding hall, these venues detach the wedding from a context of community feasting and relocate it at a convenient node of urban activity. (One wedding hall proprietor with an eye for business sighed enviously over Korea House's favorable downtown venue.) Albeit in the case of the Confucian Academy and Korea House, this node is replete with self-conscious "traditional" associations and the open-air theater, with revivalist performances. Like the commercial wedding hall, sites for the traditional wedding provide commercial services for the convenience of its enactment: costumes, prepared offering trays, photographs, and a trained officiant.

24. The Confucian Academy, where promising scholars once trained for the higher civil service examinations, is now maintained as a national monument next door to a modern university of the same name. The site includes the national shrine to Confucius where the spirit tablets of Chinese and Korean sages and worthies are honored.

In accord with the Family Ritual Code and the public's disinclination for extended ceremony, procedures which once required a full two hours have, under the solemn scrutiny of the Confucian Academy, been boiled down to an essential twenty-five minutes. The generally unintelligible Sino-Korean of the ritual manual is, at Korea House, translated into modern colloquial Korean. Korea House also incorporates elements of the "new-style" wedding: the marriage declaration from the Family Ritual Code, brief remarks by a well-wisher, and a formal presentation of the new couple to the applause of their family and friends. The Confucian Academy performs a purer traditional wedding rite, but suggests the possibility of incorporating a second officiant who follows the primary officiant's Sino-Korean declamations with a pure Korean subtitle. The Ministry of the Interior offers both versions as acceptable models (Naemubu 1986).

While the ministry's handbook allows leeway for the inclusion of "local custom," the rites at Korea House and the academy are pure and solemn ritual as embodied in the text of a ritual handbook. Ritual as structure, the dominance of an explicitly Confucian script, effaces playful elements of custom, the teasing, hazing, and spectator participation that were part of an old-fashioned Korean wedding not so very long ago. In 1972, when I finally got my wish to see a traditional wedding, lovingly recreated by a rural troupe of middle-aged folk dancers when one of their number celebrated his fourth marriage, each bow and each cup of wine was negotiated between partisans of the bride and groom. After drinking the wine, the groom was offered some food on enormous chopsticks that retreated from his raised and open mouth, repeatedly, until he seized the moment and snatched some of the food with his hands. Other observers have described similar antics:

> Then the groom bowed. "Deeper! Deeper!" shouted the crowd of boys, and some stepped forward to press his head down. . . . Inevitably the groom fell over in trying to get up. "Do it again!" insisted the boys. In all he did it four times.
>
> Then the bride poured three cups of wine. . . . [The groom] sipped the first two. At the third one the boys insisted that he drink it all. He refused, and so the youths once again took charge and forced it down his throat. . . . Then the little dish of *kimch'i* on the table before the bridegroom was seized, and a youth with a pair of chopsticks made of sizable bamboo stalks forcibly fed him with it.
>
> The ceremony was virtually over, but not the horseplay. The groom moved round to the bride's side, and they were draped with paper streamers and sprinkled with paper confetti. . . . Then a whitefaced girl stepped forward to present a wrapped mirror. She held it out. "Take it, bride-

groom!" called the boys. He grasped it through his long silk cuffs, and immediately the girl, with a ridiculously dead-pan expression, withdrew it (Rutt 1964:158–190).

They say that if he [the groom] laughs, then the first child will be a daughter, so friends from both sides keep saying that he is going to laugh to startle him into embarrassment, but he proceeds as if he did not hear them (MCIBCPP 1977 "Kyŏngnam":148).

Mischievous friends tease the couple throughout the ceremony (Chai 1962:95).

The success of traditional weddings at Korea House (now a private restaurant and theater) and at the Confucian Academy rests on a profound rethinking of the old wedding sufficient to transform a domestic celebration into a commercial service, a rite of kinship into an austere celebration of national identity. The officiant who would seem to be the very embodiment of "tradition" is himself the product of multiple transformations. The officiant at the old rite represented the distinction and erudition of the bride's community, while the *churye* of the new-style wedding, more a creature of Parsons than of Durkheim, evidenced the groom's or groom's father's ties to influential persons in the realm of public affairs, the world beyond kinship and village ties. The member of the Confucian Academy who officiates at the revived traditional wedding, far from restoring localism, links the wedding to an authorized version of Korean Confucianism in the name of an explicitly *national* heritage.

In 1986, the Ministry of the Interior initiated its own campaign to "reestablish a wedding ritual which sets a wholesome tone and which, as our national heritage, is both simple and suited to our national temperament" (Naemubu 1986, n.p.). While the directive articulated a newfound pride in national traditions, it also expressed an appropriately Confucian response to "harmful custom": "it is feared that the trend toward weddings beyond one's means, that is now so pervasive, hampers a frugal livelihood and fosters social discontent" (Naemubu 1986, n.p.). While lauding the efforts of the Confucian Academy and Korea House, the Ministry of the Interior's practical objectives were to discourage the performance of *commercial* weddings and thereby to encourage thrift. Free public space would be available in every city and county, as well as costumes, ritual equipment, and a trained officiant (*Chosŏn Ilbo*, 1986, 5, 25:6).

The logic that links traditional weddings to frugal ceremonies held in free public space bears scrutiny. If anything, the reformers of decades past had seen the new ceremony as more pragmatic, freed from the onerous burdens of feasting and time-consuming arcane procedures. Although the new-style wedding is widely associated with the commercial wedding hall, it can also be transplanted to a less costly setting. The government has, for the last two decades, encouraged frugal new-style ceremonies held in community halls or agricultural cooperatives. My village acquaintances, however, hold that these places, like the free charity weddings, are "for people who don't have much money," for people like Hangil, whose wedding was described in Chapter 1. Because weddings held in public facilities are so clearly identified with poverty, only 2 percent of the respondents to a 1985 government survey used them, in contrast to the 97 percent who patronized wedding halls (Naemubu 1986:79). Why did the Ministry of the Interior assume, in the mid-1980s, that couples would be more inclined to have a free traditional wedding than a free new-style wedding?

Where the Family Ritual Code of 1973 sought direct curtailment of specific practices, the authors of the 1986 directive speak of a more diffuse climate of extravagant spending on dowries, gifts to the husband's family, and celebration, concerns that have been addressed with increasing urgency in the media and in public campaigns by such organizations as the Korean Mother's Club and the Seoul YWCA. (The emphasis, in 1973, on excessive communal feasting versus the emphasis, in 1986, on excesses of personal and family consumption speak volumes about changes in Korea over a decade and a half.)[25] While the directive faults the wedding halls for encouraging consumerism, it faults the "Western style wedding" for superficiality, for failing to foster a sufficiently solemn and appropriately Korean attitude toward marriage (Naemubu 1986:79–80). The superficial content of the new ritual is explicitly linked to runaway consumption, insofar as the new wedding "lays bare the trend toward empty formalities and vulgar ostentation and extravagance that is a contemporary social problem" (Naemubu 1986:18–19).

Written in a climate of mounting dissent and incipient labor militancy, the directive cautions that the conspicuous consumption evidenced in lavish weddings precipitates social unrest (Naemubu 1986, n.p.). The directive situates some of the blame for extravagant weddings within the new-style rite itself; it is a blameworthy practice because it encourages a socially deleterious moral climate through its superficial treatment of a sig-

---

25. Ethnographer Yim Dawnhee (1986) equates the decline of rural wedding feasts with the reduced significance of labor exchange in a mechanized and severely depopulated countryside.

nificant human event and by fostering extravagant displays which stoke the fires of social discontent. The old Korean rite, "replete with the spirit of our ancestors," is thus deemed morally superior to the Western import. In the eyes of the reformers, it fosters better social practice and consequently better people.

WHOSE TRADITIONAL WEDDING?

In order to fashion a democratic family life for the future, we must attempt to design a new wedding ritual that illuminates the meaning of matrimony in this era. In particular, we must overcome the mistaken assumption that the democratic family is necessarily a product of Westernization.

> Pak Hyein, *Korea's Traditional Wedding Ceremony:*
> *Continuities and Ruptures* (1991:17)

[A] history of rituals is a history of reproduction, contestation, transformation, and—if we accept carnival as a ritual—deconstruction of authority.

> John D. Kelly and Martha Kaplan,
> "History, Structure, and Ritual" (1990:141)

The nationalist subtext of the government directive on "Our Traditional Wedding" echoed the mood of the moment, but failed to claim it completely. The 1980s were a decade of debate, argument, and sometimes violent protest, baptized in the blood of the Kwangju Insurrection and culminating in the torrent of popular dissent, labor strikes, and grassroots movements which ushered out the Chun Doo Hwan government in 1987. Things Korean came to be cast in opposition to things Western. The most obvious targets were postwar American patronage, held culpable in the massacre of citizens of Kwangju and more broadly for supporting several decades of dictatorship, and Western-inspired popular culture, seen as having stifled the Korean spirit. Nativistic impulses which had fueled Korean folklore scholarship in the 1920s and 1930s, and a revival of interest on university campuses in the 1970s (Janelli 1986; Robinson 1988), now blossomed into a broad-based popular culture which drew its idioms from the traditions of downtrodden peasants and outcast shamans (the *minjung*, or "masses"). Choi Chungmoo (1987, Ch. 3), Donald Baker (n.d.), Kim Kwang-ok (1994), Kim Seong-Nae (1989a, 1989b), and Sun Soon-Hwa (1991, Ch. 3) provide stunning examples of some of these activities. Where small but dedicated student groups had once learned Korean masked dances, housewives and salaried employees now hired teachers and reveled in this once déclassé art form. Student demonstrations began with an approximation of shamanic rituals, and dissident farmers and workers punctuated their chants with the cadence of Korean drums.

The revived traditional wedding ritual, and its prior association with a conservative elite, were not universally satisfying to those who would reclaim popular culture in the name of the Korean masses. In her well-researched critique of marriage practices, Pak Hyein sees the new-style wedding as the product of a profound confusion of values and mores, of an uncritical acceptance of Western culture in the colonial and postwar period, but she harbors no illusions about a return to a lost agrarian paradise. She sees attempts to revive the Confucian wedding rite as an exercise in anachronism, a mistaken conservatism that does not speak to the needs and aspirations of contemporary people. She describes the Confucian wedding rite as itself a superficial encrustation upon older indigenous customs which reflect popular aspirations for longevity, good fortune, and the birth of many sons (Pak Hyein 1991: 67, 70, 64).

In a moment of contestation, weddings, as a corpus of shared acts and symbols, became forums for diverse social statements. At a wedding for a couple who were veterans of the student and labor movements, protest songs were sung with great feeling. "Folk weddings" combine elements of the new-style and traditional wedding with farmers' music. As an example of innovation, the women's magazine *Reidi Kyŏnghyang* carried an account of "a folk wedding performance" (*minsok hollye madang*) heralded as "an experimental wedding performed for absolutely the first time under heaven" (*Reidi Kyŏnghyang* 58, 23 October 1985:260–261). This particular wedding was the creation of a folk song research society that claimed its ceremony would strip away empty formality and reconnect with the meaning "contained within the cultural life of the past." Again the rationale strikes the familiar chord of twentieth-century Confucianism, but the vision of an essential core tradition has shifted. The solemnity of *yangban* rites has been replaced by the music and dance of commoners and outcasts. Like a performance of Korean masked dance-drama, this wedding began with a procession to percussive music and ended with all the spectators joining the participants in a joyous dance. Farmers' music (*nongak*), performed with drums, gongs, and cymbals, was combined with elements of the traditional and new-style weddings, an exchange of cups and bows, and a speech by the master of ceremonies (*Reidi Kyŏnghyang* 58, 23 October 1985:260–261). The *Tonga Ilbo* described another "traditionalist wedding ceremony" (*chŏnt'ongjŏk hollyesik*) that combined elements of the old and new rite with the music of the masses (*Tonga Ilbo*, 4 May 1987:5). At least one distinguished folklorist is often asked to officiate at these traditionalist celebrations, and I understand from conversations with students that the inclusion of folk music in weddings became very popular in the late 1980s. The Folklore Research Society has issued a pamphlet of "Music for Weddings." Celebratory dancing to farmers' music occurs at wedding receptions even within the national Confucian Academy itself, albeit to the ire of the impeccably *yangban* staff. The protocol officer, whose business it is to officiate at weddings and offer instruction on correct ritual procedure, told me that sound and music, even the performance of congratulatory songs which have long been a feature of the new-style wedding, violate the appropriate solemnity of the event. He bent forward and issued the scathing pronouncement, "Music at weddings is a vulgar person's (*sangnom*) custom."

Advocates of women's rights who name Confucianism as the source of lingering patriarchal oppression are uncomfortable with the old rite, which requires the bride to bow once more than the groom in symbolic affirmation of the wife's subordination to her husband. Clearly sensitive on this point, the protocol officer at the Confucian Shrine took great care to explain to me that because the groom bows once when presenting the wooden wedding goose, the number of bows performed by bride and groom are equal.[26] In some quarters, gender symmetry has been self-consciously encoded into ritual form. The bride and groom enter the hall together rather than the groom first, followed by the bride on her father's arm. In rare instances, the kin of both families may receive the couple's bows during the *p'yebaek* rite. The master of ceremonies might be the bride's mentor, rather than the groom's, and in a few controversial weddings, the master of ceremonies might even be a woman.

Emphatically Korean elements have also begun to infiltrate the wedding hall. In a minor indication of a larger trend, fashion magazines now show, in addition to Western-style bridal gowns, Korean dresses (*hanbok*) in gauzy bridal white sprinkled with the lavender magnolias that symbolize a virtuous wife and distinguish a bridal gown from a white mourner's dress. The fashion revives a bridal costume often seen in the early years of the new-style wedding, a Korean dress and a white lace veil. Lauding the "more wholesome wedding culture" brought into being by youthful innovation, the *Tonga Ilbo* cited a ceremony in which the bridal couple

---

26. As previously indicated, in the old country weddings of living memory, youths from the bride's side may even have forced the groom to execute more bows than the bride; she, however, would soon be required to perform the arduous *p'yebaek* obeisances to his kin.

wore Korean dress and entered the wedding hall to drum beats rather than piano music. The congratulatory song was a romantic piece from a Korean ballad opera (*Tonga Ilbo,* 4 May 1987:5). As the protocol officer of the Confucian Academy told me with a mischievous twinkle in his eye, "Those wedding halls are a business. They'll do whatever makes money."

CONCLUSION

The "new wedding," when it was new, proclaimed a vision of marriage, family, and urban life-styles which are now more or less taken for granted. As a "rite of modernization," the new wedding served its purpose and is subjected to an indigenous postmodern critique. The "traditional wedding," so defined, implies both a self-conscious, selective reclamation of the past and a tacit recognition of the transformed circumstances in which that past is reclaimed and transacted. Precisely because Korean family rituals are construed as signs and instruments of social morality and because, among them, weddings constitute "the one great event of a lifetime," distinctions between new and traditional weddings—as well as innovations and manipulations of both forms—are not trivial matters of fashion.

"Wholesome family rituals" have long been a matter of state policy and government directive because rites and morality have long been considered an appropriate concern of the state. This does not mean that the Korean (and by extension the "Confucian" or "post-Confucian") state is always successful in inscribing the rites with its own hegemonic vision of good and proper behavior. Neither the new wedding nor the revival was initially a government innovation, save insofar as venerable scholars, under the auspices of the Ministry of Culture, offered instruction on the old rite of matrimony. Both the Family Ritual Code and the campaign to revive the traditional wedding appropriated concerns already present in the performance of popular ritual—infatuation with "modernization" on the one hand, a nationalistic and nostalgic return to "tradition" on the other—providing a more specific agenda and a more explicit discourse, articulated through the national media.

The Family Ritual Code of 1973 did succeed in streamlining wedding hall procedure and in fostering the notion that economies of time, money, and procedure were part of what was "new" about the new-style wedding. Because violators were subject to fines and arrest, the code was successful—for a time—in curtailing feasting, the giving of gratitude gifts, the sending of printed invitations, and other related expenses, although all of these practices had begun to reappear long before the code was repealed in the liberal climate of the late 1980s. Beyond this, the code influenced the way people thought and talked about weddings as templates for their own immediate history. The repeal of the Family Ritual Code in the late 1980s reflects a changing political climate in which the south Korean state is more cautious about meddling in the intimate aspects of people's lives, from roof styles to hair length, than it was in the 1960s and 1970s, when development campaigns and anticommunism fueled a centrist state.

The campaign to revive the traditional wedding addressed a more diffuse climate of extravagant weddings by advocating a particular style of ritual in a more economical setting. Whereas the Family Ritual Code could be enforced, with genuine legal sanctions, the later campaign merely encouraged, with limited success and in competition with both the wedding hall industry and a multiplicity of new hybrid forms. Even more dubious was the campaign's advocacy of free facilities, generally associated with poverty, for although weddings are construed as rituals of morality, they also signify social status in an expanding consumer culture (a theme that will be amply demonstrated in the following chapters). An appreciation of the "Confucian" roots of both the Family Ritual Code and the campaign to revive the traditional wedding cannot ignore profound differences in both political culture and life-style between the Korea of the late 1960s and that of the late 1980s.[27] Weddings, like so much of Korean life, are a moving target.

27. Contrasts between Korea and other post-Confucian cultures are also illuminating. While Ann Anagnost's work on Chinese popular religion (1994) reveals the common seed of some Chinese and Korean assumptions, it also underscores the very different circumstances under which policies governing ritual, and popular responses to those policies, are transacted in the Republic of Korea and the People's Republic of China today. Where the Korean state makes conscious use of Confucian homilies to foster harmony and loyalty, and even the authors of the Family Ritual Code were at pains to cast their remarks within an acceptably Confucian frame, the Chinese state claims a revolutionary rejection of an oppressive past. While Anagnost's discussion of state criticism of excessive ritual expenses, a target of the "civilized village" campaign, sounds strikingly familiar, she describes a state that wields far greater coercive power and a rural society where local identities, embodied in communal ritual, are far more compelling than in contemporary (south) Korea.

2  COURTSHIP

Now my parents want me to come home and get
married to a guy they have lined up for me—yes, we
still have arranged marriages in Korea, believe it or
not. My father can't understand why I keep putting
him off.

A character in David Lodge's *Small World*
(1984, p. 297)

4

Transformations:
The Construction of Courtship
in Twentieth-Century Korea

My sister Sukcha was in no rush to wed. When the family teased her, she said that she would marry late "like Tallae Ŏnni,"[1] claiming me, her American "sister," as a role model. Ŏmŏni, on the other hand, began to fret over the prospect of her fourth daughter's wedding from the time that Sukcha graduated from high school. How would she ever finance the dowry? Where would she find suitable "groom material"? In these conversations Ŏmŏni could claim, with gentle pride, that her fourth daughter was bright, poised, and musically talented, but then she would add with a sigh, "Sukcha has no looks." Sukcha's nose was flat, her face lacked the classic moon shape of a Korean beauty, she was short and skinny, and her cheeks were perennially spattered with acne.

When the family still lived in Enduring Pine Village, a younger Sukcha had seemed at a loss. Her high school degree, the first in the family, opened no doors after all. In the months after graduation, she moped at home, a welter of unrealistic hopes and profound frustration. In the summer of 1983, she would come to me for English lessons, bearing such astonishing queries as "Ŏnni, what is 'sloe gin'?"

In 1985, Ŏmŏni sold the village house and the two remaining dry fields and invested in a restaurant in Righteous Town with her daughter Kkach'i and Kkach'i's husband. Sukcha went to work waiting on tables and taking orders by telephone, a job well suited to her warm and sociable personality. The restaurant prospered, and it was understood that in exchange for Sukcha's labor, Kkach'i and her husband would finance most of Sukcha's wedding. In the meantime, they gave her ample pocket money and a liberal work

---

1. Sukcha calls me "elder sister" (ŏnni) because Ŏmŏni claims me as her fictive daughter *(suyangddal).*

schedule that allowed her to socialize with her many friends. She studied dance and performed with a local folk ensemble. Sukcha was happy now. Her laughter and scraps of songs would reverberate off the walls of the tiny restaurant. Her looks improved. Her complexion cleared and her figure became more womanly. Dressed in inexpensive ready-made clothing, she developed a sense of style. There was even occasional talk of "boyfriends," but never, so far as I could see, a serious relationship. By the summer of 1991, all her female friends but one were married, and that wedding was scheduled for the early fall. Sukcha would be the last of her group to marry, but she was still reluctant, saying that once married, she would just grow old. Even so, the handwriting was on the wall.

I knew that things had gotten serious when I went to see Ŏmŏni in July. She was filled with matchmaking schemes and thoroughly exasperated with Sukcha. Sukcha had already gone through with three arranged meetings (*massŏn*) with eligible bachelors, and had found each of the men unsatisfactory. One was too short, another was too ugly, the third did not have enough money. One of these men had even called her up the next day wanting to date, but Sukcha would have none of it. I could not help but wonder if, by the logic of well-intentioned matchmakers, the obvious deficiencies of these less-than-ideal candidates were intended to balance Sukcha's lack of beauty. Ŏmŏni now pinned her hopes on the next meeting; the date was soon to be set.

Ŏmŏni tends the child of a woman who works in a government office, a fertile hunting ground for "groom material" (*sillanggam*). Ŏmŏni could not resist enlisting her patron in the task of finding a promising young civil servant as a husband for Sukcha. The request had yielded up a prospect, as Ŏmŏni related in hushed and breathless tones for the benefit of myself and a neighbor: "She says that this man doesn't drink or smoke, that he's steady-going. He's already thirty-five, but then they say that women age more quickly than men. [Recalling Ŏmŏni's own circumstances, I didn't have the heart to say, "Yes, but women live longer."] I've seen his photograph. He looks very serious, wears glasses. He goes to night school, he's very busy, we can't have an arranged meeting until his vacation in August. If all goes well, we'll hold the wedding in November. Sukcha turns thirty at the end of the year. I have to marry her off before that. . . ." Ŏmŏni broke stride and tilted her head toward the open doorway. Beyond the fence I could barely discern the figure of a slim young man in a short-sleeved shirt walking down the alleyway. "It's the bachelor from the eyeglass shop," she said in a stage whisper, following the retreating figure with her eyes. When he had disappeared from view, she explained the obvious, "I'm thinking of groom material for Sukcha."

"You know, Sukcha had her nose fixed," our third sister told me with much amusement. Envious of delicate Korean noses, I marveled at the complementary insecurities that had caused my sister Sukcha to have a local plastic surgeon add a "Western"-seeming bridge to hers.[2]

"Did she do it for the arranged meetings?"

"Of course."

To this degree, Sukcha was complicit in the process that would eventually lead her to matrimony, but she was profoundly uncomfortable with Ŏmŏni's near obsessive need to bring things to a speedy resolution. When she walked me back to the subway station through the midsummer sunshine, Sukcha gave vent to her feelings.

"Ŏmŏni is driving me crazy."

"I remember what it was like."

"Are mothers like this in America?"

"Not as bad. If the daughter is an old maid, no one blames the mother. It just isn't the mother's responsibility. In fact there isn't much the mother can do, since we don't have arranged meetings."

"I wish I lived in America."

I recalled the incredulity and pity of another Korean friend, back in the 1970s, when I had explained that my mother was not going to get to roll up her sleeves and find me a husband, that her friends and relations were not likely to introduce me to a mate. I tell Sukcha, "All you need is one good man."

"There aren't enough good men."

"That's what women say in America. That must be what women say all over the world. Just find one good man and grab hold of him."

She laughs at my choice of an oddly aggressive verb, suggestive of a policeman apprehending a malefactor.

When we reach the station, I want to say something encouraging. I tell her, "You've gotten so much better looking. Your hair is prettier, your face is prettier, [I lower my voice] and your nose is prettier."

"Shh!" Eyes wide with melodramatic horror, she quickly scans the crowd in the station to verify that no significant ears have heard me and stifles her giggles behind the finger she holds to her lips.

Arranged meetings (*massŏn*)—a practice which had so far disappointed Sukcha, but had brought Pak Yŏnghŭi and Yi Chongil together in a coffee

---

2. According to one survey reported in a weekly magazine in 1989, from 20 to 30 percent of all unmarried Korean women in their early twenties have cosmetic surgery performed on their eyes, noses, mouths, or breasts (cited in Hart 1991:256).

shop and prompted their wedding—fuel conversations, advice columns, and all manner of fiction. A popular television miniseries featured "the woman who had a hundred arranged meetings." What a Korean character in a Western work of fiction describes as a condition of "still" having arranged marriages in Korea, "believe it or not," becomes, upon closer scrutiny, a feature of the social landscape which has been molded into its present shape by recent history. This chapter explores the means and circumstances through which Koreans have redefined the process of getting married in the twentieth century.

My aim is to chart something of this history and retrieve something of its contemporary manifestation in Korean popular culture. To this end, I combine the sorts of information and insight garnered from interviews and observations with writings that appeared in Korean women's magazines during the 1980s. I see women's magazines as one more source of raw data. Even so, my field assistants were horrified when they saw me begin to amass stacks of this (to their eyes unreliable) material, and one of my American readers asked piquishly if I would trust accounts of life in the United States contained in *Redbook*, *Woman's Day*, or *Cosmopolitan*. In fact, social historian Beth Bailey makes excellent use of these same American women's magazines in her study of American courtship, *From Front Porch to Back Seat* (1988), as indications not of what has literally happened but of how changing mores have been discussed and understood. Women's magazines have a wide circulation in Korea,[3] and even those who cannot afford these relatively expensive publications[4] have access to them in tearooms and beauty parlors.

I do not have a high regard for the ethnographic validity of magazine copy, any more than I would accept the literal truth of the folktales about marriage that I recorded during more conventional fieldwork and also cite in this work. I do consider women's magazines an influential source of discourse about weddings, much as myths and legends, in public citation, give shape to the ways people understand and talk about who they are and why things happen to them the way they do. The gendered visions contained in magazine copy are all but self-evident. It is far more difficult to discern the meeting ground of magazine copy, pervasive attitudes, and

3. In 1990, a consumer group estimated that the most popular women's magazines sold about seventy thousand or eighty thousand copies per monthly issue (*Newsreview*, 24 March 1990:30).

4. In 1987, I purchased women's magazines ranging in price from 3,300 *wŏn* to 4,700 *wŏn* (roughly $4 to $6.25 U.S.).

the actual choices made by young women and men. This chapter is primarily concerned with the evolution of a feminine ideal. The stories of courtship recounted in the next chapter are intended to add substance and variation to what might otherwise seem a cartoon caricature of potential brides and grooms. In subsequent chapters, I shall also return to the story of my sister Sukcha, whose life, for all its demographic inevitability, reveals a strong and buoyant personality.

ABOUT ARRANGED MEETINGS

In Korea, as elsewhere, the arranged meeting is often described as a blending of traditional wisdom (marriage is too important to be left to the young) and progressive ideals (marriage should be a matter of individual choice made on the basis of mutual attraction).[5] As an innovative marriage practice, the arranged meeting has counterparts throughout Asia. The thoroughly cosmopolitan characters in Junichiro Tanizaki's well-known novel of prewar Japan, *The Makioka Sisters*, are intensely involved in the negotiation of arranged meetings (*miai*) for their unmarried third sister, and recent ethnography suggests that the *miai* remains a vital option in Japanese matrimony.[6] Similar practices have appeared in China,[7] India (Roy 1972:76–82), and no doubt in many other places as well (Mace and Mace 1959:159–161). When I presented an account of the Korean arranged meeting to an audience of ethnologists in Hanoi, my interpreter paused in midtranslation to inform me, "It's just the same with us!"

Passage Rites Made Easy describes marriage through an arranged meeting as more "rational" (*hamnijŏk*) behavior than simply falling in love because the candidates for romance and matrimony have already been carefully scrutinized by parents and matchmakers (Ko 1982:55). Korean women's magazines also emphasize the value of prior screening in choosing a mate, suggesting by the frequency with which they address

---

5. Thus in *Marriage: East and West,* Mace and Mace (1959:159) offer the overarching generalization that "Asians" have come to acknowledge "the judgment of young people" in marriage choice as an adaptive response that may yet preserve "traditional family values" against the assault of "Western" dissolution, even as Asian societies have found it necessary to discard the most oppressive attributes of traditional patriarchy—a case of having one's cultural cake and eating it too.

6. See examples in Edwards (1989:Ch. 3), Hamabata (1990:41–42, 118–141), Hendry (1981:123), and Lebra (1984:Ch. 3, 122–123, 237).

7. See Croll (1981:26–27), Potter and Potter (1990:196–207), and Wolf (1985:153–154, 166–167).

this topic that their youthful readership is by no means convinced of the merits of matchmade matrimony:

> Today, with the trend toward frankness in sexual matters, talk of "arranged meetings" or "matchmade marriage" might sound excessively stale. Even so, in marriage the conditions of both sides enter into things. Matchmade marriage, where you can dispassionately investigate these conditions beforehand, has some advantages that cannot be ignored ("The Secrets of a Successful Arranged Meeting," *Yŏng Reidi*, 3 March 1985:347).[8]

In the social science writing of decades past, the world marched to a common drumbeat of "modernity," and like-seeming practices took on an aura of near evolutionary inevitability, as in Mace and Mace's comprehensive volume *Marriage: East and West* (1959). A Korean author of the 1950s, describing Korean life for a Western audience, could claim that "The trend now is toward a greater freedom of choice in the selection of a lifetime mate, and a companionship approaching the relationship of husband and wife in the Western world is developing throughout Korea." He assumes, uncritically, that cultural "development" must follow upon Western lines (Kim Hyontay 1957:103). In local discourses, as in an older social science, the illusion that marriage practices necessarily follow a trajectory of "modernity" elides other issues which have great bearing upon why, when, and through what sequence of procedures people marry, the reasons different people make the choices they do, and the very different consequences of these choices for different segments of the population.[9]

In her critique of early-twentieth-century Chinese "modernism," Rey Chow (1991) suggests that progressive ideologies, even when they decry women's lot under the old society, may be oblivious to the actual conditions and premises of women's lives in the new. Readings of history as a journey in the direction of progress and enlightenment have been chal-

---

8. See also "Matchmade Marriages Are Fine, Too" in *Reidi Kyŏnghyang*, 8 November 1984, 293.

9. Lisa Rofel offers the caution that while "hegemonic transnational flows of commodities and values create a powerful discourse on modernity spreading out of the West," as Baudrillard (1987) suggests, "we must nonetheless be wary of creating unified readings out of local Euro-American practices and allowing those to overpower interpretations elsewhere " (Rofel 1992:93). Discourses on modernity sound so reassuringly familiar that the different processes through which "modernity" is experienced might easily be obscured. See also the several essays in Comaroff and Comaroff (1992).

lenged in many quarters.[10] Within Asian studies, this critique has been particularly fruitful in the gendered quarter (Bernstein 1991; Chow 1991; Mani 1987).[11] The evolution of Korean courtship practices provides one excellent example of how notions of progress, of an enlightened "now" versus a repressive "then," mask the particular disadvantages for women in new forms of matrimonial negotiations, be they "matchmade" or "for love"—a mask which sometimes slips in angry conversation or social satire. Through courtship and through all of the talk about getting married, notions of ideal "man" and "woman," "husband" and "wife," "son-in-law" and "daughter-in-law" are constructed, reinforced, and resisted.

Picture, if you will, an exhibition case in the National Folklore Museum of Seoul. A bride and groom, in colorful antique costumes, face one another across a table upon which fruits and wine are arranged according to the specifications of a ritual manual. Embalmed under glass, this presentation signifies quaint old customs not only for the foreign visitor, for whom the display is briefly identified as a "Korean wedding ceremony," but with a more elaborate discussion for the gaze of a Korean audience. The Korean-language label explains that, in the past, marriage "was no individual contract, and even today it is a contract between families."

In Korean popular discourse, the evils of old-fashioned matrimony, in which near-children were forced by the will of their elders to marry total strangers, have been replaced by more enlightened practices. The "old days" are still on the horizon of living memory, but are recalled as from an utterly vanished time. In confessing that he never saw his wife's face until his wedding night, the writer Cho P'ungyŏn (1983:30) states with a touch of hyperbole that "Today's young people would consider this laughable and the faint-hearted might swoon away, but in my day these procedures were considered natural." The Janellis (1982:39) report that, in the 1970s, rural informants over the age of forty "chuckled as they told us of seeing their spouse's face for the first time on their wedding day." A woman of my acquaintance recalls the buckets of tears her sister shed

10. See Rofel (1992:94) for a discussion of sources, following the seminal work of Foucault, that "reexamine some of the most cherished Western ideals of liberty and progress."

11. Some years ago, historian Joan Kelly (1984:19) posed the rhetorical challenge, "Did women have a renaissance?", suggesting that events which liberate men from natural, social, or ideological constraints "have quite different, even opposite, effects upon women." Within Asian studies, the "narratives of progressive modernization" (Lata Mani's phrase) which have summed up the last century of national histories are now subject to a similar questioning.

more than thirty years ago over the prospect of marrying an unknown man. When I asked women who had participated in the old custom of poking holes in the paper doors of the nuptial chamber and keeping watch throughout the wedding night *(sinbangyŏtpogi, sinbangŭl chik'ida)*, they explained their activities as insurance against a terrified bride's running away.[12] Hangil's Mother could still muster anger at the memory of her first glimpse of her husband, "a short guy in a rumpled Korean coat, I never much liked him anyway." Ŏmŏni, on the other hand, smiles softly and reminisces that she thought her new husband was "just fine." She even claims to have sneaked a look at him through the long white sleeves that shielded her painted seventeen-year-old face.[13]

Images of weddings, then and now, offer a reassuring visual shorthand for fundamentally different premises of matrimony (as in fig. 6). The traditional bride—rendered anonymous under thick white makeup, marked with auspicious red dots on her cheeks and forehead, eyelids glued shut, an unseeing face, a face nearly unseen, hidden away behind the long white sleeves of her costume—becomes an icon of women's oppression under traditional Korean patriarchy. Any source book on Korean women will describe the hardship of the young bride sent off to live among strangers and serve an exacting mother-in-law. Young brides were to be "steeped in the customs of the house" as water takes on the color of tea (Lee Kwang-Kyu 1975:218).[14] The bride and groom might be no more

12. Men were more likely to invoke a grim folklore which attributed the necessity of watching over the inexperienced couple to an incompetent groom's having once peeled off the bride's skin in the act of disrobing her or a bride's former lover having once murdered a groom.

13. Ŏmŏni does have painful memories of her early married life—not as a consequence of her father's choice of a groom, but because he was forced by circumstance to send her to an impoverished rural household, where she became the sole housekeeper for her husband, father-in-law, and unmarried brother-in-law. She speaks of sneaking into the kitchen late at night to drink water laced with soy sauce in the hope of relieving her hunger pangs. Her now-deceased husband once told me that his father-in-law's misfortune was his own blessing, for how else would he have acquired so fine a wife?

14. Within the Korean family, brothers are unequal, and sequential segmentation is assumed. The eldest son is the primary heir, the son who would inherit house, ancestors, and a major share of the family's estate. Joint or grand households, where they existed, were a transitional pattern insofar as brothers other than the heir would, with maturity, establish separate households (Han 1949:81, 83; Janelli and Janelli 1982:79, 104; Lee Kwang-Kyu 1975:218; Sorensen 1984).

Figure 6.   Stereograph image, "The bridegroom's first view of his future wife," c. 1900. The bride's eyes seem to be glued shut. Keystone View Company, courtesy of the Library of Congress. National Photographic Archive #23700.

than children; their early marriage was insurance for the continuity of the line.[15]

The woman in antique dress, her face veiled behind her long sleeves, only half seen and all unseeing, her eyelids glued shut with rice paste, is

15. Several early accounts and retrospective studies remark upon the extremely young ages at which Korean children of both sexes might be wed (Han

juxtaposed with the radiant bride of contemporary advertisements, resplendent in her white lace veil. "A woman of three and twenty, her heart flutters with dreams of the future" reads the legend that accompanies one poster image of a modern bride. That potential brides and grooms, at very least, now meet face to face and give their own consent to matrimony distinguishes an enlightened "now" from an old-fashioned and repressive "then." Attraction may follow upon the family's negotiation of an arranged meeting in the case of a "matchmade" marriage *(chungmae kyŏrhon)* or precede the nervous introduction of one's "beloved" *(aein)* to the members of one's family in a "love" marriage *(yŏnae kyŏrhon)*, an event which, in Kim Eun-Shil's words, initiates "more or less serious rituals of negotiation to demonstrate the power of family rights over the person concerned" (Kim Eun-Shil 1993:48).[16]

Both trajectories are subsumed by the overwhelming statistical preference of marriage-age survey respondents for "marriage by personal choice with the approval of the family." [17] In contemporary Korean myth, modern marriage—whether by falling in love or through an arranged meeting—is a democratic transaction. But the bodies of men and women, the chips in a marriage transaction, are invested with different and gender-specific notions of what is most material, vital, and desirable, to paraphrase Foucault (1980:152). As succinctly stated in a Korean women's magazine, "A recent newspaper survey on the opinions of youth revealed that men considered a woman's beauty and women a man's earning capacity the most important criterion [of matrimony]" *(Yŏng Reidi* [Pak

---

1949:48; Han 1990:80; Lay 1913:1; Moose 1911:108–109; Pak and Gamble 1975:96; Savage-Landor 1895:151). Elite families were anxious to marry their firstborn male children early to secure the continuity of the line, while the poor sent their daughters off at early ages. In 1925, when the first modern Korean census was taken, most Korean women were marrying before the age of sixteen. The median age at marriage for women rose about one and a half years between 1925 and 1940. In 1925, the median age of marriage for men was twenty-one; by 1940, it had risen by little more than half a year (Kim 1966:77; Kwon 1977:46).

16. See, for example, the continuation of Sukcha's story in the next chapter.

17. According to a 1980 survey of unmarried men and women in Seoul, only 1.5 percent expressed a willingness to merely "follow" a parent's choice. The vast majority of those sampled, 77.7 percent, considered marriage a matter of individual choice sanctified by parental consent. When contrasted with similar surveys conducted since 1958, this survey marked not only a steady rise in the number of respondents giving this response, but also a decrease over the preceding eight years in the number advocating marriage solely on the basis of personal choice (3.2 percent, down from 10.9 percent) (Korean Women's Development Institute 1985:59).

Yŏngae], October 1984:148).[18] To the extent that men's careers are "invested in" and men are thereby invested with defining responsibilities for women's potential well-being, marriage transactions are fundamentally unequal.

It may seem commonsensical that men want pretty wives and that the burden of attraction in these encounters should be placed upon women, and yet, in Korea, beauty has not always been a criterion of matchmaking. The brides of decades past were faceless and invisible. The bridal body of contemporary Korean matchmaking is "securely anchored in a particular historical moment" (Scheper-Hughes and Lock 1987:7) and through it linked to other times and places where, beyond all rare and wondrous inspiration to art and poetry, the (highly variable) body of a beautiful woman comes to be read as a relentless standard of her worth and being (Scheper-Hughes and Lock 1987:25; Turner 1984:174, 196–197, 203).

INVISIBLE BRIDES AND PEEK-A-BOO

As elsewhere in much of the preindustrial world, Korean marriage was once exclusively a family matter, determined by those who regarded a potential bride as a source of labor, sons, and (among elite families) prestigious matrimonial alliances. A woman's labor was vital to the success of the family enterprise. Late-nineteenth-century travellers to Korea remarked upon the range and variety of women's work. Foodstuffs grown in kitchen gardens were processed through a seemingly endless round of drying, salting, or pickling. Cloth was loomed both for domestic consumption and as a medium of exchange and taxation. Women clothed the household through the industry of their needles. Padded clothing was unstitched and then reassembled with each rigorous laundering at the stream bank. Both laundry and needlework were the resources of women who covertly maintained the economic "face" of destitute households. All of these activities could be performed within the respectable confines of women's realm, but where necessity required, women in poor households also worked at transplanting rice, weeding, and harvesting. Some women were even hitched to plows in the absence of oxen.

18. In her study of the urban middle class, Yi Eunhee Kim notes that "what the man looks like is rarely important," although "In choosing a bride, the physical appearance of the woman is one of the most important facts." Because a man's university and the ranking of his department within the university are believed to determine his subsequent career success, his educational background might be the first attribute described by a matchmaker (Yi Eunhee Kim 1993:361).

A Korean wife's abilities as a hard worker and frugal manager were recognized as a measure of the prosperity, harmony, and reputation of her household.[19] *Yangban* families had additional stakes in selecting a child's spouse, insofar as their status claims were repeatedly validated in the willingness of other distinguished families to seek their daughters as brides and send in their own daughters as wives.[20] Respect for the elders in all matters, including matrimony, while celebrated as a tenet of Confucian ideology, was also the practical consequence of a social system in which the family maintained and bestowed not only critical material resources, but identity itself. The most serious sanction a community could wield was banishment. Vincent Brandt (1971:48) describes two households in the isolated coastal village he studied in the 1960s as belonging to "impoverished couples who provide a dramatic illustration of the tragic fate tradi-

19. For descriptions of women's lives in the Chosŏn period, see EWUCCHKW (1972, vol.1:pt.2), Kim Yung-Chung (1977:Ch. 9), Lee Hyo-jae (1986), and RCAWSWU (1986). For an appreciation of the transformation Confucianism wrought on women's lives in this period, see Deuchler (1977, 1992). See Kendall and Peterson (1983) for an interpretive account of early traveller and missionary observations on Korean women, with citations. See Sorensen (1988:Ch. 5) for a speculative reconstruction of women's work in preindustrial rural households.

20. The society of Chosŏn period Korea (1392–1910) was more rigorously stratified on the basis of hereditary status claims than that of late traditional China. Most critically, members of the *yangban* class, those who could demonstrate a clear line of descent from an ancestor who held high public office, held a monopoly of prestige and status enhanced by landed wealth and an education in the Confucian classics. *Yangban* were exempt from most taxes and were entitled to sit for the civil service examination, the gateway to public office (Deuchler 1992:12–13, 309, n.22; Palais 1975:6–7; Wagner 1972, 1974). At the local level, increasingly distant descendants of high officeholders maintained claims to genealogical distinction and social respect through membership in agnatic lineages which meticulously traced their descent from illustrious antecedents (Janelli 1975; Janelli and Janelli 1982). By the eighteenth century, local elites had compiled registers *(hyangan)* of the recognized *yangban* families in their area. These were the basis of endogamous marriage circles among exogamous *yangban* lineages (Kawashima 1980, 1992). Folklorists' twentieth-century accounts of regional custom invariably include orally generated lists, both of those lineages considered to be acceptable sources of brides and grooms for the local *yangban* and of families with whom such alliances would be shunned (MCIBCPP 1969–1978 cum. vols. sections on *"hollye"*). The more prestigious the lineage, the wider its marital radius (Deuchler 1977:10). Roger and Dawnhee Janelli (1982:38–39) describe a lineage that enjoyed more prestige than most of its near neighbors: "it did not take wives from adjacent villages. Instead, lineage members found suitable partners in villages within ten to twenty kilometers. Had they been more illustrious, they would have had to search even farther afield."

tionally reserved in Korea for those who marry for love against their family's wishes."

In the not-so-distant Korean past, not only would brides and grooms go to their weddings in ignorance of each other's face, but the daughters of good families were best not seen at all. In the Chosŏn period (1392–1910), women of the noble *yangban* class ventured forth from behind the high house walls in closed sedan chairs or concealed in veils that covered the head, face, and upper body. A woman of reputable origins but more modest means would always be veiled when she appeared in public. Travellers' tales from the end of the last century speak of an equation of invisibility with virtue and honor so profound that "fathers have been known to kill their daughters, husbands to kill their wives, and women to kill themselves because strangers touched them with a finger" (Bishop 1970:34; Dallet 1954:117).

At the other end of the social spectrum, slaves (who made possible the sequestered life-style of the highborn lady), peddlers' wives, and peasant women at work in the fields appear in genre paintings and early photographs with bare heads, shorter skirts, and brief jackets. Occasionally, the painter portrays the women beside a stream, bared to the waist as they bathe or wash clothes; the painter's addition of a covert male spectator enhances the voyeuristic message of the scene. Also visible were dancing girls *(sadang)*, courtesans *(kisaeng)*, and shamans *(mudang, mansin)*, all considered practitioners of "base" *(ch'ŏn)* professions who sang and danced in public.

While veils, sedan chairs, and slaves are recalled as relics of the last century, the notion that good women are best not seen persisted in rural Korea well into the middle of this century. Both Cornelius Osgood, who conducted his fieldwork just before the Korean War, and Vincent Brandt, in a relatively isolated village in the late 1960s, speak of the near impossibility of a Western man's conducting a conversation with a rural Korean woman (Brandt 1971:134; Osgood 1951:34). Women who were teenagers in the countryside after the liberation (1945) recall that it was not unusual for conservative fathers to prevent pubescent daughters from attending school to keep their reputations intact. A woman who grew up in rural Kyŏnggi Province, not far from the capital city, described her sense of victimization when an unknown young man observed her from the hillside behind her house wall and then sent her an admiring letter. "In those days [the 1960s] there would be so much talk in the village if a maiden received a letter from a man." Wary of the consequences of local gossip, she hastily accepted an early offer of matrimony from a different man introduced by a matchmaker.

As a liability of propriety, families negotiating a match were vulnerable to manipulation by deceitful matchmakers, stock villains in any recounting of old-fashioned matrimony. Moose (1911:160–161) wrote of matchmakers who married off brides who were hunchbacked, deaf, or blind and grooms who were ugly or deformed. In the 1980s, informants readily offered jokes about the matchmaker who, through verbal sleight of hand, married off the blind groom ("It's [his eyes that are] too distant") or the crippled bride ("she just sits and sews all day").[21] I heard these stories any number of times, usually with the teller's implication that this sort of thing used to happen all the time. Thus mythologized, the past is cast even further adrift from the present.[22] A retired soldier was most explicit in telling me that "In the past, even cripples could be married off because you didn't meet them in advance. That sort of thing doesn't happen nowadays because we've become enlightened [kyebaltoeda] in every respect."

The practice of matchmaking sight unseen seems to have engendered its own checks. Close acquaintances and kin were considered far more reliable matchmakers than were itinerating professionals, and village wives, married patrilocally, commanded an ideal position for pairing suitable candidates from their natal and affinal villages.[23] As a further check on mendacity, someone from the bride's or groom's family might secretly

21. "*Nŏmu mŏrŏsŏ kŏkchŏngitchi*" ("I'm concerned that it's too distant") is offered for "*nuni mŏrŏsŏ kŏkchŏngitchi*" ("I'm concerned that [the groom] is blind"). "They say she always sits around sewing" *(ŏnjena anjŏsŏ panŭjilhandae)* masks a bride who is a cripple, "a sitter" *(anjŭnbaengi).*

22. The ubiquitousness of this theme may, in part, be attributed to the success of Ŏ Yŏng-jin's play, *Wedding Day*, in which the groom puts forth the groundless rumor that he is a cripple to test his would-be in-laws' intentions. In the end, to the bride's family's chagrin, the perfectly fit and highly desirable groom insists upon marrying the good-hearted servant girl they would have covertly substituted for the bride (Ŏ 1983). This is not to deny that such abuses sometimes happened in the past, but merely to note that they have become a salient image of old-fashioned matchmaking. None of the tellers of matchmaking puns could cite me specific instances of matches made among their own circle of kin and acquaintances with blind men or cripples. An anthropologist recollecting an incident from his own childhood did describe for me his firsthand observation of a marriage made with a cripple. The family had sent a counterfeit groom to the first meeting (Lee Mun-Woong, personal communication).

23. For discussions of rural matchmaking in decades past, see Osgood (1951:42), Choong Soon Kim (1974), Han (1949:182), MCIBCPP (1978 "Kyŏng-gi":70).

investigate the other family's circumstances and catch a covert glimpse of the intended bride's or groom's appearance and demeanor.[24] In his auto-biographical novel, *The Grass Roof*, Younghill Kang (1966:45) tells how his grandmother, the matriarch of a respected *yangban* family, "disguised herself as a peddler of embroideries, in an old dress . . . so that she was not to be recognized. Then she went to the girl's house and observed for herself. She came home with a glowing report."

Tacit opportunities to view a child's potential spouse were sometimes institutionalized as local custom. In a conservative village in the Andong region, a group of lineage wives, including the mother of the person to be married, would constitute a "marriage committee" to investigate potential spouses. Without revealing their intentions, they would arrange to visit the home of a promising candidate. However, "Even though they disguise their purpose, the person's family understands the reason for the visit and is prepared to show . . . the person in question (to advantage)" (Cho 1979:130). In a filmed re-creation of marriage customs set in this same region, the would-be bride was posed behind a woven screen, demurely embroidering while the white-haired women of the groom's family cast discreet but approving glances in her direction.[25] In a less socially distinguished village near Pusan in the early 1950s, the groom's family would similarly visit the bride's house with the matchmaker: "Usually the bride-to-be may be seen by the guests at a distance industriously working" (Knez 1959:65–66). This glancing view of a young woman absorbed in her tasks, however easily staged, seems to have been the ideal image of a potential daughter-in-law.

The elders' favorable evaluations of a potential son-in-law or daughter-in-law would have turned upon the two broad sociological questions which inform parental negotiations today: "Would one's daughter have a reasonable life if she married into the groom's household?" and "Would such a bride be an asset to one's own family?" *Yangban* families might have been more concerned with the bride's deportment and knowledge of etiquette and less advantaged families more concerned with the bride's capacity for hard physical labor. A glancing view of the bride or groom would verify reasonably good health and an absence of obvious handicaps. Healthy brides could be expected to produce sturdy children, and sickly

24. See Cho (1979:130), Chun (1984:50), Han (1949:182), Knez (1959:65–66), and MCIBCPP (1977 "Chŏnnam":126).

25. The film was *Korea: The Circle of Life*, produced by the Korean Film Board and distributed by Centron Films.

grooms carried the peril of early widowhood. Elders thus read marriage candidates through a pragmatic assessment of the social field in which the bride and groom, and the elders themselves, would live out the consequences of a marriage.

Outside of folklore, the comeliness of the bride had little bearing on these readings.[26] Indeed, a folk belief held that beautiful women were predestined for misfortune: "they are thought more likely to become courtesans or shamans than . . . average or homely looking women" (Harvey 1983: 278 n.2; Kang 1966:136). In contrast to the photographs families now exchange at the beginning of matchmaking, the groom's first tangible evidence of the bride's suitability was once a garment, stitched to his measurements, as an indication of his future wife's skill with a needle.[27] The bride's ability to clothe her household was more crucial to its future happiness and well-being than was the beauty of her face.

COMING INTO VIEW

In 1938, a promising college graduate in his early twenties was allowed to meet his bride before the wedding—a bold departure from established form. The now elderly Kim Sŏngbae recalls:

> Bidding my thumping heart to be quiet I offered a few words. The woman, her head bowed with bashfulness, answered with a tiny voice like the buzz of a mosquito. It seemed as though she hadn't really gotten a good look at me. When everyone else went outside, leaving only the two of us, I couldn't bring out a word or even touch her wrist, so I took my leave in a melancholy mood (Kim Sŏngbae 1983:53–54).

This awkward encounter was a harbinger of change as young men began to claim the right to see their future wives, however briefly, before the wedding. Commonsense explanations attribute the rise and gradual spread of the arranged meeting, and the even more radical love marriage, to the diffusion of "enlightened" attitudes and Western-engendered romantic expectations from the urban intelligentsia through the general

---

26. While the "virtuous wife Ch'unhyang," the quintessential Korean heroine, was fabled for her beauty, the plot turns on her status as the daughter of a courtesan (kisaeng) who is thus unable to become the primary wife of a yangban. Ch'unhyang demonstrates an extraordinary degree of wifely fidelity and, in a happy ending for a work of fiction, becomes the acknowledged wife of the man she loves.

27. See Ko (1982:117), Kang (1966:54), MCIBCPP (1971 "Chŏnbuk":68), and Miln (1895:81).

population. The development and ultimate staying power of this practice, however, suggest a more fundamental redefinition of the groom as a new man in a new social order. From the end of the last century, young intellectuals began to advocate marriage on the basis of personal choice and mutual understanding in the name of individualism and free will. These ideas gained passionate currency through the popularity of Yi Kwangsu's early novel *Mujŏng* (Kim Yung-Chung 1977:248; Robinson 1988:65). In turn-of-the-century Korea, the most emphatic advocates of education for women were progressive men. Their logic was patriotic: educated women might better serve the nation. But these patriots must have recognized that "wise mothers" would also be more congenial mates for the members of a new professional elite (Cho Haejoang 1988:227; Kim Yung-Chung 1977:247–248). Their advocacy of women recalls Lata Mani's (1987) provocative essay on the SATI question, which argues that debates about women's rights and status in society may not be about women at all so much as they are about the stakes particular social groups have in advocating "tradition" or "modernity." In redefining "marriage" as a matter of individual choice and mutual understanding, and in advocating education for women, male visionaries had begun to redefine "wives" as women of their own choosing.

In the early decades of the twentieth century, a wave of Korean youths (like their Chinese and Vietnamese cousins) embarked upon a new style of higher education in the brave new world of the colonial city and metropole. Some left behind the brides who had already been chosen for them by their families. Ideological currents proclaiming the new morality of marriage on the basis of free choice were matters of intense personal concern for male students, who now juxtaposed the image of an unlettered wife, perhaps already with a baby on her back, against the educated and stylish "new women" *(sinyŏsŏng)* who promenaded on Seoul streets in Western clothing, their unveiled heads shielded only by coquettish parasols. Aided and abetted by the liberal divorce laws enacted under the Japanese, many men cast off their old-fashioned-seeming wives (Clark 1919:161; Kim Yung-Chung 1977:276; Robinson 1988. Ch. 3). Contemporary newspaper editorials and personal accounts suggest that, in this period, divorce and matrimony in the name of free choice provoked intense disapprobation and profound anguish among kin (Kim Yung-Chung 1977; Han 1949:49–50; Pahk 1954: Ch. 6).

The emergence of the arranged meeting among this new urban intelligentsia is sometimes described as a compromise in the struggle over free choice marriage, a "rational" attempt to have the best of both worlds.[28] It may also be understood as a response to the altered circumstances of men seeking brides and the interests of new elite families in consolidating their status claims. The period of Japanese colonial domination (1910–1945) saw the emergence of a new urban intelligentsia, a small core of white-collar managers and technicians, and the first stirrings of a native capitalist class (Eckert 1991: 253; Robinson 1988: Ch. 3). The members of this new urban elite would define themselves against their rural origins as modern people, educated in a new way, dressed in a new way, exhibiting new styles of consumption and new intellectual tastes (Eckert et al. 1990:390–392; Robinson 1988:28–29 and work in progress). While family identities remained (and still remain) a significant source of social capital, the new order provided unprecedented mobility (Eckert 1991:1). The worth of young men could be demonstrated in arenas which were independent of the old land-based family and its genealogically anchored reputation, while the carefully orchestrated marriages of sons and daughters could validate the status claims of new elite families.

The young man who met his bride in 1938 boasted in old age that he had often been "praised as a handsome man and as a teacher of noble bearing and faultless deportment who taught his students well." And so, he says, "the parents of daughters who were of age began to consider me as son-in-law material" (Kim Sŏngbae 1983:53). Because he was a promising young professional whose behavior indicated sufficient good breeding to charm the parents of a prospective bride, *his* request to view the bride would not have been lightly refused. Like this young teacher, the new professionals were in the vanguard of the many men who, beginning in the colonial period (1910–1945) and accelerating with industrial development from the 1960s, would find employment off the land and outside the family economy.

Outside the success stories of the new elite, Han Gyoung-hai suggests that, with the impoverishment of the rural economy in the colonial pe-

---

28. In *September Monkey*, the English language autobiography of a "new woman," Induk Pahk (1954:225) explains to her Western readership how, after her own disastrous love marriage, she skillfully manipulated the meeting and courtship of her daughters and suitable marriage candidates. She is explicit in her sense of having improvised a mediation between the rejected past and her own radical youth: "Knowing the old traditional way in which my mother and grandmother had been married and the headstrong manner in which I had managed my own marriage, I wanted to help them [her daughters] marry well and happily. . . . I decided to evolve a new marriage pattern for my girls to follow."

riod, families began to depend upon the nonagricultural income earned by their unmarried children and consequently found it in their interest to delay a child's marriage (Han Gyoung-hai 1990: Ch. 4).[29] Han's study of shifts in the timing of marriage suggests an accompanying shift in the definition of suitable grooms, from boys at the bosom of their families to young men prepared to earn a livelihood. In the early decades of the century, young male students might already be married, but by the 1940s, education had become a legitimate reason for postponing matrimony (Han 1990: Ch. 4). Men became "good groom material" by virtue of their own efforts; they married older, wiser, and possessed of personal attributes which gave them some leverage over the most crucial decision of their lives—even if initially that leverage was only the right to see and, if necessary, to say "no."[30]

The innovation of the arranged meeting would be resisted and negotiated over several decades until by the 1950s it was common in Seoul, and by the 1970s it had become the standard practice throughout the country.[31] The brides of yesteryear recall these meetings as something men insisted upon, as occasions for potential grooms to see and for potential brides to be seen. The first quote is from my own interviews, the second was recorded by Brian Wilson (1983:117).

---

29. Even before industrialization, the sons of disadvantaged households would have married later than the sons of prosperous homes. Recall Andrews's photograph of the married "man" and unwed, unkempt, and much older "boy" (Chapter 1, cf. Kim Taik-kyoo 1964:123–124). The daughters of impoverished families, on the other hand, might be sent out as adopted daughters-in-law *(minmyŏnŭri)* even before the age of ten (Harvey 1983).

30. Margery Wolf (1975:126) describes a similar process for Taiwan in the 1920s and 1930s, when expanded economic opportunities and better educations gave young men greater say in the selection of their wives.

31. Arranged meetings were common in some villages near Seoul by the late 1950s (Lee 1960), in villages near provincial towns (Biernatzki 1967:5), and in the Chŏllas by the 1960s (Pak and Gamble 1975:34). In Enduring Pine Village, where I did my fieldwork, arranged meetings were a normal expectation by the 1960s, and also in the north Kyŏnggi village that Yoon Hyungsook studied (Yoon 1989:23). While Chai (1962:197) reports that, in her late 1950s urban sample, many women "refused at one time or another to be looked at and watched over by a strange man and his curious relatives at a formal introductory ceremony," she does not situate these refusals in time. She describes a woman, already elderly at the time of her interview in the late 1950s, whose husband had wanted to see her before the wedding until he was informed that "if he continued insisting on seeing me, my family would refuse to proceed any further with the marriage" (Chai 1962:81). Chai's text implies that middle-class women in Seoul marrying at the time of her interviews routinely experienced first meetings.

In those days the man just had to go and see and that was all there was to it. The man would say "fine" and the woman would follow. . . . The bride's family would tell the groom to come on such-and-such a day. The family would fix food. The bride would be sitting there, all bashful. I went through this, it was just for the groom to look her over [sixty-year-old woman in 1987].

Even though I didn't like it, the matchmaker came one day and my mother persuaded me to meet the groom and his family. The groom had decided not to marry me until he had seen me. After seeing me he decided to marry me. I only glanced at him so I didn't know whether I liked him or not. I didn't feel anything at all [woman married in 1949].

Anthropologist Lee Kwang-Kyu describes the complex procedures followed by some families in Seoul in the 1950s when the potential bride and the potential groom, accompanied by their parents, would each be given a covert opportunity to view their intended spouse. Next, a meeting would be arranged at the woman's house, where she would be told to fetch some water or to perform some task so that the groom and his parents could observe her attitude, bearing, and speech (Lee 1983:1273). Sometimes men arranged to view the young women without their knowledge (Chai 1962:87; Koh 1959:77), or, in one woman's words, "the bride would pretend that she didn't know what was going on," a circumstance that could be played to the advantage of an unwilling and unusually spunky bride. Elsewhere I have described Yongsu's Mother's purported ignorance and suspiciously ungainly performance on the occasion of her first meeting with her undesirable bridegroom (Kendall 1988:20–27). Sometimes a potential bride might be caught totally unaware in the middle of an arranged meeting. A woman from the countryside near Seoul described the winter day, back in the 1960s, when she was summoned to her aunt's neighboring house, fresh from housework. She chuckles now when she recalls her surprise on seeing several pairs of shoes lined up at the threshold where they had been removed by the elders of her future husband's family.[32] At the time, she had been struck speechless by the realization that they had come to look her over. When her husband-to-be posed her a series of questions, she was too startled to answer. "I just sat there like someone who didn't know anything."

How different is the world of the 1980s and 1990s, in which experts writing in women's magazines advise their readership that "This is the

32. In Korea, as in Japan, shoes are removed before entering the intimate living space of a house.

age of self-promotion *(chagi p. r.)*. You have to get the conversation going" ("The Secrets of a Successful Arranged Meeting," *Yŏng Reidi* March 1985:348–350). "To sit and resist speaking as though 'silence is golden' makes a man want to slap you across the face. . . . Give a little smile as you look him in the eye and then tilt your head slightly, this is excellent body language *(podi raenggwiji)*" ("The Psychology of the Arranged Meeting," *Reidi Kyŏnghyang* 18 November 1984, 60:302).

In decades past, many women, although they knew they were participating in an arranged meeting, "didn't really get a good look"—they were kneeling demurely with their eyes lowered or pretending to be engrossed in their tasks. In addition to their own nervous inhibitions, the necessity of giving a good impression would have discouraged any behavior which could have been construed as brazen, including a purposeful lift of the head to examine the groom. An old woman recalled for me the time of her own courtship (the 1940s): "He'd just get a glimpse of her and she might get a glimpse of him and then he'd have to leave. In those days they couldn't go out on a date where they might actually speak to each other."

The absence of conversation seems to have been typical of early arranged meetings in rural settings. Silence may have been a blessing in disguise, considering this description of arranged meetings also in the 1940s but among educated young men and women in a northern town, where some social interaction was expected:

> Neither [the man nor the woman] knew how to start a conversation and they often sat speechless, glued to their seats, eyes fixed upon their toes, afraid to raise their heads for fear that their eyes should meet. To make matters worse, mischievous brothers and sisters giggled as they peeked through finger holes made in the papered doors (Koh 1959:77–78).

Similarly, in Seoul in the late 1950s, where the man and woman were expected to converse at an arranged meeting, Chai found that "The very nature of the meeting contributes to the discomfort and embarrassment of the couple inhibiting any freedom of observing and judging each other" (Chai 1962:97). One woman who had recently experienced an arranged meeting told her: "I felt so uncomfortable that I could not feel anything about him. If there was any first impression it was not very accurate or dependable for I could hardly even see his face. The older people who were there got to know him better than I did" (Chai 1962:97). Even so, this young woman felt pressured to make up her mind after so brief an acquaintance or her "reputation would be ruined" (Chai 1962:97).

Older informants are careful to distinguish the passing glances of early arranged meetings—the final step in an already carefully negotiated match—from the arranged meeting as it is practiced today, where "success" begins a courtship and "failure" carries no particular onus for the man and woman who had agreed to meet. Contemporary sources describe the arranged meetings of thirty or forty years ago as an opportunity for the bride and groom to affirm decisions already negotiated by their parents, to verify that there was nothing grotesquely wrong with one's future spouse (Chai 1962:99; Koh 1959:78; Osgood 1951:34). Mrs. Yi, an amateur matchmaker who is thoroughly vexed by the pickiness of today's Korean men, told me that in the old days, "there was none of this 'I don't want it!' and nearly 80 percent of those matches worked out. As long as the bride wasn't a mute or a cripple, it would work out. They would get married, just like that, without even dating." These early arranged meetings, constructed as opportunities "for the groom to see the bride," carried the rare but dangerous possibility of his rejecting her. A woman teacher in the late colonial period wrote,

> When I asked my [female] pupils what they most wanted to learn they answered, with giggles and blushes, "We want you to teach us how to conduct ourselves when we meet our prospective fiancés." Since this arranged meeting was the final step before reaching an agreement to accept one another, the engagement was assured unless something unexpected occurred during the interview. It was a terrible humiliation to be rejected (Koh 1959:78).

The ethnographic record suggests a slow acceptance of arranged meetings in the countryside from the middle of the century.[33] On the eve of the Korean War, in a village accessible to the capital city, "one of the most educated men of the village with modern views ... offered his son the opportunity to see the chosen girl before they proceeded with the engagement. He was greatly relieved when the son relinquished his privilege out of deference to his parent" (Osgood 1951:104). Cornelius Osgood noted that such opportunities were "seldom taken advantage of" (Osgood 1951:106). Knez (1959) reports that in the early 1950s, in a village not far from Pusan, a groom might very rarely accompany the elders of his fam-

---

33. Dix describes a conservative *yangban* community that had adamantly resisted love marriages and, well into the second half of the twentieth century, had banished children who held firm in their choice of mates. By the time of Dix's study in the 1970s, however, even conservative elders had begun to find it prudent to accede to a son's wishes, and to do so promptly in the hope of maintaining the illusion that the match had been of their own choosing (Dix 1977:115–116).

ily on their visit to the bride's house. It would be interesting to know more about the personal circumstances of those exceptional bridegrooms who were given the opportunity to view their brides when other men in the community were not. Were they better educated than their age mates, and through education invested in "modernity," as Osgood's anecdote suggests? Did they have good employment prospects outside the community?

Farm families were the last to accept the arranged meeting, not out of innate conservatism so much as practicality, insofar as farmers' brides were seen as entering and working for the family. Yoon Hyungsook provides a telling anecdote. In a village northwest of Seoul, in the late 1960s, a bachelor went to view a potential bride at a meeting arranged by the matchmaker. Years later, he would reminisce that "he liked her right away. He thought that she was beautiful. His widowed mother and older brother thought she was too skinny to be a good wife and mother. But he wanted to marry her and persuaded his mother and older brother" (Yoon 1989:23). Perhaps his arguments were persuasive because by the 1960s it was all too easy for a dissatisfied youth to slip away to the city. This incident illustrates not only an individual victory but also a profound shift in the reading of desirable brides. The mother and elder brother initially rejected the woman on the basis of her potential contribution to the arduous work of a rural household; they read her slim physique as skinny and inadequate. The would-be groom read these same attributes as beauty and carried the day.

ARRANGED MEETINGS TODAY

The popular etiquette book *Passage Rites Made Easy* describes the arranged meeting *(massŏn)* as "a friendly exchange with the possibility of marriage on the introduction of someone with considerable experience of social life" and contrasts it with times gone by when "female relatives from the groom's side would come to the house and look the bride over to their hearts' content while the bride's side would just have to wait for word from the groom's side. In this respect a woman of marriageable age was treated as though she were an item of commerce. But this is a tale of a bygone time" (Ko 1982:55, 61). And yet, in counterpoint, from the pages of a women's magazine, an article entitled "The Sociology of the Arranged Meeting" begins: "What co-ed of 23 or 24 hasn't said this? 'I'd rather not marry than marry on the basis of a formal arranged meeting. It's like bartering in the market, like setting out merchandise on display.

Figure 7. This drawing by the artist Kim Ch'ŏnjŏng was used by a literary magazine to illustrate a disgruntled article on arranged meetings. *Saemigip'ŭnmul* (Water from a deep spring), May 1985.

What am I supposed to do when confronted with a man who already knows everything about me?' " (*Reidi Kyŏnghyang* 60, 8 November 1984:299). Or in the words of a young woman, a Seoulite from a family of comfortable means, the veteran of more than one arranged meeting:

> You feel a thrill of anticipation and then, as soon as you sit down, the atmosphere of the arranged meeting takes over. I felt as though I was a spectacle for people to look at. ("Like an animal in a zoo!" her father inserts with a teasing cackle.) Everyone in the hotel coffee shop knows what's going on. There are the two sets of parents and there is the man and the woman. So everyone in the coffee shop whispers, "Look at those two people having an arranged meeting."
>
> And then when the parents leave, and you're alone with this man you don't know in the least, he asks you things like, "How many brothers and sisters do you have?" and "What sort of music do you like?" It's the strangest conversation. You know that you're not there because of something between the two of you. You're there because you're from two suitable families. You can't forget that. It puts a damper on conversation. You can't just talk in a normal way.[34] [See also an artist's rendering of the mood of an arranged meeting in fig. 7.]

34. In addition to her distaste for first meetings, she still hoped to marry a campus sweetheart, then in the military. She was attempting to hold out against the insistence of her parents, who wanted to see her safely married. A few months

Today, as the workplace and the coeducational university provide un-precedented opportunities for romance, increasing numbers of women and men have love marriages without a matchmaker's introduction. "Ro-mance," an expectation initially engendered by Western films and novels, has flowered in the full-blown consumer culture of contemporary Korea (Cho Haejoang 1988, 1991; Pak Hyeran 1991). If the arranged meetings of a generation past were an all-but-guaranteed affirmation of a parental choice, men and women now go to arranged meetings aware of a large pool of candidates, with the possibility and often the experience of other arranged meetings and with the knowledge of friends and relations who have made love marriages. In the words of *Passage Rites Made Easy*, "The arranged meeting is that important moment when two people meet for the first time and on the basis of this one impression alone they may tomorrow again be strangers or this may be the beginning of a hundred years together" (Ko 1982:64). According to one amateur matchmaker, "It doesn't matter whether the matchmaker speaks well or not, the two con-cerned parties have to like each other. It's not the way it was in the past when the couple just got a glimpse of each other, when it was the parents who looked the prospect over, and that was that. Nowadays, I might intro-duce them but they have to talk to each other."

The meeting is described as a reciprocal sizing up; indeed, the Korean term for these occasions, *massŏn*, literally means "mutual first." But al-though both the woman and the man are expected to convey their impres-sions, "yea" or "nay," to the matchmaker the day after the meeting, and women like my sister Sukcha have no hesitancy in saying "no," the man's side holds the initiative, both at the meeting and in the subsequent court-ship. As Mrs. Yim, the mother of a marriageable daughter, explained, "The groom's side leads. It isn't for the bride's side to set the mood or in any sense lead the discussion. This would be considered inappropriate. They would say that the bride's side lacks etiquette. . . . If the bride's side is too assertive, then the match fails." According to my friend, Mrs. Oh:

> In Korea it's still like this, the woman might make up her mind first but she can't say, "Hey, let's get married." In Korea she has to pretend that she's indifferent. So the groom is the one who says "Let's get mar-ried." The woman can't let on by agreeing until he says things like "I can't live without you." [The anthropologist recalls that in the land of her birth, back in the 1960's, this was known as "playing hard to get."]

---

after this conversation, I learned in a letter from her younger sister that she was going to marry a man she had met through a first meeting, and that she was now very happy.

Mrs. Yi, an avid amateur, recounted every matchmaker's nightmare of the arrogant young man who simply walks out of the coffee shop if the woman he has come to meet is not so beautiful as he had been led to believe.

If Korean brides are now more than pawns in the matrimonial schemes of their elders, they are less than equal players in a marital enterprise constructed on the premise that women attract and men choose. Young women measure themselves, and matchmakers measure their candidates, against a projected image of feminine attractiveness fostered by the media. Korean women's magazines reinforce these perceptions with their "surveys" of what men really want, suggesting that "deep in their hearts, most men consider beauty the most important criterion in choosing a bride" (*Yŏng Reidi* July 1984:121):

> "Who is First-rate Bride material? 1000 Bachelors Reveal their thoughts on First-rate Brides" (*Yŏng Reidi* July 1984:113–123)

or

> "100 Unmarried Men State: 'My Marriage Specifications' " (*Yŏsŏng Chasin* October 1984:239–248)

or

> "Above all, the Prospective Bride must be pretty" (*Yŏsŏng Paengnyu* September 1984:136–141).

The published desires of eligible bachelors would parody an extremely demanding personals column in the United States:

> First, she should be 165 cm (at least) and athletic. She must also be able to understand men, including me of course. She should have at least average looks, and if she's beautiful, so much the better. For the sake of the next generation, she should have fair skin and a good character. She must be a woman who appreciates traditional Korean customs but be equipped with Westernized notions for these rapidly modernizing times (*Yŏng Reidi* July 1984:115).

Individual fantasies are complex and often contradictory: "In my opinion the woman who is first rate bride material has an outgoing personality but is not overpowering. She is dedicated to her family but instead of being obsessed with it, she is also active in society" (*Yŏng Reidi* July 1984:118), "a professional woman able to contribute to society who believes that the extended family is important and can maintain a great

family atmosphere" (*Yŏng Reidi* July 1984:116), or "a woman with traditional style who adapts to new trends" (*Yŏng Reidi* July 1984:118). These
sentiments recall the advertisements for Korean commercial wedding halls
promising "all new facilities with the flavor of our traditional customs."

TO BE CHOSEN

Whether or not such media treatments reflect the actual marital aspirations of a vast universe of flesh and blood men, they reinforce the pervasive middle-class notion that "good groom material" *(chohŭn sillanggam)*
is a rare and precious commodity.[35] Sukcha's feeling "that there aren't
enough good men" was echoed in conversation after conversation with
amateur matchmakers whose intentions had been thwarted by a critical
man shortage *(namjaga mojarada)*. Although the matchmakers I interviewed would probably all consider themselves "middle class," they represent a spectrum of economic and social resources. Yet they hold in common the complaint that "good men" are in a position to set exacting terms
in matchmaking. Mrs. Paek, a successful businesswoman with excellent
social connections, is frequently asked to matchmake. She told me, "The
most difficult thing about matchmaking is if the woman's side likes the
man but . . . he doesn't think she's attractive. You can't say *that*. This
happened to me once. . . ." "Was the man himself so good-looking?" [My
question was intentionally naive.] "In our country, that's not a matter of
concern. It's the man who chooses."

Mrs. Yi, impatient to make more matches, waxed indignant over the
unrealistic standards imposed by young men.

> If the bride is a little bit plump, that won't do, and they say it's no
> good if the woman isn't a stylish dresser. Show them a fat woman and
> they get angry. . . . If the man has money and educational background
> and health, then he wants an educated woman with a pretty face and a
> tall slender body of more than 160 centimeters [5'3"]. A man without
> money wants someone who can help make a living, someone who can
> teach piano or be a pharmacist—and she's got to be attractive on top of
> that. It isn't easy. If the groom says "She isn't very glamorous," I say
> "Why does she have to be glamorous? She has a good education, she's
> healthy, that should be sufficient. Why do you insist on glamour?" . . .
> This sort of thing really makes me mad.

35. As noted in Chapter 1, quite the opposite perception holds among rural
bachelors, who have great difficulty in finding wives willing to share in the hard
work of country life. Yoon Hyungsook (1991) makes explicit note of this comparison in her study of matrimony in a peri-urban village.

Mrs. Pak, a soldier's wife and well-intentioned amateur matchmaker of modest means, spoke in despairing tones of her attempts to match a plain-faced woman. "In Korea, a pretty face is important. I've taken this woman with me to several arranged meetings but it doesn't work out because they say that she isn't very good-looking." She had tried to match her younger brother to a friend's younger sister, a woman she considered a good choice as a home economics major who would be an excellent homemaker. She concluded, "Men don't want that anymore, they don't value it. They want someone who's gone out, seen something of the world." This echoes *Yŏsŏng Paengnyu*'s proclamation, from its survey of eligible bachelors, that "The wise mother, good wife, the most important criterion even in the 1960's, has lost her popularity" (*Yŏsŏng Paengnyu* September 1984:136).

Too much sophistication, however, is a liability. Ms. Ch'oe, a young intellectual, the veteran of no less than thirteen arranged meetings, told me that she thought men found her forthright personality "difficult." A mutual friend confirmed, "She's too bright, Korean men don't want a bright clever woman, they want a womanly woman" (*yŏjadaungŏt*). Ms. Ch'oe herself accepted this; she had played matchmaker for her male cousin and a female friend who is "refined and genteel, a home economics major, not at all like me." The shifting currency of a home economics degree suggests not that masculine ideals are absolute so much as that they can be invoked as a measure of any woman's inadequacy.

At the arranged meeting, as in a job interview, a woman is under tremendous pressure to convey a positive impression of her looks and personality in a brief period of time under awkward circumstances. Women's magazines, with their wealth of instruction on how to surmount the difficulties of the arranged meeting, contribute to the pitch of anxiety:

> What must I do to go to an arranged meeting and find someone who suits me exactly? All the things you must know for each step of the negotiation, before going to the arranged meeting, at the meeting place, all the essential secrets of a successful arranged meeting, all the tips (are here) just for you ("The Secrets of a Successful Arranged Meeting," *Yŏng Reidi* 3 March 1985:347).

> If you know your adversary and know yourself, you'll win one hundred per cent of the time ("The Psychology of the Arranged Meeting," *Reidi Kyŏnghyang* 18 November 1984:302).

Tips on beauty and charm are staples of the genre: choose a dress and makeup that aren't too extreme. Avoid excessively trendy, wild, or suggestive clothing, and try out your costume and makeup beforehand. Leave your cigarettes at home so you won't even be tempted to light up, and remove your gum before leaving the house. Follow *Reidi Kyŏnghyang's* "5-part Course on How To Succeed," and organize your preparations according to a checklist culminating in "D-day." On D-day itself, "Insofar as possible, think only happy thoughts and wear a pleasant expression" ("Matchmaking, Arranged Meetings, Marriage: A 5-part Course on How To Succeed," *Reidi Kyŏnghyang* 8 November 1984, 60:288–304). Don't stare at the ceiling, and guard against nervous gestures such as drumming your fingers or shaking your legs. Avoid getting lipstick smears on your glass since this disgusts some people. Even if you normally drink coffee black, order the same drink as the man ("The Secrets of a Successful Arranged Meeting," *Yŏng Reidi* 3 March 1985:348). "When ordering food, avoid things that require you to open the mouth wide or use your hands . . . when you are tense it is easy to make silly mistakes" (Ko 1982:60). *Passage Rites Made Easy* cautions against bringing a gorgeous elder sister or young aunt as a member of the prospective bride's party: "If the man finds her attractive and then makes a comparison, it's one hundred demerits and no benefit. The chaperons should let the concerned party shine to advantage." The bride's side should position themselves where the prospective bride can be seen to advantage, ideally against a nice background and with sunlight streaming on her hair (Ko 1982:62–63).

The prospective bride's conversational style, both in response to questions posed by the prospective groom's kin and when left alone with the man himself, engenders much anxiety. According to Mrs. Yi, the active amateur matchmaker, "The woman is asked things like 'What school did you graduate from?' and 'What are your hobbies?' If she isn't able to answer well, she seems cold and indifferent or not very bright, and where is the man to match with a woman like that?" The sophisticated, cigarette-smoking readership conjured by the glossy magazines is belied by the amount of space such journals devote to advice on how to hold a simple conversation at the arranged meeting. The author of one commentary notes the inadequacy of such standard exchanges as "What is your hobby?" "Mountain climbing." "What kind of music do you like?" "Jazz."

> Whenever I attend an arranged meeting, I find myself thinking "Young people today haven't the foggiest notion of how to hold a sensible conversation." Of course one appreciates that meeting for the first time in the presence of parents and other concerned parties is a stressful situation. Nevertheless asking the sort of questions that an elementary

school student writes in a diary is a sign of immaturity ("The Secrets of a Successful Arranged Meeting," *Yŏng Reidi* 3 March 1985:366).

According to the experts, a woman must reject the demure stereotype of decades past, not just sit with the neck bowed and the eyes lowered, not just answer, when spoken to, "with a voice as soft as a mosquito" (Ko 1982:64). On the other hand, a woman is advised to avoid asking too many questions and to refrain from unsolicited, aimless chatter, giggling, boasting of her accomplishments, or sprinkling her conversation with foreign words (*Yŏng Reidi* 3 March 1985:348–350). The ideal woman is a welter of contradictions: poised without being too assertive, a good conversationalist who allows the man to lead, a savvy self-promoter who submits to her partner's choice of beverage. Such texts have obvious counterparts closer to home where the stakes may be no higher than a date to the prom. As a genre, they compound the stressful circumstances they claim to remedy and thereby underscore the message that women are to be chosen. The journal *Reidi Kyŏnghyang*, offering tips on how to select a professional marriage bureau, purports to re-create an oft-rejected woman's dejected state of mind: "One by one, my maternal aunts, paternal aunts, and mother's friends had all worn themselves out in their efforts to make me a match. One month and then another have passed without an invitation to an arranged meeting. In my anxious state, all sorts of thoughts go through my head. Why am I so ugly?" ("How To Succeed at a Marriage Bureau," *Reidi Kyŏnghyang* 8 November 1984, 60:294).

MARRIAGE AND THE NEW MIDDLE CLASS

Discourses about matchmaking are overt and explicit statements of desirability; as such they inform the perceptions of women and men, whether they find their partners through arranged meetings or by romantic serendipity. The man's prerogative to choose a pretty wife, and the woman's preoccupation with being chosen, have emerged full blown in recent decades with the rise of a significant Korean middle class and a well-developed consumer culture. The matchmaking practices described here, in tandem with the prevalence of "love marriages," index a significant transformation in how Koreans live and marry in the closing decades of the twentieth century. The story of Korea's economic development, of an interventionist state favoring large corporations and stifling labor unrest among an educated and highly motivated new proletariat, has been told and debated.[36] The social consequences of Korea's rapid transformation from an agricultural to an urban and highly industrialized society have only just begun to be digested. The Korean rural population is half of what it was in 1960 and is probably at its lowest level in this century.[37] In its place, one finds a large working class and a class of white-collar technocrats, professionals, and managers, as well as an increase in the ranks of the petit bourgeoisie (Koo 1987). A majority of Koreans describe themselves as "middle class," as evidenced, in part, by their new ability to participate in a comfortable level of material consumption.[38]

Given that the Korean population is mostly urban, young, and mobile, in all statistical probability a bride and groom will establish a nuclear family.[39] The household they inhabit is no longer a collective agricultural enterprise, but rather a site of capitalist consumption, of "life-style" (an English expression borrowed into Korean speech) as a condition predicated upon the husband's occupation outside the home. In the ideal middle-class Korean family, as in so many other places, the wife is perceived as the manager of domestic consumption, a sharp contrast with the wife of generations past who, however abused, was never considered an *unproductive* member of the household. A good worker was good wife material—the

36. See Amsden (1989), Eckert et al. (1990:Ch. 20), Haggard, Kim, and Moon (1991), Koo and Kim (1992), and Moskowitz (1982). The consequences of three decades of rapid industrialization, beginning in the 1960s with the Park Chung Hee (Pak Chŏnghŭi) regime's five-year plans, were both visible and dramatic, giving the impression that an essentially agricultural society had been transformed into a highly urbanized newly industrialized country in the space of one generation (Koo 1990:672). It is also clear that some kind of demographic transformation began as early as the 1930s, was interrupted by the Pacific War and the Korean War, and resumed in the 1950s (*Census of Korea* 1949, 1959, 1968–1969; Kwon 1977:181, table 8.4, 196–197; Park Chae Bin 1962). I am indebted to Homer Williams for most of the information contained in this note.

37. See the Agricultural Census (1960:80–81), Korea Statistical Yearbook (1990:99), and Williams (1982:tables).

38. See Hart (1991:137–139), Kim Seung-Kuk (1987), and Koo (1987).

39. In 1980, extended three-generation households constituted 16.46 percent of all Korean households, with an additional .59 percent of all households including a married couple and one or more parent. Households including both parents of the senior generation are rare, about 2 percent of all households, with possible additions in the aggregate census category for "other types" of two- and three-generation households (ROK, EPB, NBS 1982:12–1, whole country). This pattern suggests that in Korea today, extended families are most often established to accommodate the needs of an aging parent, rather than as a continuous corporate enterprise in the manner of farmer families in generations past (Sorensen 1986a, 1988; Yi Eunhee Kim 1993:281–283).

preference of the rural mother and elder brother in the story cited previously.

Today, a woman's domestic responsibilities might include some very shrewd investments or nearly covert outside labor to sustain the family's standard of living, and recent statistics indicate that significant numbers of young married women returned to the work force in the late 1980s.[40] Even so, domestic ideology holds that a woman's life-style is set by the position and ability of the man she marries, the man who chooses her (Hart 1991:Ch. 5). This ideal is fostered not only by media imagery, but by employers' explicit policies, which force married women into less desirable forms of work (Cho Hyoung 1986:165–166; Kim Seung-Kyung 1990). One need not romanticize the rural past; it was a hard life and one that Korean women have largely rejected, as evidenced in the "social problem" of rural bachelors. One might recognize, however, the extent to which new marriage practices and their attendant ideologies are bound up with the reconfiguration of the Korean family under industrial capitalism, and that this process has not been an unambiguous blessing for women.

The very openness of contemporary courtship, the possibility of shopping around, suggests to members of the feminist "Alternative Culture Group" *(Tto hanaйi munhwa)* the commodification *(sangp'umhwa)* of matrimony in Korea's capitalist market economy.[41] Anthropologist and feminist Cho Haejoang sees the idealism of contemporary matrimony as encapsulated in media-engendered aphorisms: *"beloved wife and successful husband"* *(sarangbannŭn anae sŏnggonghanŭn namp'yŏn)*, in women who seek the companionship of a husband who "doesn't forget his wedding anniversary," and in men who seek "cute, dependent wives" *(kwiyŏpko ŭijonjŏgin anae)*. This, she maintains, is the banal gender ideology which sustains the Korean middle-class family, of men in grey flannel suits marching in lockstep up the corporate ladder and of women who consume, both as a measure of the husband's success and as the means and evidence of their being "beloved wives" (Cho Haejoang 1988:106–107). One recent television drama offered a mild satire in its portrayal of

40. See Kim Myung-hye (1992), *Korea Statistical Yearbook* (1981, 1990), Lee Hyo-jae (1971:63–64), Moon (1990), and Yi Eunhee Kim (1993:Ch. 11). I am indebted to Homer Williams for recent labor force participation data.

41. See for example the several essays in their special publication *Chabonjuйi sijanggyŏngjewa honin* (The capitalist market economy and marriage) (Lee Hyo-jae et al. 1991) as well as the essays by Cho Haejoang and Kim Ch'anho in the special issue of *Tto hanaйi munhwa* (1991) on "New ways of talking about love."

two ad men intending to promote a certain brand of refrigerator as evidence of a woman's being a "beloved wife."[42]

Kim Ch'anho (1991:58), in a feminist critique of contemporary Korean matrimony, describes the young and beautiful woman as a "commodity" *(sangp'um)* to be chosen by a young man with a good position. She would seem to echo, in another time and place, Beth Bailey's (1988:58) observation that American public culture of the 1950s portrayed both men and women as commodities, "she for her physical attractiveness, he for the size of his wallet." However, Kim Ch'anho and other writers from the Alternative Culture Group are careful to describe contemporary Korean matrimony as one particular consequence of Korean history, culture, and economics, as a pernicious confluence of capitalism (human relations are commodified, materialistic values predominate), an older patriarchy (masculine authority is esteemed, sons are valued, daughters are seen as being absorbed into the husband's family), and an abiding familism (questions of "face" and family interests structure marriage choice and negotiations over subsequent matrimonial exchanges) (An 1991; Lee Hyo-jae et al. 1991; Pak Hyein 1991). It is also clear that contemporary Korean gender ideology burdens men as well as women (Cho Haejoong 1988), that the notion of "good groom material" also implies commodification. Yet however mercenary contemporary assessments of "good groom material" may be, the stakes in matrimony are not the same for women and men where a man's worth is defined by his career and a woman's future is defined by the man she marries.

CONCLUSION

The "beautiful bride" and the "beloved wife" are emergent notions, constructed through and around new courtship practices in an emergent political economy. We see the evolution of new perceptions of gender in tandem with a reconfiguration of the Korean family under capitalism. Because the arranged meeting is self-consciously orchestrated and enacted, discussions about the arranged meeting starkly expose new notions of desirability.

A number of studies link histories of emergent individualism in the West to a heightened awareness of the body as an object of romantic

---

42. See Dennis Michael Hart's (1991:Ch. 6) interesting discussion of the role of advertising in reconfiguring the Korean family as a site of consumption and, in particular, the frequent association of dowry goods with images of a romantic married life.

attraction,[43] a process which may also be discerned in some Third World contexts (Abu-Lughod 1990:48–53; Ong 1987:134–136). A Western European (Stone 1979) or North American (Lystra 1989) experience would lead us to anticipate that as individualism (realized through the social and economic independence of men) and new work and educational opportunities (for both unmarried women and men) undermine the moral and economic authority of kinship, romantic attraction necessarily displaces family choice in matrimony. The rise of arranged meetings and love marriages affirms individual preference as a prerequisite of matrimony, but "preference" should not eclipse the larger Korean social field in which choice and subsequent matrimonial preparations are transacted. The very existence of arranged meetings assumes a matrimonial process embedded in the concerns and responsibilities of families who would see their children wed, and love marriages invert the process of prior screening in acknowledging the need for family approval of a son's or daughter's chosen spouse.

As we shall see in subsequent chapters, the entire marriage process draws upon the resources of kin and underscores abiding relationships among kin above and beyond family involvement in any American wedding.[44] In this, the contemporary Korean marriage process is a transformation of older ways of doing things, above and beyond any "Western" borrowing. Across the social spectrum, Korean couples can expect to have socially appropriate weddings when they have the social and material support of their families. The counterexamples, men and women who cohabit without weddings for lack of parental support or collective family resources, are objects of pity and social concern sufficient to have inspired several social programs on their behalf.

We might ask whether real-life brides and grooms themselves are so bluntly calculating as their caricatures in women's magazines. The tales of courtship contained in the next chapter reveal that, while gender ideology might help us to understand the emergent structure of marriage practices and their rationale, human responses to the business of getting married are more complex and variable than any generalized account or magazine survey might suggest. I think, for example, of a young physician, a man who, true to type, had been extremely exacting in his request

43. See for example Foucault (1980:107), Scheper-Hughes and Lock (1987:14, 25), and Turner (1984:174, 202–203).
44. Cho Hyoung (1975) was perhaps the first social scientist to identify the significance of kinship networks and support among middle-class Koreans, despite the predominance of nuclear households, and to underscore the role of women in maintaing these connections.

for a beautiful bride until, at the end of one arranged meeting, a quiet and unremarkable young woman recognized his weariness and insisted that it was not necessary for him to escort her home to a distant neighborhood. Touched by her thoughtfulness, he asked to date her, and a few months later, they were blissfully married.

As an antidote to any assumption of automatonlike brides, let us return to my sister Sukcha, aware that the time has come to get married, complicit in altering the shape of her nose, but vocal in her discontent. Despite lifelong reminders that she is the plain-faced daughter for whom it will be difficult to find a spouse, Sukcha herself is being choosy, and Sukcha keeps her sense of humor. Her story continues.

5

Requesting Marriage

In the end, Sukcha would marry for love. I was travelling in Southeast Asia when Ŏmŏni, true to her promise, telephoned my home in New York. From the laughing, excited, and only partially comprehended voices at the other end of the line, my husband intuited that the day had been set for Sukcha's wedding. Happily, I had already arranged to stop in Korea on my way home. Before many days have passed, I am sitting on the warm floor of Ŏmŏni's house in Righteous Town, impatient for all to be revealed. Had the much-anticipated arranged meeting borne fruit? "That wasn't how it happened." Yangja's Father, my fictive senior brother-in-law, begins to explain in his deep but gentle voice: "Sukcha went to her friend's wedding, she was a friend of the bride and the man was a friend of the groom. They got to know each other over drinks. . . ."

"No brother-in-law, you've got it all wrong, that wasn't how it happened." My third sister commandeers the narrative. "Her friend had someone she wanted her to meet, one of her husband's friends. Sukcha was already going to an arranged meeting, but her friend said, 'If that one doesn't work, try this.' Sukcha didn't like the first man, so she met the second. They were instantly attracted to one another."

Indeed they were. Ŏmŏni makes a chuckling show of annoyance, describing how during this brief courtship a call from Sukcha's beloved would send Sukcha flying from the restaurant to meet him for lunch or coffee. But when the potential groom came to pay his respects to Ŏmŏni during the Mid-Autumn Festival, Ŏmŏni had not been impressed and had tried to discourage Sukcha. "She didn't like his looks," the sisters tell me, "but when she saw how fond they were of each other, she gradually came around." Since Ŏmŏni now describes Sukcha's intended as "tall, well-bred, and with a good job in a government office," this report of her initially cool reception surprises me. Sukcha's betrothed, while not a paragon of Korean male beauty, is by no means ugly. Perhaps Ŏmŏni read something into his features, a ruddy complexion that suggested a propensity to drink, or some other ominous sign of a character flaw not readily grasped by one illiterate in the subtle art of reading Korean faces. More likely she assumed that the courtship would fail precisely because the man was an attractive marriage candidate. She describes the groom's family as better off than her own and the groom's mother as having justifiably wanted "a senior daughter-in-law who was tall and had a nice round face, not someone like Sukcha. It was the groom who insisted that he would have no one else." Capitulating, the mother-in-law acknowledged that her son and Sukcha "looked alike," a further measure of their compatibility. The groom's persistence may have won Ŏmŏni's confidence as well. Besides, the clock was now ticking in Sukcha's favor as each day brought her closer to the new year that would mark her transition to the awkward age of thirty. It was in Ŏmŏni's interest to have the courtship succeed; it would soon become even more difficult to arrange a new match for her uncooperative daughter.[1]

Ŏmŏni began in earnest to meet with the groom's family in tearooms to negotiate the wedding arrangements. She insisted on a December wedding, against the mother-in-law's preference for a wedding in the spring marriage season.[2] And now the day has been set, December 22. "Can you stay in Korea for the wedding?" Ŏmŏni wants to know. "I want you to come to the wedding hall and take pictures. The other side will have a photographer. It would be nice if our side had one too. I want you to take my picture when I light the candles with the groom's mother," and she pantomimes in anticipation, slowly raising her arm as if about to dance.[3]

"Not Tallae!" my sister Kkach'i snickers. "Not a single one of the pictures she took at my wedding turned out. Don't you remember?"

1. Yi Eunhee Kim (1993:279) notes how often parental opposition may be effective in causing a child to reconsider his or her marital choice, in part because decisions to marry are made after only a very short period of association, as in Sukcha's case, and attachments are usually not very deep.

2. Ŏmŏni's haste was a reversal of a common middle-class expectation that the bride's side desires a later date because their preparations are more onerous and their extensive shopping requires a mustering of financial resources. Beyond pragmatics, the bride's side may postpone a daughter's departure for reasons of sentiment, although brides' mothers seem to feel that an overlong engagement is not good insofar as the couple may lose interest in each other before the wedding.

3. The lighting of marriage candles by the mothers of the bride and groom is a recent innovation in the Righteous Town wedding halls. It was not a part of the new-style ceremonies I observed in 1983 and 1985, although I saw it performed in Seoul church weddings in the early 1980s. The new and fancy wedding halls of Righteous Town have the conceit that they provide services in the "Seoul style," following the latest fashions in the wedding hall business.

"My camera was broken." I make a lame reply as we all laugh at the memory. With sincere regret, I explain that I have been away from home for three weeks and must return to prepare for Christmas. Diana Lee has accompanied me to Ŏmŏni's house, and I offer her services as a videoteur. Against polite demurrals from the family, I successfully convince them that it is in Diana's and my professional interest to film Sukcha's wedding, important to our "studying" Korean customs. Diana thinks she can find a friend to take still photographs in the wedding hall.

The groom arrives, a robust but quiet-seeming young man. He is thoroughly bewildered to find the house filled not only with Sukcha's sisters and affines, now in a jolly and raucous mood, but with two American women as well. One of these asks impertinent and poorly phrased questions. The other, the younger one, looks more reassuringly Korean, but doesn't say very much and sports a video camera. It seems she wants to film him while the other one asks questions, and the family all thinks this is great fun. Ŏmŏni hastens to ask if his family would mind if their side has its own videoteur at the wedding. Of course, he agrees.

Mercifully, for the groom's sake, Sukcha arrives. She has been to the beauty parlor because tonight she will have her first meal with the groom's family in their home. Her hair is a complicated mass of permanented curls and waves, her face carefully made up, and she is wearing a smartly tailored brown winter dress. "I look like an *ajuma*, like a middle-aged woman," she says with mock disbelief as she catches her reflection in a mirror. I am amused by this thorough transformation of the girlish presence I remember from only a few months past. Sukcha hastens to take her place close beside the man she is to marry.

Sukcha will marry for love, although her marriage could as easily have been arranged. The very fact that a friend "introduced" the couple blurs the boundaries of any rigid categorization. This chapter is concerned with how matches are made. It presents a spectrum of personal dramas and the attendant subtle status implications subsumed under the broad dichotomy of "matchmade" versus "love" marriages. It is also concerned with the women (mostly women) who make marriages for other people and with why these practitioners of an acknowledged "good work" are necessarily both praised and distrusted.

LOVE AMONG THE WORKERS

Sukcha would marry late and in a style that suggested middle-class respectability. How different was Sukcha's wedding from the hurried and humble celebration for her sister Kkach'i fourteen years before, an ironic contrast insofar as the entrepreneurship of Kkach'i and her husband had now transported Sukcha's family into the lower rungs of the middle class and would finance Sukcha's wedding. I had first met Kkach'i on lunar New Year's eve in 1977, the day I joined Ŏmŏni's household as a visiting anthropologist in need of room and board. Kkach'i was twenty-four years old and pregnant. "There's a baby inside," Ŏmŏni kept saying, pointing to Kkach'i's belly and pantomiming fullness. "She understands, *Ŏmma!*" Kkach'i was giggling. "She isn't a deaf mute." "And the wedding is going to be this spring," Ŏmŏni beamed. Had I heard correctly? I smiled, which seemed to fit the mood. Here was Ŏmŏni, bursting with delight at the prospect of a new grandchild, anxious to introduce me to "Kkach'i's be-loved" when he arrived at the house later that evening. I would soon learn that Kkach'i's situation was by no means unusual, accepted with a chuckle in this village on the outskirts of industrial Seoul.

Other studies from other communities permit the generalization that by the 1970s cohabitation before marriage was common among village children who worked off the land and among rural migrants to the cities (Cho Oakla 1987a:72–73; Chung 1977:77; Yoon 1991). It remains a common practice among urban workers (Kim Eun-Shil 1993:186–203; Kim Seung-Kyung 1990:156–158; Pak Sukcha 1991). With no stake in the old life but with no claims to status in the new, young workers, both male and female, had little to lose in these arrangements. With limited ability to finance their children's weddings and subsequent livelihood, families would acquiesce. Indeed, by the 1980s, the parents of the man who would inherit the family farm would have the most cause to be delighted if their son found himself a wife, by whatever means. Households with bachelor farmers would not shun any tactic that brought in a daughter-in-law, including a son's temporary sojourn in urban employment (Yoon 1991:131).

Like so many village daughters of her generation, Kkach'i had gone to work in a factory, and living in the big city, she had met a man. Initially, her father stridently opposed the relationship. Kkach'i's lover had come up to Seoul from the impoverished southwest, a Chŏllado man against whom residents of central Korea would hold a profound regional preju-dice. Kkach'i seemed to be her father's favorite daughter, a factor that contributed both to his opposition and to his eventual capitulation. "So," Kkach'i told me years later, "I ran away with my baby's father, until there was a baby in my belly, and then we got married." Ŏmŏni was determined that there would be a real wedding. Kkach'i and her lover would have preferred to wait until they had built up some savings and could hold a better ceremony. Ŏmŏni harumphed, "Are you going to wait until the kid's three feet tall?" Then she called in the different bits of money she had lent out at interest and began her closely calculated preparations. An American boarder was a welcome addition to her household in that season of stretched resources; indeed, the impending crisis of an early wedding was probably the reason why the village elders had decided to send me to Ŏmŏni's house.

Sixteen of the twenty-nine couples from Righteous Town wedding halls for whom I have detailed case material—just over half—married for love rather than on a matchmaker's introduction. Like Kkach'i's parents, many of the parents were displeased, at least at first, that their children had initiated relationships. Some thought the couple too young, the groom unhealthy looking, or the couple's behavior inappropriate. When I asked one mother whether she had known about her daughter's boyfriend in the early days of their relationship, she answered me with humorous ire: "Why should she have told us? We would have just gotten all hot and bothered about it."

Some of these love brides were, like Kkach'i, pregnant when they marched down the aisle of the wedding hall. Indeed, my first round of interviewing took place in the sultry summer months, when it was as-sumed only urgency would cause a wedding to be scheduled in advance of pleasant autumn weather, and all three love brides, out of an in-depth sample of ten weddings, were pregnant. Because I found my interview subjects *in* wedding halls, my sample was restricted to couples who *had* weddings, financed out of pocket and with at least a token mustering of family support and representation. Many others are less fortunate.[4] Even among the fourteen "love" marriages in my total sample of twenty-nine weddings, three couples had waited until their children were at least of school age before they could finance this critical ritual. When one bride defied her widowed mother and moved in with her husband's impover-ished family, she was to wait for more than a decade before she could finance a wedding, largely through the force of her own resolve. Her story

4. Studies by Cho Oakla (1987a:72–73) and Pak Sukcha (1991) describe how the working poor initiate cohabitation and legally register their marriages on the assumption that they will someday be able to afford a wedding. Yoon Hyungsook (1991:128) describes the situation in "K Village," where parents, lacking the resources to approximate the matchmaking practices and formal gift exchanges of the urban middle class, rationalize consensual unions as a "sign of the times."

gives a human face to the practice of working-class cohabitation and reveals the consequences of "love marriage" in the absence of social and material resources.

MRS. CH'OE'S STORY

She is a robust and swarthy woman with a pleasant face that crinkles up with chuckles. She walked into the tearoom with the rolling gait of a woman used to carrying heavy loads. She had come up from the countryside more than fifteen years ago to work in a garment factory. Because her father was dead and her family poor, she had initially sent her wages home to help them get by. Unlike many other brides, her family's circumstances did not permit her to set aside money for her own wedding. She met her husband on an outing and liked him because he "seemed to have the strength to make a living." She described her husband as a heavy drinker and a bit of a flirt, but not wasteful.

"I was born in the year of the cow. They say that you should marry a man who is three years older than you. That's what I did, but it doesn't seem to have worked out so well anyway." She said this with her characteristic chuckle. Her husband was the eldest son of a poor laborer's family, an eldest son with numerous siblings, the burden of whose well-being would rest upon his shoulders. To make matters worse, his mother was paralyzed, thus compounding the tasks that would fall to a new daughter-in-law. When Mrs. Ch'oe made her first visit to the family and saw how they were living, she thought, "How can I endure this?"

Because of the inevitable hardship the young woman would face, her mother was vehemently opposed to the marriage. "You see, my mother was treated brutally by my father. My father was the only son for four generations, and [because he was considered so precious] my mother had a bad relationship with her mother-in-law. She always told me, 'You go and marry into a household where there's no mother-in-law,' and then she told my husband, 'Care for my daughter, don't strike her.'"

When Mrs. Ch'oe joined her husband's family, she gave her earnings to them instead of to her own mother, with whom she had quarreled and broken off relations. Even had her mother approved of the marriage and not begrudged the loss of her daughter's income, it is unlikely that these two poor families could have contemplated hosting a wedding. When her first child was born, the marriage was registered, and Mrs. Ch'oe also sought out her own mother to mend their relationship. "I'd had a baby, so of course I was desperate to see my mother."

Over the years, through hard work, her family's situation has improved. Her husband did contract work in Saudi Arabia, and Mrs. Ch'oe, who has continued to work in a neighborhood factory, invested her own earnings in rotating credit associations. She told us with pride that, in the neighborhood and among her kin, she has a reputation for being frugal and hardworking. A year after the death of her invalid mother-in-law and twelve years after registering her marriage, Mrs. Ch'oe used the profit on her investments to organize a wedding: to pay for the wedding hall, a feast, new suits for her husband and father-in-law, and a new Korean dress for herself. The standard wedding jewelry she considered unnecessary, since her husband had already bought watches during his time abroad. They had met their needs over time and she was proud. "We don't lack for anything at home, even jewelry."

Since her mother was dead, her brother and his wife represented her family. Their only contribution was the food for the final p'yebaek rite, when the bride greets her parents-in-law and serves them wine and meat. Her own children tactfully pretended to be ignorant of their parents' wedding, preserving the fiction that the quantities of food the neighborhood women were preparing in the kitchen were "for grandfather's birthday." But on Parents' Day, a national holiday that came a few days later, they gave their parents a card that read "Congratulations on your marriage! Father, please drink less so that you don't abuse Mother."

When we asked Mrs. Ch'oe how she felt, having accomplished a wedding, she said, "I don't feel anything in particular. It's something that one determines to do; I felt uneasy without it." My assistant described her as someone "suddenly relieved of a long and painful muscle cramp."

I have wondered, in retrospect, what "love marriage"[5] means for Mrs. Ch'oe. Hers is not a tale of romantic reminiscence, but a frank account of a hard life. Did she choose to "endure it" because she felt compromised, if not already pregnant, then as damaged goods?[6] Did she simply accept,

---

5. The English language concept of "love" is an overly broad translation of yŏnae, which connotes romantic attraction, desire, or erotic love. Yŏnaerŭl kŏlda, "to become romantically involved"—the term used by Kkach'i, Mrs. Ch'oe, and Mrs. Sŏ to describe their relationships—has a strong sexual connotation and could easily be applied to an adulterous relationship.

6. Writing of life among the urban poor in the early 1970s, Chung Cha-Whan notes that a rebuffed suitor might rape the woman he wished to marry, "soiling" her in the eyes of other men (Chung 1977:136–138). Many of the women who described their relationships to Kim Eun-Shil (1993) spoke almost fatalistically of entering into cohabitation because they felt it was time to leave their families.

on the strength of her mother's example, that marriage was meant to be difficult? Whatever her motivations long ago, she has persevered.

Mrs. Ch'oe's story suggests the limited options of those who meet and marry in the absence of family support. How much more difficult are the circumstances of those who have no family at all. Only after meeting Mrs. Sŏ did I understand the bone-deep significance of every Korean cliché that I have ever heard regarding the importance of family ties.

MRS. SŎ: THE STORY OF AN ORPHAN BRIDE

My assistant and I photographed Mrs. Sŏ's wedding in the agricultural cooperative on a weekday morning. The attendance was spare, fewer than twenty people, but it was, after all, the middle of the week. The bride was slim and looked so glamorous in her bride's makeup and upswept hair that we began to refer to her as "the beautiful bride" *(miin sinbu)*. Armed with a small stack of photographs and an address that someone in the wedding party had hastily scribbled for us, we attempted to find her house.[7] When we asked in the neighborhood for "the new bride, the beautiful bride," the neighbors were unresponsive. When we showed them the wedding photographs, we still drew no response. By chance, we posed our query to the groom's sister, who led us to Mrs. Sŏ.

When she came out to greet us, we could barely recognize her, so great had been the transformation worked by the wedding hall's illusions of costume and makeup. The face that had been radiant with cosmetics now seemed pale and worn, but not otherwise unpleasant. The slim figure that had been elegant in white lace now seemed a bony frame for baggy work clothes. Weary though she seemed, she was pleased to see us and beckoned us into a small dark apartment, under lines of laundry, to sit beside two small children sleeping soundly on the floor.

Our questions brought forth her story, which she told while choking back tears. She was an orphan raised in an orphanage. She never knew her parents and has only vague memories of an old man who delivered her to the orphanage on a rainy day. After completing middle school, she went to work in a factory, and when she was twenty-five years old, she met her husband. They began to live together, and the bride put her small savings toward the key money on their rented room. At first, she was

7. Korean houses are numbered by the sequence of their construction rather than by their spatial relationship to other houses on the street. Finding an address can be challenging.

ashamed to admit she was an orphan. She thought that her lover would abandon her once he knew the truth. Eventually she told him, "This is the sort of person I am. If you want to live with me, stay, and if you don't, leave me." He stayed. The groom's father sought them out where they were selling produce beside the road and invited the couple into the family home. Her mother-in-law was critical at first, but once the bride became pregnant, the mother-in-law treated her with kindness.

The groom's parents emigrated to the United States, and for five years the younger couple tried their luck at various jobs, meeting with little success. The parents' venture flourished, however, and they were now able to invite their son and his wife to join them. It was the mother-in-law who decided that there would be a wedding; she wanted her eldest son to "put up his hair," to become an adult. She returned to Korea and took care of everything: the wedding hall, watches and rings for the couple, a suit for the groom, and a Korean dress for the bride. The bride was overwhelmed with gratitude. She summed up her life with tears in her eyes.

> I'm really no better than chaff (because I have no family). There isn't anyone who would want a woman like me for a daughter-in-law, but my mother-in-law provided everything. There isn't anyone like my mother-in-law. She's helped us out, both with money and affection. As long as she lives, I intend to serve her to the best of my ability.
>
> I used to bear a grudge against my own parents (for abandoning me), but now that my life has changed, I feel that it was fated and I don't bear a grudge against anyone. It was my good fate that I met such a fine husband and mother-in-law. I don't envy people with parents of their own anymore.

TYPOLOGIES AND STORIES

While women with lives akin to those of Mrs. Sŏ and Mrs. Ch'oe might have worked beside Kkach'i in the factory, their stories are far removed from her sister Sukcha's world. In the early 1990s, Sukcha would restate with pride what government labor statisticians regarded with alarm: that "Koreans today don't want to work in dirty, dangerous factories." The term "love marriage" subsumes Sukcha's story with Kkach'i's story, and with Mrs. Sŏ's and Mrs. Ch'oe's stories. It homogenizes their experiences with those of the "campus couple," the couple who met in a church youth group, the couple who were introduced by an almost intentionally matchmaking professor, the friend's sister and the brother's friend, and the couple who grew up together in the same neighborhood on a street not far from Sukcha's house. It blends their story with that of the clerk and the secretary from a small trading company who had smiled coyly at each other but were constrained from speaking—"We liked each other but we had too much pride"—until a mutual friend invited them both to dinner, the story of the smitten fruit vendor who invited a pretty woman for a cup of coffee, and the couple who found each other through their common commitment to the labor movement (their *churye* was the lawyer who had represented the bride when she was arrested).

One couple thoroughly bent the demarcation between "love" and "matchmade" marriage. Because Ms. Kim's father was ill on the day of her arranged meeting with Mr. Pak, she had gone to the meeting without an accompanying adult. This had made a bad impression on Mr. Pak's parents, who intended to have nothing more to do with Ms. Kim. Mr. Pak had other ideas. In his own words, "I really chased after her." After a whirlwind twenty-day courtship, they decided to marry. When I interviewed them shortly after their honeymoon, they were quite obviously squeezing and patting each other under the table. If this was technically an arranged match, it certainly resembled love. Other matchmade couples who felt a similar, if not so thoroughly intense, attraction sometimes describe their marriages as "half-half" *(panban),* half "love" and half "arranged," particularly if the conversational context (an interview with an American, for example) would seem to privilege romance. Indeed, some commentators describe all contemporary matchmaking, with its provision for arranged meetings and personal consent, as "half-half." Conversely, parents have described their children's marriages to me as "half-half" when a friend, not a matchmaker from the parental generation, introduced the couple, a common happenstance which my marriage-age assistants and my sister Sukcha regarded as "love marriage."

The notion of a "matchmade marriage" similarly elides a great range of stories, from the high-powered pairings of the sons and daughters of Korea's business and political elites, a subject of intense media coverage, to the well-intentioned negotiations of neighbors and aunts, to the dreary commercial marriage bureaus which promise wives for elderly widowers and foreign husbands for women on the run.

MAKING MATCHES

Although recent studies of both the urban middle class (Pak Minja 1991) and the urban poor (Pak Sukcha 1991) indicate a steady rise in the number of love marriages over the course of recent decades, matchmaking, in its modern transformation, is very much a part of the contemporary Korean scene.[8] It is a topic of constant conversation among women like Ŏmŏni, who have sons or daughters of marriageable age, and a popular subject for television soap operas. This course remains a universal possibility for the unwed, offering anxious mothers like Ŏmŏni an honorable means of marrying off a recalcitrant child before age becomes a serious deficit to matrimonial prospects. In the words of Mrs. Yi, an active amateur matchmaker: "These days, if people don't fall in love while they're still in school, it would be difficult for them to get married without matchmaking. Once they leave school, they don't have many opportunities to meet people of the opposite sex and fall in love. You soon grow to dislike the people you see at work everyday, so, you see, there's a real need for matchmaking."

Kkach'i is certain, from her own experience and observations, that love marriages are on the rise and matchmaking is dying out, that only a scant minority need ever consult a matchmaker. Some of the well-connected and well-endowed women I spoke with, on the other hand, insisted that they wanted matchmade marriages for their own children and that in their circles matchmaking was regaining lost ground. They confessed that they had begun to negotiate the marriages of daughters newly graduated from college. Some women claimed to have learned by bitter experience the disappointments of marriages naively premised upon romantic attraction, and having learned their lesson or witnessed the disillusionment of friends or relations, they would protect their children from the perils of romance. One woman felt that today's youth, raised in an affluent society, had lost the purity of motive which love unions required, particularly when a potential partner was the child of a wealthy home. Others frankly suggested that, among their set, the social and material stakes in matrimony were too significant to be left to blind chance and potential exploitation.

Both casual discussions and media portrayals of matchmaking often evoke the image of ambitious mothers and daughters desperate to win an illustrious match, either as an affirmation of status or as a means of advancement. Well known is Chohŭi, the heroine of Pak Wansŏ's popular

8. The National Statistical Office reported that 39.4 percent of all marriages in 1989 were matchmade (*Newsreview*, 26 October 1991:8) while a survey conducted by the Korea Institute for Health and Social Affairs revealed that seven out of ten married Korean women met their husbands through a matchmaker's introduction (*Newsreview*, 23 March 1991:11). The data in the two surveys are inconsistent but permit the generalization that while matchmaking is no longer the dominant form of Korean matrimony, it is for many Koreans a significant means to finding a spouse.

novel, then movie, *Staggering Afternoon* (*Hwich'ŏnggŏrinŭn ohu*). Cho-hŭi barters her youth and beauty for the hand of a wealthy widower.

More than one woman mentioned the proliferation in recent years of commercial matchmaking services. There were professional matchmakers (*maep'a*) in the past, usually described as itinerant female peddlers ever on the lookout for bachelors and maidens. Today newspapers and telephone books carry advertisements for licensed marriage bureaus (*kyŏrhon sangdamso*), some offering computerized matching, while a legion of unlicensed professional matchmakers (usually referred to as Madam Ttu or *pok puin*) pedal their encyclopedic knowledge of suitable mates. Women married twenty or more years ago assure me that both of these services were either unknown or extremely rare when their own matches were made.

Sociologist Lee Hyo-jae (1983:175) links the emergence of the licensed marriage bureau to the industrial transformation of Korean society. The many young men and women who left the Korean countryside in the 1960s and 1970s to seek their fortunes in the cities were often removed from networks of supportive kin when the time came to make their marriages. By implication, those who used these early marriage bureaus had a social or personal deficit. The rise of the Madam Ttu, by contrast, is commonly perceived as linked to the rise of an affluent and socially ambitious industrial elite (*Han'guk Ilbo*, 26 February 1984). Even so, most matchmaking in Korea is performed by well-intentioned amateurs.

Insofar as marriage constitutes the "one great event of a lifetime," the quintessential attribute of adulthood, facilitating the marriages of others is considered a "good work." If even the proprietors of public wedding halls and purveyors of dowry goods can claim the luster of humanitarian motivations for their work, how praiseworthy the ordinary aunt or everyday neighbor who, for no obvious personal gain, brings an unmarried man and an unmarried woman together, face to face, in a hotel coffee shop. To be asked to matchmake for others confirms matronly stature, insofar as the well-regarded amateur is well spoken, has an excellent range of connections, and can be trusted to take one's own interests to heart. "Find me a daughter-in-law just like you" is how fellow churchwomen asked Mrs. Pak to matchmake for their children, and she relates this to me with great pride.

Successful matchmaking engenders profound, sometimes lifelong gratitude. But at the same time, matchmakers are widely portrayed as avaricious and deceitful villains or, at best, akin to the proverbial American used car salesman whose glowing recommendations are ever to be taken with a grain of salt. A popular women's magazine, commenting upon the propensity of matchmakers to exaggerate their candidates' attributes, advises that, in the matchmaker's telling, "A 'deputy section chief' becomes a 'section chief' and a monthly salary of 500,000 *wŏn* is expanded to 800,000 *wŏn*" ("The Secrets of a Successful First Meeting," *Yŏng Reidi* 3 March 1985:347).

I have found it instructive to pursue the topic of matchmaking through a matchmakers'-eye view, to examine why matchmakers must necessarily be both praised and distrusted. My subjects are thirteen amateur matchmakers and five employees of different licensed marriage bureaus (one of these was a man).[9] The amateurs were old acquaintances of mine or the relatives and mothers' friends of three marriage-age research assistants. Each of the amateur matchmakers had concluded at least one successful match; a few were avid in their continuing efforts. These women speak of the significance of the matchmaker's task, the strategies they employ, the satisfactions they gain, and the frustrations they suffer. I also spoke with vast numbers of friends and acquaintances on the subject of matchmaking, which most had experienced firsthand as brides, potential brides, or the parents of marriageable children. Although the multiple voices contained in this chapter were recorded during several separate interviews and conversations, they emerge here in rapid juxtaposition, as from a round-table discussion, affirming and sometimes contradicting each other. This is how I imagined my subjects, these women of different ages and backgrounds, when I reencountered them on reviewing my field notes from 1987. I saw them seated comfortably around me, perhaps in a semicircle of chairs in my office in New York, even as the notes that contained the fragments of our encounters were scattered round my desk. I have posed my questions and listened, trying to apprehend what these several voices had to tell me about Korean matchmaking.

WICKED MATCHMAKERS AND MYTHICAL MADAM TTU

When the topic is matrimony, stories abound concerning the deceitful matchmakers of long ago. Some tales are personal recollections from the not-too-distant past, of the crippled groom who appeared at the bride's house on the wedding day or of the bride who, counter to the matchmaker's assurances, found that her new home would be a beggar's hovel. Some

---

9. Interviews in marriage bureaus were requested in advance by telephone. The bureaus were located through newspaper advertisements.

tales are pure folklore, and these were told to me with thigh-slapping amusement throughout my fieldwork (see Chapter 4). Both folklore and reminiscence emphasize the old-fashioned matchmaker's capacity to deceive when the bride and groom did not look upon one another's faces until the wedding day. For at least a generation, no Korean bride or groom has gone to a wedding sight unseen, and the telling of wicked matchmaker tales affirms the broad distance between the still remembered past and the seemingly enlightened present. That these tales of bygone times are so readily elicited when the conversation turns to matchmaking also suggests an abiding distrust of the matchmaker's words.

The folklore of contemporary matchmaking has engendered its own stock villain in the unlicensed professional matchmaker, the "Madam Ttu" who, for an extortionate fee and sometimes with the threat of blackmail, schemes the matches of the rich and powerful.[10] In these "bad matchmaker" stories, the irresponsible matchmaker typically exaggerates the bride's family's wealth, and when the mercenary groom is subsequently disappointed, he mistreats and abuses his disillusioned bride.[11] Or the bride finds that her husband's position and his family's circumstances have been woefully misrepresented.

The name Madam Ttu, or "Madam Procuress," came into popular usage through the apt and outrageous characterization of a professional matchmaker in Pak Wansŏ's novel of contemporary matrimony, *Staggering Afternoon* (Yim Dawnhee, personal communication). "A woman with a wrinkled face and short bobbed hair, a strange seeming woman loaded with earrings, necklace, bracelets, and broach who inspired an uneasy sense of dislocation in those who encountered her," Madam Ttu appears as a sharp-talking businesswoman with a penchant for black market Kent cigarettes (Pak Wansŏ 1985:vol. 1, 213). She seals the doom of the

10. In 1980, after Chun Doo Hwan's (Chŏn Tuhwan's) coup, the new government identified illegal matchmakers as "elements corrupting society" and began a major crackdown. In 1981, some eighty matchmakers were arrested for violating the Family Ritual Code, which prohibits arranging marriages for cash (*Korea Times*, 6 March 1982:8). Seoul gossip held that the list of marriage prospects carried by a Madam Ttu brought to judgment included the name of the unmarried judge who presided at her trial. The Madam Ttu have, by all accounts, continued to flourish.

11. In a notorious case, the groom physically abused not only his wife, but also her parents. This extreme breach of propriety won press coverage and a spate of commentary condemning the mercenary odor of contemporary marriage negotiations, but I heard other tales of disappointed husbands and battered wives as common gossip.

ambitious and beautiful heroine by encouraging her aspirations for a wealthy but otherwise disappointing husband. The popular novel became a film, and other Madam Ttu began to appear in television soap operas and media exposés: "The Resurrection of Madam Ttu" (*Han'guk Ilbo*, 26 February 1984), "Tears and Laughter at the Trickery of 'Madam Ttu' " (*Tonga Ilbo* 7 April 1987:5). In 1984, the *Han'guk Ilbo* would describe the Madam Ttu as women who carried on their persons great lists of high civil service exam passers, recent graduates, and the unmarried children of prominent families. The handbag of a certain Mrs. Um was said to contain a list of one hundred ninety marriage prospects and their personal data, written, so the newspaper claimed, "in a script as tiny as sesame seeds" (*Han'guk Ilbo*, 29 February 1984). One young woman of marriageable age told me, "Those women are so scary. They have long lists in their purses and they know absolutely everything about everyone." Like Dora's reticule, the purse of the Madam Ttu is magical, fertile, charged with power and danger; Freud would be pleased.

A woman at the top end of Seoul's middle class, living in a well-apportioned apartment south of the river, was surprised when she received a telephone call from a total stranger: "You have an unmarried daughter, don't you?" Because this mother was already beginning to fret about her twenty-four-year-old daughter's marriage prospects, because she had already wondered "Shall I really go that far? Shall I consult a professional matchmaker?" she agreed to meet the woman in a tearoom and selected three candidates from her file for further scrutiny. When she had checked their horoscopes and none was auspicious, she let the matter drop: "Because the matchmaker was a professional, it didn't feel right." Similarly, Mrs. Kim, an elegant matron in her late forties, received a telephone call from, in her words, "a real Madam Ttu" (*wŏllae Madam Ttu*) who had found her daughter's name in the school registry. Wary of the Madam Ttu's high fees, she did not pursue it.[12] In retrospect, Mrs. Kim muses that some Madam Ttu are acceptable, particularly when they are

12. The *Han'guk Ilbo* exposé claimed that the Madam Ttu received between 200,000 and 500,000 *wŏn* (approximately $250 to $625 U.S.) for a single introduction, with far larger sums anticipated if the match were to be successful. Some, it was said, received private cars and small apartments. One professional matchmaker nicknamed "Queen Min" was said to have received properties valued at $150,000 for matching the daughter of the head of a certain auto company with a graduate from a prominent medical school (*Han'guk Ilbo*, 29 February 1984). By 1987, the rumored fee of a Madam Ttu ranged from one to ten million *wŏn*, although a secondhand report of an actual transaction claimed that the matchmaker was bargained down from a million to 650,000 *wŏn*.

negotiating a marriage between two prominent families (who are also sufficiently well connected to verify her claims). She mentioned one illustrious marriage among her circle of acquaintances in which the professional matchmaker negotiated a very lavish exchange of wedding gifts.[13]

Had I interviewed more extensively in upper-middle-class neighborhoods, I would undoubtedly have heard of more direct encounters with Madam Ttu; I might even have been able to meet and interview one. Students assure me that "they are all over," lurking near the restrooms of better women's colleges or scrutinizing the marriageable maidens who study flower arranging. In 1987, I was struck by how thoroughly the Madam Ttu's negative image had penetrated the consciousness of women who knew of professional matchmaking primarily from television dramas. Among women of modest means, like my fictive sister Kkach'i, talk of Madam Ttu is taken as further confirmation of the extravagant foibles of the very wealthy, a constant theme of soap operas and the popular press. In at least one editorial, the Madam Ttu's popularity was taken as symptomatic of the thoroughly materialist flavor of contemporary Korean life (*Korea Newsreview* [Joh] 4 November 1989:33). The Madam Ttu epitomizes the wicked matchmaker, the matchmaker whose motivations are mercenary rather than altruistic, who lies and deceives to further the match that brings her a rich reward, regardless of the consequences for those who marry. My matchmaker informants, both amateur and professional, disdain the Madam Ttu's machinations as the antithesis of their own well-intentioned work.

The closest I came to interviewing an unlicensed professional matchmaker was Mrs. Yi, a gracious grandmother who describes matchmaking as her "hobby" (*chaemi*), but who would like to expand her operations and earn a bit more cash. Her ambitions are modest and her motivation admirable; she hopes to subsidize her husband's nonremunerative work as an inventor. Mrs. Yi would be horrified to find herself in the same paragraph with a Madam Ttu. She speaks with comic animation about the cost and relentless activity of intensive matchmaking:

> It's such a bother, always rushing off to hotels, and my son gives me trouble over the taxi fares. We don't have very much money, and here I am spending 10,000 to 20,000 *wŏn* on telephone bills. I go out every day. I make a telephone call and then I go out. Of course, I have to have my

---

13. She considered this delicate negotiation and its splendid results a good conclusion, but many others consider excessive ceremonial exchanges to be one of the liabilities of matchmade marriages. See n. 14.

hair done, and if I'm bringing someone to a first meeting, I can't just show up wearing any old thing. I have to get dressed up. It takes about 200,000 or 300,000 *wŏn* a month. I don't have that kind of money. But I keep getting telephone calls, this friend has a daughter, that friend has a son. . . .

THE GOOD MATCHMAKER

The women I talked to, both women who make matches and women concerned with the marriages of their own children (by no means exclusive categories), gave me a clear and fairly consistent image of the "good" matchmaker. Most often, the good matchmaker is described as a "good talker," "someone who speaks well" (*mal chalhanŭn saram*) and so presents her subjects in a very favorable light. The good matchmaker does not lie, but she might bend the facts—shaving a year or two off of the bride's age, for example, or minimizing past improprieties—so that the two parties, in her eyes an ideal match, will at least agree to an arranged meeting. As my friend Mrs. Oh explained:

> The matchmaker must be eloquent. She goes to the groom's house, and if the groom's house is interested, then she goes to the bride's house and states her case so well, speaks of him in such glowing terms, that of course they want to look him over. . . . She goes back and forth, talking up her subjects until each side says, "Now I want to see for myself!" The matchmaker has to go back and forth and back and forth again. "When shall we meet and where?" And then to the other side, "When shall we meet and where?" back and forth, right up to the meeting, that's the matchmaker's role.

Having invested time, energy, and personal capital in effecting the first meeting, the matchmaker risks profound disappointment when one or another of the parties is simply not interested. Mrs. Kim, who rebuffed a Madam Ttu, speaks of amateur matchmaking from bitter personal experience: "The most difficult thing about matchmaking is when you think you've made an auspicious introduction, but then it turns out that the two parties aren't pleased with each other. I was really vexed. I felt, 'So now I've failed.' "

It is the matchmaker who must report a negative judgement to the other side. Mrs. Kim feels that "If you don't like to tell people disagreeable things, then you can't be a matchmaker," and for this reason, she gave it up. Mrs. Paek, a successful businesswoman, is more comfortable with the necessity of finessing a negative response:

Although the two families were ideally matched, the man didn't think that the woman was sufficiently pretty. I couldn't say that. They asked me not to give that as a reason, so I said that the groom was busy preparing to go away for foreign study, that he would call her during his next vacation.
You told a white lie.
I told a necessary lie. I had to do it gently.

How often, in the course of these conversations, did I hear the match-maker's proverb "Do well, then three cups of wine; if you fail, then three slaps on the face" (*chalhamyŏn suli sŏkchan, mothamyŏn ppyami sŏk-tae*)? Even after the meeting, successful matchmakers find themselves embroiled in delicate negotiations over wedding gifts, affirmations of status which will set the future tone of the relationship between the two families.[14] And even after the wedding, the matchmaker might be called upon to mediate family matters. The couple quarrels. The mother-in-law complains that the bride takes too many naps ("In my day, daughters-in-law never took naps"). The bride's family thinks that their daughter has lived too long under her mother-in-law's roof, that she has lost weight and looks stressed, that the time has come for a promised separate residence. In such circumstances, the matchmaker might be called upon to finesse a satisfactory outcome.

The good matchmaker is, in every sense, an extrovert. She is described as the sort of person who concerns herself with other people's affairs and consequently has intimate knowledge of her subjects. In the United States, we might call her a busybody, but in her own milieu, she is valued for her willingness to involve herself in the exhausting business of arranging marriages for other people's children. The good matchmaker cares about her subjects. Mrs. Yi, the matchmaking enthusiast, offered a negative image of the person who cannot and will not be a matchmaker: "The person who thinks, 'I'm living well, my family is all right, why should I concern myself with other people?'—that sort of person cannot be a matchmaker." Mrs. Pak, active in her church, described the matchmaker as having a sense of "service" (*pongsa*) and good connections. A YWCA employee and sometime-matchmaker lamented the emotional "coldness" of con-

14. It is commonly assumed that matchmade marriages require a greater outlay of ceremonial goods, in part because the matchmakers are thought to inflate each side's intentions and expectations for the sake of their own "face." See, for example, Kim Yugyŏng's (1984) essay "My Daughter's Wedding Expenses," which several women pointed out to me as a sensitive portrayal of the dynamics of ceremonial exchanges.

temporary people, now less inclined to undertake the "good work" of matchmaking. The amateurs, she feared, were surrendering the field to the professional matchmakers.[15]

Amateur matchmakers spoke of the nervous tension they felt (*sin'-gyŏngŭl ssŭda*) while negotiating a match, of the ceaseless ringing of the telephone as one or another mother vented her concerns, and of the bruising realization that those who had sought their assistance now questioned their judgement or honesty. Mrs. Han, a warmhearted woman in her late thirties, describes a matchmaking experience that was still immediate at the time of our interview. Her story captures the delicacy, the strain, and the rewards of matchmaking:

> I was at my neighbor's house. Some relatives were visiting. We were sitting around talking and, thinking of my friend's unmarried brother—my friend was concerned about him—I just happened to mention that I knew of some good "groom material" [*sillanggam*]. Did anyone know of a bride? "Yes, there is a bride." I asked where she had gone to school and about her family. It just came about like that. Their educations, their economic circumstance, and their family backgrounds all matched perfectly. The man and the woman were both high school graduates, and they had both been raised without a father.
>
> Should I talk about this? [Encouraged by her nephew, a sociology student who has already grilled me concerning the scholarly intentions of my study, she continues.] The bride's father, well, you see, he fooled around. [She giggles with embarrassment.] This was a long time ago. He abandoned his wife and daughter. When the little girl was three years old, her mother took her back to her natal home, and when the daughter graduated from high school, the mother remarried. She couldn't take the daughter with her; the daughter stayed with her grandmother. Now she teaches in a piano institute. The mother claimed that she would have been pleased if her daughter had made a love match, but now the daughter was twenty-six and it hadn't happened. The mother thought it was all because of that business with her father. It's difficult for her daughter to trust a man. She wasn't able to meet and get to know someone.
>
> It's hard to talk about these things when you are a matchmaker. . . . A professional would probably lie, but I was honest; I told the groom's side about the divorce. I also told them that the stepfather is a fine person with five children of his own, that the mother treats her stepchildren well, that she is also a fine person, and that the daughter herself is a fine

---

15. While the women overwhelmingly identified the good matchmaker with a particular personality type, the one male matchmaker I interviewed equated the good matchmaker with those roles requiring intense social interaction: teachers, clergymen, and civil servants, the sorts of men who in fact do sometimes become involved in amateur matchmaking.

person, someone that they should have for their daughter-in-law. The man's mother agreed to overlook the divorce.

We arranged a meeting in a hotel coffee shop. The man and the woman ordered juice, but both of them were so bashful that they didn't even drink it. Since I represented the groom's side, the bride's side contacted me the next day. They were pleased with the man, but thought that he was too good to be true. Because it was dark in the coffee shop, they thought that he might be hiding some defect. The woman's stepfather arranged to meet him for dinner the next day in a brightly lit place, and since dinner lasts a long time, the stepfather had ample opportunity to examine the groom. He liked what he saw. The next day, the telephone calls started coming in. The woman's side wanted to know if the man was interested.

The couple started to date, but they were both very shy at first. The man hadn't had much experience with women. The woman was extremely self-conscious because she was already twenty-six. A younger woman might say whatever came to her mind, but she thought that the man would dislike her if she said the wrong thing. Neither of them said very much. And then after each date, a call would come from the woman's side wanting to know how the man felt about things after the date. That mother! She was so impatient for an engagement. Because of her own history and because her daughter had never known a father's love, she brooded over the man's intentions. I had to keep reassuring her that yes, he really was fond of her daughter, that he enjoyed meeting her even though he didn't express his feelings.

The bride's side still thought that the groom was too good to be true. Thirty is old for a man to be unmarried. They wondered if maybe he hadn't had an affair in the past. I said that it was all because he'd been so busy, working by day and studying by night. He goes to night school. Even now that they're engaged, he isn't able to meet her very often. I told the woman's side that he has absolutely no talent for romance. [We giggle at her turn of phrase.]

. . . . I stated the facts, although I tried to say things in a way that would be agreeable to both sides. Right up to the engagement, the bride's side kept contacting me, and I had to keep giving them some response. It wasn't as though I could simply ask the groom's side, "What do you want to do?" I had to move things along obliquely by saying, "How would it be if I were to say such and such?" The difficult thing about matchmaking is that you are matching two people who know absolutely nothing about each other. There are times when the matchmaker just wants to be done with it. That's probably why they sometimes lie. . . . I could understand the mother's feelings, but when she went to extremes, it was really disagreeable. She would call and grill me about this and that. Sometimes I found my anger rising, thinking to myself, "Why, why can't you trust me?"

. . . . So now they're engaged. I feel a great sense of accomplishment having served as a bridge between two such bashful people, otherwise unknown to each other, who will marry and have a good life.

This was Mrs. Han's first matchmaking. Mrs. Yi, the matchmaking hobbyist, distills her broader experience into this description of match-making's satisfactions and disappointments:

> So many worthwhile things come out of it. When the date is set and then the wedding is held, I think to myself, "Well now, this is all happening because I made the match, they are pleased with each other, it's all come about with great good fortune." Then, when a son is born, I have the same feeling. These are the two fruits of my endeavor; I made the match, and now it's turned out to be so auspicious. That's what I really like. Now there's a son, and that's happiness. They come and express their gratitude to me.
>
> The greatest difficulty? The most difficult thing is arranging the meeting and wondering if they are going to like each other. I bring the groom's side with me, and he says, "She isn't very attractive." I say, "Why does she have to be attractive? She's got a good education, she's healthy, she has a job, she's got a good disposition. . . ." [Here she launches into a full tirade against the unreasonably high standards of today's young men, some of whom might callously turn on their heels and march out of the coffee shop if the woman they find there displeases them.]

Matchmakers like Mrs. Yi so identify themselves with the subsequent fate of the couple that they may regard their own involvement as having a lucky or ill-fated influence upon the couple's married life. Most of the amateurs who described their matches concluded with the happily-ever-after formula "and the couple is living well," noting in particular the birth of sons. Kkach'i is proud that the couple she matched "had a son right away!" Ŏmŏni, on the other hand, regrets that when she introduced a couple many years ago, the groom died young. "Now," she says, "people don't ask me." Yongsu's Mother, the shaman, having endured the embarrassment of arranging a match that was broken off at the last possible moment, feels a perverse justification in noting that the bride, married to someone else's candidate, has been worked to the bone and returns to the village looking worn and haggard. Her colleague, the Songjuk Mansin, experienced a similar disappointment, even having gone so far as to deliver the betrothal gifts to the bride's side. "They were crazy, crazy to break it off," she said. "The groom they chose drank himself to death at an early age and didn't leave any property. The bride would have had a good life with my choice, my own natal kin."[16]

16. The coincidence of two shamans having been similarly ill used as match-makers might suggest that, as both shamans and matchmakers, their intentions were doubly suspect.

Mrs. Chŏn, another amateur, claims the satisfaction of one couple "living well" but suffers remorse over a failed marriage that she arranged without adequate knowledge of the groom's family background:

The groom didn't have a (legitimate) father, but that didn't come out until after the wedding. The groom's mother was just like a maiden; she had never been married. When the boy's father was in the army, he'd had an affair with her. She got pregnant and raised the baby all by herself in her own parents' house. The boy's father went somewhere else to marry and have children. The groom was never registered as his father's child because there were other children. [Because he was not registered as his father's child] there were complications about registering the marriage, and because of that, they separated.[17] The groom's mother came crying to me and said, "I've done wrong." She was so apologetic. I had known that woman for a long time, she had been my friend for ten years, and in all that time she had never said a word about this history. . . . It's hard when you want people to live together well and happily, but instead they get together, fall out, and divorce. That's difficult.[18]

For most of the women who shared their thoughts with me, the good matchmaker is an amateur, never a professional. Kinswomen, neighbors, former classmates, and other longtime associates are sympathetic and understand one's own situation. An intimate acquaintance can represent the circumstances of both families fairly and accurately, and she understands the personalities of the man and woman whom she suggests as life partners. (Although, as we have seen in the case of Mrs. Chŏn, it is possible to know someone long and well and still remain ignorant of crucial background information.) And because the relationship with an amateur matchmaker preceded and will continue after the matchmaking, because this relationship is ultimately more valuable than the gold ring or set of clothing the successful matchmaker receives as an expression of gratitude

17. A father has the option of recognizing a child born out of wedlock on his family register, and the mother has the option of petitioning to have her child so recognized. Even when entered on a family register, the child's out-of-wedlock status is so recorded, unless the legal wife agrees to falsify the child's status as that of her own issue (Lee Tai-Young 1981:Ch. 5).

18. In retrospect, she feels that the groom was too concerned with beauty and that this was insufficient to sustain the match. When the bride failed to conceive, the couple began quarreling, and the marriage remained unregistered. Because the marriage was never registered, the groom's side was under no legal obligation to compensate the bride. Mrs. Chŏn believes that the groom and his family behaved honorably in allowing the bride to keep the apartment purchased for the couple, but it is worth noting, with respect to the relative disadvantages of men and women in failed marriages, that at the time of this interview the groom had remarried but the bride had not.

(*tamnye*), the amateur is trusted over the professional who works for cold cash. Mrs. An, one of the women who had rejected the overtures of a professional matchmaker, found a happier solution: "I only had that one experience. My daughter's marriage was arranged by a relative, my elder sister. Her daughter had a friend, and the groom was the friend's elder brother. Since the two girls were close, we already knew something about the family."

Mrs. Yim, preoccupied with the marriage negotiations for her own daughter, lamented,

> It's so difficult. You raise your daughter prettily and educate her well. Now you must worry about the decision that will determine whether she lives well or badly. It's so unsettling to go through this business of matchmaking. . . . You rely on friends. You go to the friend you feel has your own interests at heart, the sort of friend you can believe in. [And she gently squeezed my arm to illustrate the warmth of her regard toward the sort of friend she would ask to matchmake for her own child.]

Her daughter's match was being arranged by a neighbor, someone she has known for more than a decade through their apartment stairwell association. For years, she has encountered her neighbor's relations in the elevator and feels comfortable with this family as potential in-laws. Trust, however, did not stop her from conducting a thorough background check on the potential groom:

> The young man works for the T—— Corporation; I knew which section. I had my husband ask his friend, who also works for the T—— Corporation, to quietly check him out. The report was favorable. The groom's father is in the National Assembly and so is the father of one of my daughter's friends. I asked the friend's mother to ask her husband what he thinks of the groom's father. His opinion was also favorable. I knew that the family was all right. I wanted to know more about the groom's personality, since this will have the most bearing on my daughter's future happiness. The easiest way to do this would be to find someone who knew the groom from high school and who could say what he was like back then. That's very difficult. It would be easier to find someone who knows one of his former teachers. A friend's child is a teacher on rotation, so he knows several people in several schools. At the appropriate time, he can ask to have the record pulled, but this requires finesse so as not to incur a major obligation.

Mrs. Yim is very well connected. Although covert verifications of the matchmaker's words are a long-standing tradition in Korean matchmaking, relatively few urban women could command the social resources that Mrs. Yim mustered for her investigation. The family of the bride whom

Mrs. Chŏn unwittingly matched to an illegitimate son clearly did not. Also disadvantaged are those who would use matchmakers to further their own status and material well-being, the ambitious social climbers of Pak Wansŏ's novel and common gossip, or the factory women Seung-Kyung Kim writes of who hope their hard-earned dowries will win them a middle-class marriage (Kim 1990). The most pathetic matchmaker story I heard in the field was recounted by a tearful, demoralized, battered wife. Her mother-in-law had hoped that a wedding would cause her reprobate son to mend his dissolute ways. The bride, brought up to Seoul from the deep country, remained innocent of the family circumstances until after her wedding, when she learned, to her horror, that her husband was a drug addict with a violent and brutal temper.

THE PROFESSIONAL MARRIAGE BUREAU

Although marriage bureaus were known in the 1960s,[19] the government legalized and began to license them in 1973 to control the extortionate activities of unlicensed professionals whose "business caused all kinds of social ills with dirty, unfair behind-the-scenes scandals" (*Korea Times*, 17 March 1974:4). All other matchmaking for pay was illegal, an activity banned under the Family Ritual Code.[20]

The counselors who work in licensed marriage bureaus see themselves as "good matchmakers," as the sort of people who are intimately concerned with human affairs and are motivated by an altruistic desire to help people wed.[21] Mrs. Yu, the seventy-year-old proprietress of a venerable

19. They were reported as a curiosity in the English-language *Korea Herald* (30 June 1966:3, 2 May 1968:9).

20. In 1973, there were some 23 licensed marriage bureaus in Seoul. In 1982, the number had risen to 65, in the wake of a crackdown against unlicensed professionals (*Korea Times*, 6 March 1982:8). It had nearly doubled by 1986, one year prior to my interviews. At that time, the 118 licensed marriage bureaus in Seoul conducted 10,160 consultations resulting in 1,251 successful unions (*Tonga Ilbo*, 23 April 1987:9). If these figures are correct, then only slightly more than 1 in 10 consultations yielded a successful union, and each marriage bureau would have averaged only slightly more than 10 marriages among their clients per year.

21. At the time of these interviews, the Seoul city government's requirements for marriage bureau counselors simply stated that they be "morally and academically respected." In 1988, more specific requirements were enacted: counselors must be at least thirty-five years old, have a college-level education in psychology, social welfare, or education, or have worked for more than five years in a government or educational institution, or be a licensed social worker, or have had five years or more experience counseling in social welfare or religious organizations and be more than forty years old (*Korea Herald*, 4 February 1988:3).

marriage bureau, describes herself as a former educator who became a full-time professional matchmaker by popular demand for her services. The educator's persona, as a moral guide and social critic, shines through in Mrs. Yu's interview as she explicates her marital philosophy while stridently asserting the need for social reform. She sees her own efforts as one foundation stone in an enterprise that will eventually elevate the popular image of the professional marriage bureau.[22] For the present, she bitterly regrets the fact that most of her clients will never acknowledge how they met,[23] and most do not invite her to their weddings.[24] (Today, however, she rushes from our interview to a client's wedding.) Mrs. Yu goes to great lengths to distinguish herself from the Madam Ttu who, she opines, are motivated by greed rather than by a sincere desire to help people. The Madam Ttu, she claims, "just matchmake by telephone," without adequate background checks and home visits. For this, they receive fees many times the government-regulated amount charged by a licensed marriage bureau (in 1987, 5,000 *wŏn* for a consultation, an additional 45,000 *wŏn* for a meeting, and another 100,000 *wŏn* if the match led to marriage).[25] Mrs. Yu blames the Madam Ttu for the bad image that falls upon all professional matchmakers, including those who work for licensed marriage bureaus.

Counselors employed in professional marriage bureaus claim that many modern people lack precisely those sorts of intimate contacts women value in the amateur matchmaker. The counselors I spoke with

22. Similarly, Mr. Kim, the one male matchmaker I interviewed, described the marriage bureau as an institution for a "developed society." He observed that since both Japan and the United States had them, the institution would inevitably gain in esteem within Korea. Mrs. Cho and Mrs. Pae were both keenly aware of sophisticated matching services in Japan, Europe, and the United States which use computers and videos. They offer this information to indicate that Korea's marriage bureaus are moving along a trajectory of "development."

23. Marriage bureau clients are often seen as having a social or economic deficit. Counselors counter this perception by claiming professors, doctors, and graduates of top-ranking universities among their clients (*Tonga Ilbo*, 23 April 1987:9). Working against a positive image are the many marriage bureaus which specialize in "international marriage" or "second marriage"—neither of which is an auspicious union.

24. These sentiments were also expressed by a matchmaker for the Korea Federation of Housewives' Clubs, who told the *Korea Times:* "I only want to see the happy scene from a corner of the hall, not wearing an arm band of the Korea Federation of Housewives' Clubs, but praying for their future happiness" (*Korea Times*, 5 December 1976).

25. Mrs. Yu was one of the marriage counselors who acknowledged that clients routinely gave additional sums as an expression of gratitude.

described themselves as offering a service better suited to the practical necessities of modern life. In one counselor's words, "People don't have the time for matchmaking, and they live in apartments, not houses. They aren't connected to other people's lives the way they were in the past." Mrs. Pae, the smartly dressed young counselor at a stylishly appointed computer matching service, peppers her speech with social science jargon: "Our society has changed. People live a corporate life-style, as in foreign countries. People don't have time to fret about matchmaking. Besides, we don't live in villages where everyone knows everything about everyone anymore. We live in nuclear families, not with the whole big extended family gathered around us. If a mother's friend does the matchmaking, how can she really know the two families or the personalities of the potential couple?"

Mrs. Cho, a gracious counselor in a licensed marriage bureau, affirms the amateur ideal that the good matchmaker "must know both parties thoroughly" but claims this is precisely what the skilled counselor in a marriage bureau sets out to do:

> If, for example, I were to make a match for Miss An [She names my marriageable research assistant to whom she has already handed three promotional brochures. She uses the English-derived title *"missŭ"*], why then I would have to know everything there is to know about Miss An. I would have to know her as well as my own younger sister. And then, suppose I was going to introduce Miss An to Mr. Ch'oe, I would have to know Mr. Ch'oe as well as his mother or sister might know him. I would have to know everything, be like a member of the family making the introduction. If you don't know it all, then you don't succeed. You learn these things through the process of counseling, all the family relations, everything. You form an impression, a feeling for what this person is like. On that basis, you think, "Now who would be a suitable mate?" Fifty percent of our first meetings are successful.

Mrs. Cho holds that amateur matchmaking is inherently flawed. "If matchmaking is done in the neighborhood (on the basis of relationships), then family and friends cover things up because they feel a sense of obligation, but there is no such obligation in a marriage bureau." The marriage bureau requires its clients to provide a copy of the family registry (information which would have spared Mrs. Chŏn her embarrassment over the absent father), a certificate of graduation, a statement of employment, and a health certificate. Some counselors insist on home visits. More often, a counselor makes a random call to the place of employment to verify that the information is correct: "You ask if 'so and so' is there and see if they answer with the title he gave. One call, and everything is revealed." But not all professional counselors make these calls; the one male marriage counselor I interviewed considered them an invasion of privacy, possibly to his clients' peril. An editorial in the *Tonga Ilbo's* series, "Marriage Practices: Is This the Right Way?", told of women who worked confidence rackets by presenting themselves to the marriage bureaus as potential spouses and then bilking their would-be partners out of large sums of money.[26]

The A—— Marriage Service, Mrs. Pae's employer, locates compatible personalities through a "scientifically tested" marriage survey used internationally but adapted to the conditions of Korean matrimony (for example, "Would you be willing to become an adopted-in son-in-law?" "Would you be willing to co-reside with your husband's parents?"). New clients take a "color test" wherein they indicate their color preferences on a scale of one to eight and fill out a detailed data sheet beginning with background information on their personal appearance, health, family background, and employment. They complete a checklist of their hobbies and interests and indicate their preferences for "dogs or cats, television or radio, bread or rice, love call or love letter." They check "agree strongly, agree, disagree, disagree strongly, don't know" in reply to such statements as, "Even if one is poor, one can live happily if there is love" and "A husband should always listen to his wife."

The A—— Marriage Service is one among a small but growing number of matchmaking services which employ computers in an upmarket appeal to young professionals seeking appropriate mates on their own initiative.[27] Detailed surveys and computer printouts are only the beginning, however, and Mrs. Pae, no less than Mrs. Cho and Mrs. Yu, insists on the value of intensive counseling. "An introvert can't do this job," she says. "It takes an extrovert, people who make conversation easily do well."

---

26. The article also claimed that unethical bureaus might charge fees in excess of the nominal sums set by law (*Tonga Ilbo*, 23 April 1987:9). Some of the employees of marriage bureaus told me that clients often gave them cash above the (in their eyes woefully small) set fee "to help us with our work."

27. The A—— describes itself as a "matrimonial enterprise" (*kyŏrhon sangŏp*) of which clients become "members," a circumvention of the negative connotations of "marriage bureau" and also of the marriage bureaus' fee schedule. In 1987, women paid the A—— an annual "membership fee" (*hoebi*) of 330,000 wŏn and men 220,000 wŏn. The difference in fees, Mrs. Pae frankly acknowledged, reflects a shortage of desirable men, the common complaint of matchmakers. The A——'s members are entitled not only to the matchmaking services, but also to discounts on wedding goods and honeymoon package tours. Nowhere in the A——'s literature is the term "marriage bureau" used.

In sum, amateur and professional matchmakers share a common image of the "good matchmaker," the altruistic extrovert who concerns herself with other people's lives, the good talker who moves the match along. They measure each other against perceptions of reliability. The professionals claim the amateurs are incapable of garnering sufficient background information and are more likely to falsify out of personal obligation; nonprofessionals distrust the intentions of a stranger who receives a fee for her work, a larger fee when the introduction yields a successful match. Through this mirror imagery of professional and amateur, effective and untrustworthy, we begin to understand the ambiguity of matchmakers. They are simultaneously good at what they do and suspect for doing it because their enterprise is built upon words.

THE MATCHMAKER'S WORDS

The power of words, the skill of the good matchmaker at wielding her words, is already evident in the ways she has been described: she talks up her candidates until neither side can resist the desire to see for themselves. She must be able to say "disagreeable" things; Mrs. Paek is adept at breaking bad news gently; Mrs. Kim found she had no stomach for it and gave up matchmaking. Mrs. Paek, with characteristic frankness, suggests that if someone is too honest, if they run back and forth with everything they hear, then the match fails; but if they engage in too much falsehood, they lose trust, and the match fails. If necessary, the matchmaker tells "white lies" (*hayan kŏjinmal*) to bring an otherwise ideal couple together. Several women thought it harmless to shave a few years from a prospective bride's age, although Mrs. Yi has refused to falsify an inauspicious horoscope. Mrs. Cho thinks nothing of reducing a woman's age, but claims she would never misrepresent a man's job or family situation, circumstances which color a woman's expectations of her future life. "White lies" are seen as necessary strategies in the good work of facilitating matrimony, in no way akin to the deceits of a bad matchmaker.

Nevertheless, the matchmaker's judgement calls are not always shared by the subjects of her matchmaking. The friend who matchmade for Mrs. Pak misrepresented the groom's family as Christian; the matchmaker did not consider this detail important since the groom, at least, was Christian. The bride was horrified when she first saw her mother-in-law making offerings to the household gods and still musters anger at the friend who "lied about something so important." Oggyŏng's Mother, a matchmaking shaman, considers it acceptable to cover up minor indiscretions, so long as they are never revealed. Fearing such obfuscation, the bride's family in Mrs. Han's negotiation was suspicious of an honest matchmaker.

Bending the truth, when expedient, is only one dimension of matchmakerly representations as the courtship unfolds. Mrs. Han, the matchmaker almost by accident, claims she succeeded because she presented the facts of the case—including the blemish of a divorce—simply and honestly, and so won trust. But honest Mrs. Han also became a sort of female Cyrano de Bergerac, scripting the inarticulate groom's responses to the bride: "How would it be if I were to say such and such?" The expressive Mrs. Paek holds that the most successful matchmaker would be "someone like a professor who has been lecturing for a long time, or a movie director, someone who is good at explaining things, at setting the scene, someone who can keep the meeting moving along, a shaman could do it well. These are the sort of people who can create the right situation for a successful match." She gives me an example from her own successful matching of two illustrious families:

The man was attracted to the woman because she was a youngest child, she seemed uninhibited, interesting, an art student who had studied abroad. . . . There was another woman, a rival candidate, the daughter of a wealthy family who had grown up in a provincial city. She was a pharmacist, very serious. The man was attracted to the Seoul woman, my candidate; he thought that she had more charm, knew how to talk and act. I think she had the edge . . . but he couldn't make up his mind. In a case like that, the mother can be very forceful, and she would have wanted the prettier and wealthier daughter-in-law. Even so, she trusted me; she knew that I would not deceive her, so she allowed her son to go on meeting the woman I had introduced. . . .

But then a month went by without a call from the man's side. The woman and her mother were anxious; they were in a terrible state. They were the ones who had asked me to make the match, and they kept after me. By now, the couple had met three times. The woman's side would lose face if the man broke it off. I told the man's side that they would have to make up their minds. . . . Now this is really snobbish. The man's side thinks of themselves as an extremely successful, socially prominent family. I told them, "Think about Diana, Queen Elizabeth's daughter-in-law in the United Kingdom. After they got Diana, their entire image brightened up. She is so famous; she has so much popular appeal. It's true, your other candidate is a nice young lady who has studied hard, but you need a fresh new atmosphere in your family life. Now the art student, that's an attractive woman; everything she does is appealing. When the mood strikes her, she goes out to sketch."

I had to come up with something to help my candidate because the woman's position in matchmaking is always so weak. I was in a difficult position. The woman's mother, my friend, was losing patience with me. What do I know about Diana? I just read an article in some magazine. [This was in 1987, when the royal marriage still retained some of its fairy-tale aura.]. . . . That's why I think a shaman or a movie director would be an excellent matchmaker; they know how to turn a situation around.

The stories told by Mrs. Han and Mrs. Paek reveal an intense involvement in the process of courtship, a weaving of words to cast their subjects' actions in a favorable light. If we are to believe their own accounts, their actions fulfilled the urgent expectations of their subjects' families. Professional marriage counselors would probably deny that they engage in verbal persuasion; those I interviewed claimed that once they had made an introduction, the rest was up to the couple. Yet in their counseling, they try to shape the client's image of a possible spouse. Counselors' responses to my standard question, "What is the most difficult thing about matchmaking?", implied that they invest much verbal energy in disabusing clients of unrealistic expectations: "Wealth and beauty aren't as important as compatibility because marriage lasts your whole life long."

Some of their answers seemed to be standard homilies. For example, both elderly Mrs. Yu and youthful Mrs. Pae volunteered their pocket lectures in support of marriage to a firstborn son. These matches are unpopular because of the eldest son's weighty familial responsibilities. As "problem" matches, firstborn sons might be well represented among a marriage bureau's clients. Mrs. Pae assures her clients that "it isn't the way it was in the past," that extended families are no longer tyrannical, that many first sons now live apart from their parents, that firstborn sons have good characters and the success of their marriages is verified in statistics. Mrs. Yu advocates co-residence with a first sons' parents so that the working wife can rely on her mother-in-law for child care; she echoes the logic of Margaret Mead's lectures in Korea in the 1960s.

Words, then, make the matchmaker—words to investigate, mediate, and convince—but words can also falsify. The matchmaker's work recalls another enterprise built upon words, that of the professional shaman (*mudang, mansin, posal*), a comparison Mrs. Paek made explicit when she talked about the matchmaker's verbal mastery of a situation. The shaman's utterances are also regarded as both vital and suspect, and for a similar reason. Both matchmaker and shaman mediate between the known and the unknown, between one's own household and the spirits in the case of a shaman, and between one's own household and potential in-laws in the case of a matchmaker. For both the matchmaker and the shaman, this capacity to bridge the known and the unknown is the essence of power and the source of suspicion, of danger. The matchmaker's words create a credible vision of the future in the empty space between two strangers, but such an empty space is also necessarily filled with uncertainty and doubt. Perhaps the matchmaker represents one's own interests, but perhaps she sacrifices them to the unknown agendas of the other side. She is dangerous in the sense that ambiguous creatures are often perceived as dangerous (Douglas 1966). She is one among those who inhabit the ill-defined space between two states of being or who are vested with contradictory intentions: anomalous beasts, tricksters, witches, shamans (and anthropologists).

CONCLUSION

The stories told in this chapter begin to suggest how a common vocabulary of matrimonial procedures, of "love" versus "arranged" marriages, of matchmakers who match their clients by age, family background (*kamun*), and education (*hakpŏl*) mask profound differences in the circumstances of those who marry. Yet through this common vocabulary, profound distinctions of status are also articulated. At a bare minimum, a family struggles to provide a wedding for a pregnant daughter and so distinguishes itself from the many other families whose children cohabit (and legally register their marriages) without the benefit of a wedding. At the other extreme, elite families frankly acknowledge that they favor matchmade unions as a means of articulating their own status. The capitalist, military, and political interests comprising the Korean elite today are an awkward replacement for the landed Confucian nobility who were politically dispossessed under Japanese rule, then saw the land reform that followed liberation complete the erosion of their economic dominance in the countryside (Cho Oakla 1987b; Eckert 1991; Koo 1987). When a privileged family considers marital candidates on the basis of education, breeding, and family background, it evokes the ethos of archaic *yangban* culture and takes this mantle as its own, asserting the claim that its own elevated status is not merely a function of wealth or naked power.

The stories recounted in this chapter reveal women as enmeshed in the pragmatics of making marriages, not only as skillful matchmakers, but as mothers who set the process in motion and who effect the complex exchanges of proper weddings. Ŏmŏni has begun her discussions of wedding goods with the mother of Sukcha's intended. Fifteen years ago, she brought about Kkach'i's wedding on a shoestring. Mrs. Sŏ's mother-in-law determined that the time had come for her son to "put up his hair," and Mrs. Ch'oe, in the absence of a mother, struggled to accomplish her own wedding. Chapters 6 and 7 concern the ritual exchanges offered by the brides' and grooms' households, the business of dowries, bridewealth, and other gifts given in acknowledgement of affinity. We shall see how the pivotal role of women in these exchanges, like the pivotal role of the matchmaker, earns both esteem and disapprobation.

3  EXCHANGE

Yongsu's Mother, anticipating Oksuk's wedding in 1977: When her daughter marries, a mother is lucky if she's left with her own navel.

Yongsu's Mother, anticipating her son's marriage in 1985: These days, the brides bring everything.
Old man: They earn money so they can do it.
Yongsu's Mother: These days no maiden can afford to just stay at home and play.

6

Ceremonious Goods

MY SISTER SUKCHA, 1991

On this late autumn day, Sukcha is full of wedding plans. She has found an inexpensive honeymoon package, a four-day, three-night trip to scenic Sorak Mountain and to the ancient capital of Kyŏngju. "My sisters-in-law don't understand it," she giggles. "They tell me 'Honeymooners fly to Cheju Island. Nowadays, people even go to foreign countries, and you're just going to Kyŏngju?' " Sukcha is pleased with herself, unconventional and self-righteous at the same time: "Why spend all that money on a honeymoon? We'll need it for other things later on."

Our third sister gives me a knowing smile. "Won't she be a terrific housekeeper?"

Sukcha insists that the dowry (*honsu*) will include only the basic and essential items she needs to set up housekeeping. She will do her shopping at a leisurely pace in the weeks that remain before the wedding. Her matter-of-factness in contemplating this task is in contrast to a common stereotype of upper-middle-class mothers and daughters who spend months, possibly even years, assembling a dowry.[1] She tells me that young people today are not interested in a lot of extravagance. I smile, recalling the volumes of diatribe maintaining just the opposite, and mark Sukcha's borrowing of the sloganeer's vocabulary to proclaim her own values. I smile because Sukcha so often takes it upon herself to correct my understandings of "young people today."

---

1. See, for example, Kim Yugyŏng's (1984) essay "My Daughter's Wedding Expenses." Several women in Korean anthropology circles suggested this work to me as a telling portrayal of dowry obsessions among the middle class.

As in many Korean weddings, the assembling of Sukcha's dowry would be a collective effort. Most of the money for her wedding, a sum of ten million *wŏn* (between $12,000 and $13,000 U.S.), would be covered by Kkach'i's successful investments in informal rotating credit associations (*kye*), using the sum Sukcha had earned working in the family restaurant. Ŏmŏni would use her own baby-sitting money, similarly invested, to buy Sukcha a washing machine and a thick winter quilt. The household of Sukcha's oldest sister would provide her refrigerator, and her third sister's household would buy her television set. Months after the wedding, Ŏmŏni would describe Sukcha as the one among her four married daughters who had gone off with the greatest style, a function of the household's improved circumstances and the fact that Ŏmŏni's married daughters' households were now well established.

However "basic and essential" Sukcha's dowry was by the standards of their new life, the refrigerator, television set, and washing machine Sukcha brought to her new home had been beyond the wildest dreams of her sister Kkach'i fifteen years before. The pregnant Kkach'i's own dowry had been a hasty and inexpensive assembly of quilts, pallet, cabinet, mirror stand, rice pots, wash basin, and chamber pot.[2] Even in that simpler time, Kkach'i's dowry stood in marked contrast to the great array of goods assembled by Oksuk, the stepdaughter of the shaman Yongsu's Mother. Oksuk had worked in a factory until, at age twenty-six, she decided it was time to marry. She placed her fate in the hands of Yongsu's Mother, moving into her stepmother's house and delivering over to her stepmother's hands the sum of her savings and severance pay. In only a few months' time, Yongsu's Mother had found a suitable groom, a young man whose family would set him up as the proprietor of a small shop.

Yongsu's Mother hosted the expensive engagement party which serves as a formal meeting for the extended kin of both sides in a matchmade union.[3] Once this event was successfully completed and the groom's family's intentions affirmed in the handsome present of jewelry they made to

---

2. According to the proprietor of a shop specializing in dowry goods, the essential "five happinesses" (*ohaeang*) of a dowry are a marriage quilt, a pillow, a pair of rice bowls, a wash basin, and a chamber pot; but in 1985 he was providing this list as folklore rather than as contemporary practice.

3. The wedding process of a love marriage may also be punctuated by an engagement party (Sukcha's third sister had one), but parties are easily omitted in the name of haste or practicality, as with Sukcha's wedding. With matchmade marriages, however, the bride's family is under far more pressure to observe propriety and host an engagement party.

Oksuk, Yongsu's Mother and Oksuk embarked upon a seemingly interminable series of shopping expeditions. A small mountain of dishes, electrical appliances, and clothing began to grow in Yongsu's Mother's house, and each time I visited them, I was regaled with a tale of the day's accomplishments in the marketplace. Sometimes Yongsu's Mother took delight in her own grand gestures of generosity, buying ruffled white aprons for Oksuk and insisting that they give the groom a bathrobe as an innovative and sophisticated addition to his gift of clothing, "They wear these in foreign countries." Sometimes she offered good-humored complaints that Oksuk was a "robber woman" (*todungnyŏ*) whose marriage would be her stepmother's ruin. "And she even wants one of those things, you must know what it is, a *mik'ŭssŭ*, it spins things around" (a blender, I surmised).

When the shopping was done, Oksuk's household goods and furniture were piled high in her stepmother's house, displayed for the wonderment of her neighbors, some of whom, like me, had already heard a detailed accounting of each shopping expedition. This was, by the contemporary standards of Enduring Pine Village, a splendid and much-remarked-upon wedding. Village gossip held that Oksuk had given her stepmother between 600,000 and 800,000 *wŏn* (between $1,200 and $1,600 U.S.) to purchase her dowry. Barely five years later, this would be considered too paltry a sum for even a modest dowry, but in those days, it was big money. For her part, Yongsu's Mother sniffed that Oksuk had squandered her factory earnings on clothing and cosmetics, that the bride's contribution to the expensive wedding was minimal. By then, I was accustomed to both the gossips' love of exaggeration and village women's routine denial that they or their children earned any significant sums of money. I was also aware of Yongsu's Mother's desire to underscore how well she had done by her stepdaughter. I assumed Oksuk's contribution had been considerable, but that even if Oksuk had contributed a full 800,000 *wŏn*, the cost of her dowry, the gifts, feasts, and customary fees would have exceeded this amount.[4]

Yongsu's Mother also prevailed upon her dead husband's kin to con-

4. In 1978, the families of urban brides spent, on average, 1,490,000 *wŏn* (*Korea Times*, 5 February 1978: 8). It would be reasonable to assume that Oksuk's above average rural wedding cost at least one million *wŏn* (in 1978 Korean *wŏn*, approximately $2,000 U.S.). In the month preceding Oksuk's wedding, I tallied the expenses of several shopping expeditions, the engagement feast, and other ceremonial expenses. Although my tally was only partial, it easily exceeded the 600,000 *wŏn* low-range estimate for Oksuk's own money.

tribute to their niece's dowry. I remember sitting quietly in the corner of a restaurant just after Oksuk's engagement party, playing deaf and dumb, while Yongsu's Mother tried plaintively to persuade Oksuk's uncle to buy the nice large storage cabinet (*chang*) she had chosen. The uncle bluntly stated that people who lack money should not spend it, suggesting that Yongsu's Mother was attempting to impress the groom's family with a wedding beyond her means. It would be wrong to give these new affines the impression that the bride's stepmother had money to spare. Yongsu's Mother spoke glowingly of the groom's bright prospects, implying both that she had acquitted herself admirably as a matchmaking stepmother and that the bride's side could ill afford to skimp on dowry goods. Then she spoke at great length about her youngest son's school fees. Finally, with the hint of a sob in her voice, she described the burden of marrying off a stepdaughter as more than she, a poor widow, could bear. Her efforts were rewarded when Oksuk's middle-aged senior cousin agreed to contribute 20,000 *wŏn* ($40 U.S.) to the furniture and a widowed aunt promised a quilt. The parsimonious junior uncle, however, remained to be convinced.[5]

The experiences of Sukcha, Kkach'i, and Oksuk, combined with the stories of the impoverished working-class brides encountered in Chapter 5, begin to suggest several things. Exchanges of ceremonious goods are an essential component of the contemporary Korean wedding. That many Korean women work before marriage provides some with the means to effect these status-enhancing exchanges, but contributions from close kin to the dowry of a daughter, sister, or niece are often a necessary component of a respectable wedding. Finally, as a contradiction at the core of contemporary Korean matrimonial practice, while the association between dowries and prestige is obvious and widely recognized, by the time of Sukcha's wedding, popular morality also held that extravagant dowries were unnecessary and harmful. Korean weddings, like weddings in many other stratified societies, are an arena of social display and status assertion. While Confucian moralizers have long enjoined thrift, they valued proper ritual performance, and doing the rites properly has always meant doing them well. In contemporary Korea, the contradiction is intensified by rising expectations of conspicuous consumption on the one hand and a rising pitch of public concern on the other.

In this chapter, I examine the interconnectedness of women's work and

---

5. I assume that for the sake of family feeling, he did eventually make a contribution, but I never learned how close it came to Yongsu's Mother's expectations.

weddings and see how the marriage goods which money buys signify in a shifting social milieu. The idea of thrift as a moral issue, already introduced in Chapter 3, will be taken up again.

WOMEN WHO WORK FOR WAGES

The financing of weddings is necessarily bound up with larger issues of the Korean political economy. Although small numbers of young unmarried women have worked in Korean factories and in the service sector since the colonial period (Eckert 1991:198), from the late 1960s, the "woman worker" (*yŏgong*) or "factory girl" (*kongsuni*) has been prominent in the cast of characters for Korea's drama of rapid industrialization. Without a pool of cheap, educated, and initially docile female labor, the Korean "economic miracle" would not have taken place (Amsden 1989; Cho Hyoung 1987; Koo Hagen 1987).[6]

Increasingly, unmarried women like Sukcha favor the better pay and more respectable image of clerical or service sector work, but they continue to work in large numbers (Koo 1990:676). All but one among my 1980s sample of twenty-nine brides worked at extradomestic labor before their marriages.[7] The one exception had tended a widowed father and brought a poor dowry to an arranged match with a government warehouse employee. Three, like Sukcha, had worked for family businesses in anticipation of future family support for their weddings, one as a cashier in her mother's tearoom, one as a receptionist for her uncle's company, and the third in her aunt's supermarket. A fourth bride had been a self-employed vendor.[8] All of the wage-earning brides indicated that some of

6. The assumed docility of Korean womanhood was unabashedly touted in the 1970s to encourage investment in Korean industry, although before the decade was out, women workers would have occasion to disabuse the promoters of the stereotype. The late 1970s saw numerous strikes and protests by women workers, many led by women. The death of a young woman worker during the forceful removal of striking women from the Y. H. Trade Company ignited a firestorm of protest which contributed to the collapse of the Park Chung Hee regime (Yi Ujŏng 1986). Unions have been most effective in organizing women in the textile and garment industries. The late 1970s were peak years for women's union membership and activity, followed by severe suppression of labor activities in the early 1980s. Kim Seung-Kyung (1990) describes labor agitation by women in the Masan Export Processing Zone during a new high tide of labor activity in 1987.

7. Two brides were entering second marriages; their work experiences predated their first marriages.

8. Those who married in 1985 were earning an average monthly wage of 188,000 *wŏn* ($235 U.S.), or slightly more than the national average woman's wage in 1985 of 180,000 *wŏn* ($225 U.S.). Brides' wages just before marriage

their earnings had been set aside for their weddings, either on their own initiative or by their mothers. Not only do many Korean daughters expect to work until they marry; like Sukcha, Oksuk, and many others interviewed in the course of this study, whenever possible they work to finance a status-enhancing wedding whose component exchanges have increased in both cost and kind.[9] Indeed, dowry elaboration runs in tandem with the widespread employment of unmarried women over the last two decades (Kendall 1985b).

I began my research in 1983 with vivid memories of Kkach'i's and Oksuk's weddings. I was impressed by the initiative each had shown in the very different courses which led them to matrimony. I wondered if the experience of wage work gave Korean women new leverage in one of the most crucial decisions of their lives. The expectations of social scientists regarding the consequences of wage work on young women's status and consciousness are both varied and contradictory. A daughter's experience as a wage worker is sometimes seen as intensifying her exploitation and, in other circumstances, as destabilizing family authority (Elson and Pearson 1981:158). Joan Scott and Louise Tilly (1975) have argued that far from emancipating European women, a daughter's participation in the early industrial work force was constructed as a strategy of household survival. Daughters worked to support the household economy, and in this their efforts were thoroughly consistent with preindustrial values. The timing of children's marriages was part of a larger domestic strategy wherein daughters subordinated their own wishes to the family's need for their wages.

There is much that would recommend the domestic strategy model to students of Korean society. Observers of Korean life, myself included, have highlighted the importance of the household[10] as a social, economic,

---

reflect their peak earning capacity after several years of employment. When the peak earnings of the 1983 brides are included in the total, the average is lower, 164,000 wŏn ($205 U.S), but the "average" is skewed by significant inflation over the intervening two years.

9. See Chang-Michell (1984:62), Kim Eun-Shil (1993:206), Kim Seung-Kyung (1990:113–114, 159–161), Spencer (1988:20, 63), and Yoon (1989a:71). The lure of factory work as a means of enhancing a dowry was already recognized by the women who went to work in Korea's first factories during the colonial period, but as Carter Eckert (1991:198) notes, poor pay allowed scant opportunity for significant savings.

10. "Household" and "family" are used almost interchangeably in ethnographic writing on Korea, in part because the common social science understand-

and ritual unit (Janelli and Janelli 1982:Ch. 2; Kendall 1985a:Ch. 8; Yoon 1989a). Clark Sorensen (1988) has made an explicit application of Chayanov's model of the rational peasant farm, arguing that the conscious strategies adopted by Korean rural households enabled the rural sector to make a successful transition to a new, highly capitalized economy.

Diane Wolf faults the domestic strategy model for masking profound inequalities within families under the rubric of a "common good," for blinding researchers to generational and gendered conflict within domestic groups, and above all, for ignoring the significance of agency where individual family members "may engage in behaviors that are passive, nonstrategic, overtly resistant, antagonistic, ambivalent, antistrategic, or even multistrategic" (Wolf 1990, 1992:14). She faults Sorensen in particular for his unproven assumption that the Korean household runs smoothly under the rational guidance of a solitary patriarch (Wolf 1990, 1992:15–16). When early industrial experiences are examined in a variety of settings, the results permit no easy generalization.

Tamara Haraven (1982) argues that, in a manner consistent with Scott and Tilly's expectations, the working daughters of a nineteenth-century American factory town lived at home and faithfully contributed their wages to their families of origin, maintaining a relationship of continued interdependence. She adds, however, that they gained a limited sense of independence, a condition of "semi-autonomy" through the experience of spending their days outside the family in industrial time, time dominated by the workday clock and spent among the extrafamilial peer culture of the workplace.

Aihwa Ong (1987) argues that the employment status of working daughters in Malaysia weakened the control of fathers and brothers, ultimately transforming the culture and expectations of the family as women workers "engaged in constituting their own subjectivity or in occasional

---

ing of either term, in isolation from the other, does not provide a precise translation of the Korean *chip*. "Household" might be literally rendered in Korean as *sikku* (those who eat together, those who share a common domestic budget), but the word lacks the emotional resonance of *chip*, which connotes the physical structure of the house and those who dwell there, those who once resided in the house, and, by very broad extension, all those who are (agnatic) descendants of a common ancestral house (Lee Kwang-Kyu 1975:29–30, 33–34). That married daughters or junior uncles might be called upon to subsidize the wedding of a daughter of the *chip* reflects notions of intimate kinship broader than any precise definition of "household" as a single domestic economy.

acts of defiance," saved for their own weddings, and chose their own husbands.[11]

Diane Wolf (1992) found that, counter to expectations she had garnered from the sociological literature, Javanese factory women set the course of their own employment, often over family protest. They made only negligible contributions to the family economy and married on the basis of "impetuousness, risk, luck, accidents, and some hormonal reactions rather than a series of rational calculations" (D. Wolf 1992:219). Wolf acknowledges that while the assertiveness of Javanese women workers might be recognizable to their Malaysian cousins as described by Ong, a very different image of the working daughter appears in studies set in Taiwan and Hong Kong (Arrigo 1984; Kung 1983; Salaff 1981), where family authority over working daughters remains strong. Observers cite the abiding strength of "Chinese patriarchy." Familist ideology, sometimes described as "Confucian," regards individual advancement as a function of family advancement (Salaff 1981:258, 392) and holds that working daughters must honor their overwhelming debt to the parents who gave them life and raised them (Kung 1983:56). Salaff's portrait of Hong Kong working daughters recalls Haraven's image of the semiautonomous children of the Amoskeag mill town, bound by familial obligations but with expanded social horizons, new opportunities for personal fulfillment, and choice in the matter of a marriage partner, if not in the timing of a wedding.

With a common heritage of strong familism made explicit in shared Confucian homilies, one would expect the experiences of Korean working daughters to resemble those of Taiwanese or Hong Kong women. Indeed, factory women often claim they are working to help their families, to support a brother's education, or to supplement a sister's wedding expenses.[12] But then there are the stories of Kkach'i and Oksuk. One boldly defied her family in order to marry the man of her choice, the other—perhaps because she distrusted her stepmother's intentions—amassed a personal nest egg without making any significant contribution to her family until she relinquished the entire sum of wedding money to Yongsu's Mother, with the full knowledge of the community. Kkach'i and Oksuk, participants in the world of work and wages, removed from the village

11. At the same time, Malaysian working women experienced new systems of domination, including "industrial discipline, social surveillance, and religious vigilance" (Ong 1987, 1988:83).

12. See Chang-Michell (1984), Kim Seung-Kyung (1990:113–114), Spencer (1988:22–23, 28), and Yoon (1991:134–135).

where they had grown up, made independent choices. But recall also that their stories had happy endings because their families were both willing and able to sponsor their weddings.

Many other working women, like Mrs. Ch'oe, whose story was told in Chapter 5, were not so fortunate. Their stories are common among the working poor who cohabit without weddings, as an act of rebellion or with the nearly fatalistic acquiescence of families who cannot give them weddings.[13] Clearly, the condition of Korean working women cannot be reduced to a simple dichotomy of "dutiful daughter" versus "autonomous woman." An examination of how a daughter's wages, particularly her marriage money, are managed suggests a delicate balance between family obligation and personal entitlement, between long-term strategies and romantic impulses.

Most of the twenty-nine Righteous Town brides gave their wages to their parents, usually to mothers, and held only small amounts for their own expenses. Five brides, like Oksuk, managed all of their own savings and investments, while others invested some of their earnings in rotating credit associations. Like Oksuk, most of the twenty-nine brides relinquished their savings to parental management at the time of their weddings.[14] The involvement of mothers in purchasing ceremonious goods for a daughter's wedding bespeaks their managerial knowledge, but it also carries a cultural assumption that families provide daughters with weddings and that mothers bear a particular responsibility for bringing this event to a successful completion.

The amount a woman may save toward her own wedding seems to accelerate with her wages as she approaches marriageable age, but there is considerable variation. As the years pass, a working daughter may be under less pressure to support younger siblings at home, and younger daughters may be entirely free of such obligations (Kim Seung-Kyung 1990:113–114; Spencer 1988:81). There is seldom a precise relationship between the bride's earned money and the bride's marriage expenses. Daughters usually contribute more money to the family than is invested on their behalf, and investments of the daughter's own money are usually supplemented by parental resources, often also by siblings or parents' siblings, as in Oksuk's and Sukcha's weddings. In a manner that would please

13. See Kim Eun-Shil (1993:205–223), Kim Seung-Kyung (1990:156–159), Pak Sukcha (1991), and Yoon Hyungsook (1991).

14. Exceptions, brides who had no savings, included two brides who had married for love without parental approval, significantly delaying their weddings, and Mrs. Sŏ, who had no family and used her savings as key money on an apartment.

the domestic strategy theorists, both earnings and wedding expenses are transacted within the domestic economy and supplemented within the broader frame of family obligations; a daughter's wages are a family resource as her wedding is a family responsibility.[15] Even where a daughter's earnings are all saved toward her wedding and not used to defray other family expenses, her parents acknowledge that a daughter's wages relieve them of this significant financial burden (Yoon Hyungsook 1989a:71, 1989b).

But if, as the domestic strategy theorists would expect, the working daughter's wages are absorbed into the domestic economy, even as savings for her wedding, do they not then lose some sense of being "hers," and does she not risk losing them in marrying when and whom she might choose? Daughters' claims on a dowry are least ambiguous when, like Oksuk, they save and invest all or part of their own money. However, this assumes both autonomy (in this case, the autonomy of a stepdaughter who had no strong emotional attachment to her widowed stepmother's household) and an absence of family need. Brides' claims are most ambiguous when family need consumes all of their earnings.

No bride accused her family of opposing her marriage because they needed her wages or service, but need could have been a subtext for some of the stated opposition to early marriages. Two of the women who married over serious family opposition had given all of their wages to needy families headed by widowed mothers. One bride, after some delay, had a modest wedding, largely subsidized by a married sister. The second was Mrs. Ch'oe, who waited more than a decade before she could finance her own wedding. The daughter's significant contribution to her own wedding is most explicitly recognized where mothers' investments of daughters' money are specifically earmarked for wedding expenses, and several of the women I interviewed had a very clear idea of the size of investments made on their behalf. When one mother invested her daughter's money imprudently and "lost it all," the mother made good the loss and financed the daughter's wedding with the proceeds from her ginseng crop.

Even though a daughter has legitimate expectations of a wedding, and these claims are generally recognized among families who can afford weddings, she has little recourse when her wedding money is reappropriated within the family. One bride explained that she had sent her mother savings of 70,000 to 80,000 *wŏn* (about $100 U.S.) each month to be invested

15. Lydia Kung (1983) describes a similar dynamic for working daughters in rural Taiwan.

for her dowry. After the mother's death, the money "was put to a different use." Her father opposed her subsequent marriage plans and made only a minimal contribution to the wedding that was held when she became pregnant. He scowled when he led her down the aisle and continued to scowl throughout the wedding feast. Despite her father's relative affluence as the owner of a small company in a provincial town, this bride was disadvantaged because there was no one like Kkach'i's mother to take her part and see that she had a proper wedding.

Similarly disadvantaged was a bride who worked for a family enterprise, her mother's tearoom, and consequently received no wage. Mrs. Yun claims to have been very popular with the customers until she fell in love with a driver who worked for her father, a man of whom her mother disapproved because she considered him to be lower class. The young woman was indifferent to the driver until she suffered an attack of acute appendicitis, and he carried her to the hospital in his arms. This won her heart. To escape her mother's beatings, the pretty cashier ran away with the brawny driver. (The mother may have been particularly vehement, and the daughter particularly vulnerable, because the mother was herself a concubine.) Mrs. Yun's wedding occurred five years after her flight, before her own daughter entered school. The little girl's appearance in the wedding hall, where my assistant photographed her modeling the Korean bridal crown her mother would wear for the *p'yebaek*, was cause for much tongue clucking since parents' late weddings are usually hidden from children (as in Mrs. Ch'oe's story in Chapter 5). There had been a family reconciliation, and the bride's mother and brother provided the ritual gifts of jewelry and clothing.

Conversations with Korean mothers anticipating the marriages of daughters and sons reveal a careful sense of planning. Mothers are attuned to when their investments in rotating credit associations come due or when a working child is likely to receive a bonus. Events, however, often conspire against them as a consequence of the "impetuousness, risk, luck, accidents, and some hormonal reactions" cited by Wolf (1992:219). Several brides indicated they had married sooner than anticipated and before reaching their targeted sum of marriage money. As a consequence, they settled for modest dowries. These were almost inevitably love marriages, and some, like Kkach'i's marriage, were the marriages of pregnant brides. Pregnancy forced at least one bride to take an unfavorable return on money invested in a rotating credit association.

The combination of work, wages, and family support made it possible for most of the twenty-nine brides to have respectable weddings and for their families to bask in the satisfaction of having seen a daughter well wed (the thrust of Yongsu's Mother's argument to her husband's kin). For these brides and their families, as for Yongsu's Mother, "well wed" meant not only with proper ceremony but with adequate dowries, both in household goods *(honsu)* and in gifts given to the groom and his family *(yedan,* "ritual silks"). Even as working daughters have gained an ability to subsidize weddings, the requirements expected of them in wedding goods have increased in both cost and kind. Indeed, the very nature of ceremonious goods has shifted over the last century.

ABOUT DOWRIES

After all, marriage is marriage, and money's money—both useful
things in their way. . . .

Edith Wharton, The Age of Innocence

A contemporary Korean wedding process is marked by exchanges of cash and ceremonious goods *(yemul)*[16]: household goods, cabinets, and appliances *(honsu)*; gifts of cloth, clothing, and jewelry exchanged between the bride and groom *(yedan, ch'aedan, p'aemul)*; gifts of cloth, clothing, quilts, or blankets given to the groom's significant kin *(yedan)*; gifts of cash from the groom's kin to the bride *(chŏlgap)* and from the bride's family to the groom's friends *(hamgap)*; and exchanges of food and wine between the two families *(sangsu)*.[17]

Kopytoff (1986) suggests, in distinguishing "gift" from "commodity," that while the objects of these transactions may be things normally viewed as commodities, the bestowal of ceremonious goods is not a discrete transaction in the manner of a commodity exchange. Rather, each gift becomes one more link in a chain of transactions, the sum of which effects a significant social process—in this case, the making of a marriage (Kopytoff 1986:69). Or in John Comaroff's (1980:36) words, "marriage

16. The common gloss of *yemul* as "gift" seems to me more neutral than the Chinese character components of this word and its common association with marriage goods imply.

17. Minor cash payments and small gifts are also made, with varying degrees of ritualization, to different categories of wedding participants. The *churye* who presides at the wedding and the moderator sometimes receive gifts from the groom's family, and the groom's friends who deliver his gift of cloth and clothing to the bride receive a substantial sum of cash *(hamgap,* described in the next chapter), some of which may be given over to the bride's friends in exchange for her bouquet *(kkokkap)*. Wedding guests bring gifts of cash, and friends of the bride and groom may bring inexpensive presents.

prestations are not ontologically separable from marriage. Rather, they are complementary elements of the same thing: a meaningful order with reference to which the physical fact of cohabitation is transformed into a social fact of marriage."

To this end, Kkach'i's family struggled to provide ceremonious goods, and Oksuk's stepmother reveled in her own ability (aided by Oksuk's earnings) to do them well. Even Mrs. Ch'oe, who held a wedding after years of cohabitation, made a minimal provision of ritual goods in the new formal clothing that she, her husband, and her father-in-law wore. Mrs. Sŏ's mother-in-law gave her son and his orphan bride both clothing and rings. Couples who participate in charity weddings (described in Chapter 1) receive rings and small gifts of dishes, pots, and pans as material markers of a significant social event. The provision of at least minimal ritual goods, no less than the ceremony, would seem to make a wedding. Conversely, those who are unable to provide even a minimum of ritual goods, those who lack personal and familial resources, do not have "weddings," although they may be legally "married" for having registered their marriages at the ward office. The dowry goods give testimony not simply to the amount of wealth invested in them; they testify to family support. When the sharp-eyed shaman Yongsu's Mother surveyed the spare rented room of a new client, she told me that the bride must have bad relations with her own family, that they do nothing for her. "How did you know?" "Didn't you see that tiny little cardboard storage cabinet? No real wardrobe cabinet to speak of."

The groom's betrothal gifts to the bride are expected to include more jewelry, and thus to be more costly, than the gifts of clothing, watch, and ring he receives from the bride. The bride, on the other hand, has the considerable burden of a dowry of household goods and the obligation to provide gifts of "ritual silk" to the groom's significant kin. While the groom's side is expected to provide the couple with a place to live, a significant expenditure in this age of neolocal residence, this investment is still seen as a family resource, in no sense given over in exchange like ceremonious goods. The bride's family's obligation is thus widely recognized as the more burdensome since ultimately, even the betrothal gifts sent to the bride come back to the groom's side with her person.[18]

18. Koreans do not seem to have followed the Chinese practice of taking cash betrothal gifts as a form of "indirect dowry," to be spent by the bride's family in furnishing a wedding, although betrothal gifts of cloth, transformed by the bride into clothing, could be said to constitute a kind of minimalist indirect dowry. A survey of regional folk customs records a local practice whereby cash was included

Marriage exchanges in Korea have been accelerating in both cost and complexity, in pace with Korea's industrial transformation. In 1990, weddings, with all their attendant exchanges, cost the average couple and their families 18.32 million *wŏn* (roughly $26,000 U.S.). Brides' families spent, on average, 10.57 million *wŏn* ($15,100 U.S.)—between a quarter and a third again as much as grooms' families. These estimates more than doubled the results of a 1985 survey (Chŏch'uk Ch'ujin Chungang Wiwŏn Hoe 1985; *Korea Newsreview*, 3 March 1990:7). The expectations placed upon women and their families have also been elaborated in marriage "customs" with only brief and tenuous genealogies, as in the giving of a large cash fee to the friends of the groom when they deliver betrothal gifts (described in the next chapter) and the giving of "ritual silk"—gifts of cloth or clothing—to members of the groom's extended family.

Many of my informants share with many Western-trained anthropologists the notion that the dowry is an instrument of status maintenance and manipulation.[19] In everyday conversations and in the popular press, one hears a great deal about the economic bartering which transpires over weddings among the upper middle class. I soon learned the urban folklore of the "three keys," that if one wishes to marry one of the three *sa* (the three professions of doctor *ŭisa*, lawyer *pyŏnhosa*, or professor *paksa*),[20] then one must provide the house key, the car key, and the office key (purchase a professional practice). In the early 1980s, Yim Dawnhee (personal communication) conducted an informal survey of recently married physicians and dentists and found that, while their brides had brought generous dowries to their marriages, none of the men had received "the three keys." The ubiquitousness of this folklore is indicative, rather, of a cynical and hyperbolic humor regarding matchmaking. I learned recently, when I made reference to the three keys in a public lecture, that at least in the popular imagination, the ante has now been upped to five keys, including the golf club key and the vacation condominium key.

The bride's side is seen as investing in their daughter's future happiness and security by marrying her to a young man with a promising

---

with the betrothal gifts as a "sewing fee" intended for the bride's use (MCIBCPP 1977 "Kyŏngnam": 145–146). As we shall see, in another community, accepting gifts of cash from the groom's side was considered tantamount to selling a daughter.

19. See Bourdieu (1977:171), Goody and Tambiah (1973), Harrell and Dickey (1985), and Schlegel and Eloul (1988).

20. Although professors were a favored match a few decades ago, they remain in the aphorism only for the sake of alliteration.

future. This point, implicit in the transformation of courtship practices, is made explicit by some of the matchmaking women encountered in the last chapter. Mrs. Yim, so concerned about the prospective marriage of her own daughter, told me, "With sons who are doctors and lawyers, the family feels that they've invested in their son's education and that it's a good, solid career, a source of lifelong security. If the young professional happens to be from a poor family, they may even ask the matchmaker to find them a wealthy family, but I don't like this idea of a large obligation at the time of marriage." According to Mrs. Paek, the relentlessly pragmatic boutique proprietress, "It isn't enough that the woman be beautiful. Her family must prepare; they must have the economic resources for a good match." Similarly, Yi Eunhee Kim's middle-class informants regard the dowry as "compensation" or an expression of "gratitude" given to the groom's parents for their having raised a successful son (Yi 1993:288). With more modest prospects, some of the factory women studied by Kim Seung-Kyung (1990:171–173) hope that their savings, converted into dowries, will win them middle-class marriages.

In 1983, the basic dowry for working women in my sample included a large wardrobe cabinet, a dressing table, a dish cabinet, quilts and sleeping pallets, dishes and cooking equipment, a small television set, a rice warmer, and, if done well, an electric rice cooker and a small refrigerator—a dowry which could furnish an independent household and transform the working daughter into a housewife. By the time of Sukcha's wedding, eight years later, refrigerators and washing machines were common components of the dowry among her friends and former classmates. By then, upper-middle-class dowries could include suites of furniture, automobiles, pianos, savings in the form of cash or stocks, and even sums of cash sufficient to purchase the couple's first apartment. The groom's (and bride's) clothing might bear designer labels, his close kin might receive head-to-toe sets of Korean or Western clothing, and grooms' mothers might even sport mink coats and diamond jewelry as their ritual silk (Pak Minja 1991:164; Yi Eunhee Kim 1993:293).

Feminist commentator An Chŏngnam (1991) and I agree that Korean marriage practices have assumed their present shape because marriage so often ends a woman's most remunerated work years and more generally because married women are regarded as the less productive members of the new industrial and service economy. An underscores a further contrast between the dowry, brought to the groom's side but intended for the bride's own use, and the ritual silk, given to the groom, his mother, and members of his family, an expense from which the bride derives no direct benefit (An 1991:194).[21] The elaboration of dowries of household goods follows upon the celebration of conjugality as a romantic ideal and a new mode of consumption widely accessible through the purchase of new Korean-made products. The very recent rise and elaboration of gifts in ritual silk, with no such obvious rationale, indicates a more profound devaluation of brides and brides' families.

ABOUT RITUAL SILK

The following incident, recorded during my first field trip, highlights the quicksilver quality of "new customs" in the countryside near Seoul. On an early autumn day in the fall of 1977, two village women bemoaned the costs of marrying off their daughters while the anthropologist offered appropriate murmurs of amazement and sympathy and scribbled field notes. One of these women was Munae's Mother, who had recently seen her daughter wed, and the other was Yongsu's Mother, then busy with arrangements for Oksuk's wedding. She began to elaborate her list of anticipated expenses for the gifts the bride's side would provide, estimating the cost of buying a suit,[22] a ring, and a watch for the groom and a Korean dress for the groom's mother—at least the groom's father was dead and would not require a new suit. Now Munae's Mother burst forth. When her daughter had married, the bride's family gave a Korean dress to every father's sister and brother's wife in the family and a dress shirt, a pair of socks, and a necktie to each of the uncles. Yongsu's Mother was incredulous. This was the first and perhaps the only time I have ever seen her acknowledge ignorance of a social phenomenon. She seemed to match the anthropologist in her unfamiliarity with this "custom," but beyond any ethnographic curiosity, she was immediately anxious that this would be yet another expense, not only substantial but also unanticipated. Her friend explained, "They do it that way in Seoul now. It's a new style, a new custom (*sinsik, sinbŏp*)."

Yongsu's Mother eventually recovered her usual shrewdness and fulfilled her newly inflated obligation by bestowing one thick plush blanket

21. Caplan (1984) describes an analogous development in urban India, where, in addition to the daughter's own wedding settlement, the groom's family receives a large cash transfer as a sign of the groom's worth.

22. "Suit" is shorthand here for the full complement of dress shirt, necktie, and additional sets of clothing the bride's side would provide. Yongsu's Mother did not, however, provide shoes since, as she explained, an old belief equates the giving of shoes with the groom's walking out on the marriage.

upon each of the many pairs of aunts and uncles in her new son-in-law's family. By the summer of 1983, her neighbors had come to assume that brides' families send "ritual silk" (*yedan, yemul*) in the form of clothing, cloth, or quilts not only to the groom and his immediate family, but often to his aunts and uncles as well. When I reviewed my notes, taken on that autumn day in 1977, it was with the eerie realization that I had serendipitously recorded one small turning in a larger transformation in the bride's family's obligation to send ritual silk.

In Righteous Town weddings, clothing for the groom and his parents seems to be the fundamental, nearly irreducible unit of ritual silk.[23] Even the hard-working Mrs. Ch'oe managed to provide her father-in-law with a new suit for the wedding. In the wedding hall, the groom wears his full dress suit, shirt, and necktie, his mother, a Korean dress, and his father, a Western suit or Korean suit and topcoat. This public display of ritual silk is one small sign that the two families have conducted an appropriate and worthy wedding process. One elderly woman with a practical bent claimed that, counter to common practice, she sent her daughters' ritual silk after their weddings, after the brides' side had received the betrothal gifts sent by the grooms' families. This sequence of exchanges is in fact closer to normative accounts of the "traditional wedding," where the bride would present gifts of cloth or examples of needlework to the groom's parents when she made her first salutation, long after the betrothal gifts have been received.[24] The early provision of ritual silks places the bride's family at a disadvantage; they must assume in good faith that the groom's side will respond with comparable gifts to the bride when they send the gift box, on or near the eve of the wedding. In *Staggering Afternoon*, Pak Wansŏ's 1977 novel of middle-class matrimony, the groom's family crudely asks for the early delivery of a large sum of cash so they can prepare their wedding day clothing. In their turn, however, the groom's side sends only inferior synthetic fabric as betrothal gifts. The bride's long-suffering father finds it particularly galling to see his disreputable new affines in the wedding hall, nicely attired in clothing purchased at his expense.

Siblings and married siblings' spouses usually also receive clothing or

23. In one very poor wedding, the groom received only a dress shirt and necktie, although his widowed mother received a Korean dress.

24. The notion that the bride offers gifts when she is first presented to the groom's parents may be traced to Chu Hsi's twelfth-century manual on family rituals: "She ascends the stairs and lays down a token of silk. The mother-in-law picks it up and gives it to a servant" (Ebrey 1991a:62).

Range of possible ritual
silk recipients (29 weddings)

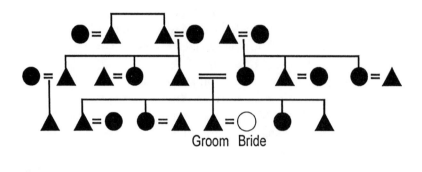

Groom Bride

● ▲ Recipients

Figure 8. Recipients of ritual silk.

lengths of cloth suitable for festive clothing, although a poor bride might give her husband's married siblings a quilt or a blanket. In one instance, a very poor bride had promised quilts but, in the end, provided only token gifts of socks and stockings—a fact her sister-in-law told me without overt criticism, although she clearly considered the stockings a paltry gift. The cloth which the groom's siblings or other kin receives can also be made up for wedding wear, but this is less likely when the gift does not include the cost of tailoring. Lengths of cloth may languish in the depths of cabinets for years because the fabric was not to the wearer's taste or because thrift or simple inertia caused the recipient to postpone a trip to the tailor until the fabric was out of fashion.

As revealed in the conversation between Yongsu's Mother and Munae's Mother, the father-in-law's and mother-in-law's married siblings and their surviving parents may also expect to receive significant ritual silk in the form of clothing, lengths of cloth, quilts, or blankets (see fig. 8). In addition, several sets of socks and stockings may be given to the mother-in-law, to be distributed among the groom's distant kin.[25] The

25. In the early 1980s, women received white Korean-style socks to wear with Korean slippers. Since then, it has become more common to wear heeled dress shoes with Korean clothing, and I suspect that the giving of Korean-style socks

question of who receives ritual silk rests both on the bride's family's ability to provide these goods and on their perception of significant kin in the groom's family. Those who receive ritual silk, like those who receive the bride's salutation and give kow-tow money to the bride in the *p'yebaek* ritual, violate strict Korean definitions of agnatic kinship.

From the perspective of the groom as ego, these relations come from a bilateral universe of kinship that includes out-married sisters and the significant kin of both mother and father. In my interviews, I was struck by the frequency with which women would list the recipients of ritual silk by female relationship, for example, "husband's brother's wife" (*tongsŏ*) or "husband's senior uncle's wife" (*k'ŭnŏmŏni*)—even when the gift of a blanket or quilt was intended for a couple's use. The giving of ritual silk celebrates *patrilocality* insofar as the bride's gifts are intended to nurture benevolence among her husband's kin, but the paths which gifts travel do not replicate an expressed ideology of *patrilineal* kinship. Ritual silks map significant familial interactions in a society of atomized and mostly urban households where women have come to do the practical work of kinship maintenance (Cho Hyoung 1975; Moon 1990).[26]

For the Righteous Town brides, the question of who receives ritual silk seems to have been smoothly resolved in consultation with the bridegroom or with the kinswoman or acquaintance who made the match, and gifts were limited to clothing, cloth, or quilts. Bridegrooms, with the predictability of a cliché, insisted upon "just the bare essentials" (*p'iryohanŭn'gŏnman*), and one bride's father candidly explained that a future son-in-law is easier to deal with than a matchmaker, who may pursue more impressive gifts. Among the upper middle class, however, where the stakes in both cost and prestige are high, gifts to the groom's kin become statements of both wealth and distinction (Bourdieu 1984; Douglas and Isherwood 1979:66, 96), and these negotiations can be cause for acute anxiety. Some of the amateur matchmakers introduced in Chapter 5 described negotiations over the ritual silk as both time-consuming and stressful, the

---

has largely been supplanted by stockings, a common small item of gift exchange even apart from weddings.

26. This shift may be a matter of degree rather than kind, particularly for non-*yangban* Koreans. Even in rural Korea, ties maintained by out-married women were critical to marriage negotiations (Han 1977:60; Kim Choong Soon 1974; Osgood 1951:42), and affines could be a source of financial or political support (Lee Mangap 1960:210; Han 1977:91–92, 107). In shaman rituals, out-married women and mothers' kin frequently appear as ancestors, and a woman's natal home may be a source of potent (and usually troublesome) household gods (Kendall 1985a).

stress accelerating with the prestige of the match. One matron explained to me that because her daughter's match had been made by one of the groom's relatives, it would be awkward to expect this woman to advise the bride's side regarding the groom's family's expectations in ritual silk. Instead, the bride's mother had hired a professional matchmaker for the solitary purpose of negotiating the ritual silk, a task the woman resolved expeditiously to the boundless gratitude of the bride's mother.

Her experience was in marked contrast to the pervasive feeling that matchmakers, particularly professional matchmakers, inflate the expectations of both sides as a measure of their own face in negotiating an illustrious match. In Kim Yugyŏng's sensitive essay "My Daughter's Wedding Expenses," her narrator describes being goaded by the matchmaker into preparing a far more elaborate gift of ritual silks than she had originally intended.

> The matchmaker insinuated her advice, "You should take great pains with the ritual silk." She told me that the first daughter-in-law had given the mother-in-law a full set of traditional cushions, so how would it be if we gave them a folding screen? She claimed that the parents and siblings are all well off, that they have a "refined eye" and wouldn't so much as deign to look at things bought in the market. "Once you receive their gift box, then you will understand. The groom's side is taking great pains with everything. You must try to meet their standard."
>
> For the first time, I was pierced with the realization that it would have been so different had my daughter made a love match (Kim Yugyŏng 1984:163).

A rare plucky woman might subvert the process. A friend who managed the marriage of her younger brother described to me how the matchmaker would come to her with reports of the splendid gifts the bride's side was preparing, urging the groom's side to respond in kind. "We aren't going to do anything," my friend told her, stonewalling to prevent the matchmaker from rushing back to the bride's side with a fresh report to inflate the ante. My friend seemed to relish her memory of the matchmaker's frustration: "Of course we were going to give appropriate gifts, but this way I could protect my future sister-in-law."

The parents of Righteous Town brides affirmed again and again that the giving of ritual silk is a "new custom" and, as such, is antithetical to the indigenous practices of Kyŏnggi Province. Although Lay spoke of the obligation of "gentle-folk" in this same region to "keep the groom in raiment" for years after the wedding, women married in the impoverished Kyŏnggi countryside of the 1930s and 1940s maintained that, at the time of their weddings, only the very wealthy would have sent even a single set of clothes to the groom. While their own weddings lacked this potentially status-enhancing practice, these same brides did bring humble dowries: "In those days, there wasn't any giving of ritual silk. I just brought my own clothes in a little basket, and even though it was the custom to look everything over, I really didn't have much to show."[27]

In their retrospective accounts, the bride's clothing, what she brought with her and what she received as betrothal gifts, was the most remarked upon item of ceremonious goods. The groom's kin, both close and distant, received only simple gifts of Korean socks, and women giggled to recall how all the women of the family would gather to produce a great stack of white cotton socks in a short time. Speaking of fieldwork done in this same province in the 1950s, Pak and Gamble report that "brides seldom send presents to the groom's relations or take much clothing or bed clothes" (Pak and Gamble 1975:135). Also in Kyŏnggi Province, Yoon Hyungsook relates how women over the age of sixty describe their marriages: "I just brought my body."[28] In the 1960s, a bride brought her own clothes, a quilt for the groom's parents, and cabinets. In this village, as in Enduring Pine Village, the elaboration of dowry rose with women's employment in the 1970s (Yoon 1989a.:35, 1991:133).

Thus within living memory, an elite custom whereby the bride fashioned with her own fingers the groom's "first garment made after adult fashion" (Miln 1895:81) has been transformed into the nearly universal practice of providing the groom with a tailored suit to wear on his wedding day and some additional clothing. By 1977, the obligation extended to wedding day clothes for the groom's parents, and rural households were just beginning to follow the "new custom," found in the capital city, of sending significant gifts to the groom's other significant kin.[29]

A seamstress of my acquaintance in Seoul blames it all on "those people from the Chŏllas" who raise a fuss if you refuse to give them ritual

27. Women married just after the liberation or around the time of the Korean War, like this woman, speak of extreme scarcity: "there wasn't any cloth to be had."

28. Many of these women were adopted daughters-in-law (*minmyŏnŭri*) who would not have brought gifts under any circumstance.

29. I have heard only one person, the proprietor of an elegant and expensive silk shop in Seoul, claim that less ritual silk is given now than in the past, that it was once properly given to relatives up to the seventh or eighth degree of relationship, the broadest extension of family (*fafafafasosososo*). This expansive vision of the past would, of course, have matched the silk shop proprietor's business interests.

silk, and an elderly farmer spoke with some heat about the deleterious effects of internal migrations that brought this jumble of custom in their wake. A regional stereotype, firmly held by long-term residents of central Korea, holds that persons from southwestern Korea (the provinces of North and South Chŏlla) are aggressive and loutish. Some twenty years ago, these perceptions were confirmed for the seamstress when the mother of her future son-in-law demanded a silk blouse and skirt as part of the marriage negotiations.

This imposition still rankles despite the inflated obligations of the present day. The diffusion of a regional custom, even an elite regional custom, could have accelerated with the pace of urban migration as residents of the southwest entered into marriage negotiations with other Koreans in the capital city. Insofar as gifts of cloth or clothing have long been "good to think" (following Douglas and Isherwood 1979:62) as items of ceremonious exchange, status-conscious residents of Seoul may have been inspired to request and send ritual silks in the wake of older token exchanges (Lee 1974:74). Whatever its origin, when this practice reached the Kyŏnggi countryside around 1977, it was not done to keep "those people" from the Chŏllas quiet, but assumed as a new and compelling obligation for local residents caught in a cycle of ritual inflation.[30]

When one asks *why* people send ritual silks, the question is less likely to engender reconstructions of cultural history than to elicit a basic premise: the bride who brings a lot to her husband's family will receive better treatment, and a bride who brings only a little will suffer scorn. In the cautious circumlocutions of one upper-middle-class matron: "Owing to the peculiarities of fashion, one has to be extremely cautious concerning one's daughter's position." I could better understand these anxieties when I hired a newly married university graduate to transcribe some of my tapes. Thin and pale, she proved to be sickly and was seldom available for work. I thought she might be pregnant until her classmate (also in my employ) asked me, during a discussion of the relative caloric values of Korean and Western food, if I did not think that Yŏnghŭi was extremely slender. "It's all because of the ritual silk," she confided. "Her husband's family has given her a bad time. They've made her nervous and ill. Her friends joke that we should all get married if we want to lose weight. The

---

30. A very few grooms have begun to give cloth or clothing to the bride's mother and siblings, a practice which seems to be slightly more common in the capital city.

matchmakers talk about 'family background' and 'educational attainment,' but economics is what it's really all about."

Fifty-four percent of the female respondents to a survey conducted by the Consumer Protection Board in the fall of 1990 claimed that the giving of ritual silk was the most burdensome feature of their weddings (*Korea Newsreview*, 27 March 1991:30). The unhappiness of a woman like Yŏnghŭi becomes a cautionary tale fanning the sense of necessity with which brides' families invest the ritual silk. At the same time, Pak Minja's (1991) study of marriage practices among the urban middle class reveals that, for most respondents, neither the dowry nor the ritual silk has any significant bearing upon a woman's subsequent married life, neither as a positive influence upon the bride's position nor as a theme in domestic quarrels. Pak ascribes to "false consciousness" the middle-class perception that a good dowry and elaborate *yedan* will win for a daughter a strong position in her husband's family (Pak Minja 1991:172). Conversely, mothers-in-law are encouraged to exact their will upon future daughters-in-law by requesting ritual silk. One independent-minded Korean woman long resident in the United States returned to Korea for her son's wedding. She was shocked when her friends insisted she request a substantial gift of ritual silk, warning her that, unless she made this demand, she would never control her daughter-in-law. She held firm in resisting the ritual silk, but acknowledged her privileged position insofar as she was "going to escape from Korea the day after the wedding."

A distinguished professor found himself in an equally embarrassing position when he returned to Korea for a nephew's wedding, filling the role of the groom's deceased father. The bride made a polite query as to when he would like to schedule a fitting for his suit. He had been gone from Korea for so long that he was taken unawares. At first he did not know what she meant, and when it was explained to him, his first impulse was to spare her an unnecessary expense. He told her emphatically that he did not need a suit and saw her face collapse into an expression of acute unhappiness. His nephew suggested that perhaps the professor could use a new pair of shoes. Still acting on his own sense of consideration for the bride, he said that an extra pair of shoes would just weigh heavily in his suitcase. The couple explained to him that the bride's gift was now the custom. The professor said he welcomed her into the family as she was, for her own sake, but the bride was still visibly unhappy. When he mentioned this encounter to two Korean anthropologists, they immediately understood the bride's distress: "She thinks that you are either saying

Figure 9.   This decal, in the shape of an antique coin, advertises the Korean Mothers' Club's "Moderate Wedding and Dowry Movement." It appeared in 1987.

you are displeased with her, or that you want something more." They advised him to accept the suit as the better part of valor.

In the late 1980s, some Koreans actively concerned with social reform attempted to hold firm against the custom of giving ritual silk (see fig. 9). The director of a YWCA program aimed at encouraging thrifty weddings was adamant, when her own son married, that she would not receive ritual silk since it was imperative that she should set a good example. The subordinate who told me this story vested her employer's action with the import of an exemplary tale. With great feeling, one of my assistants described the wedding preparations of two labor activists, children of the middle class who had chosen to devote their lives to the movement. As a gift for her mother-in-law, the bride had knit a sweater with her own hands, "a gift from the heart." The couple was adamant that no other ritual silks would be given to the groom's relations. To spare her future daughter-in-law any ill feeling in her new family, the mother-in-law herself purchased appropriate gifts and said that the bride had provided them. The mother-in-law's gesture could be given multiple readings. When I told this story to Mrs. Yim, who was so concerned for her own daughter's future, her eyes misted over and she said, "That's a beautiful story." When I told this same story to the pragmatic Mrs. Paek, she said, "Of course, the mother-in-law did it to save her own face."

Not surprisingly, Korean feminists attribute the burdensome dowry obligations imposed upon women and their families to the abiding strength of a Confucian patriarchal tradition, an ideology that values sons over daughters and makes brides most immediately accountable to their husbands' kin (An 1991). While this assumption has an ultimate logic in the relative social and economic disadvantages of Korean women, it also obscures the complex history of Korean wedding rituals by reducing historical choices to an assumed cultural inevitability. As scholars who have researched the weddings of dynastic times, neither Martina Deuchler (personal communication) nor Pak Hyein (1991) believes that "dowry"—any material wealth, however small, brought by the bride to her marriage (following Ebrey 1991a:7)—was a significant component of Korean weddings before recent times, much less a defining feature of matrimony.[31]

LOOKING BACKWARD

As both Deuchler and Pak illustrate, emic categories of matrimonial procedures and folk terminology confound the ordered sequences of Confucian matrimonial rites as described in ritual manuals (Deuchler 1992:251–257; Pak Hyein 1991). Deuchler (1992:252) wryly notes that because there were also distinct regional variations in marriage customs, "it is impossible to describe a 'typical' Chosŏn dynasty *yangban* wedding, although some basic and irreducible elements may be discerned." In Korean adapta-

31. Pak Hyein (1991) argues that pre-Confucian custom required only a minimal exchange of ritual meats, but Martina Deuchler (1992:65–66) finds evidence in Koryŏ times (918–1392) of an exchange of gifts and a display of fine silk fabrics and precious utensils. Deuchler (1992:245) notes a long history of prohibitions against extravagant weddings in Korea from as early as the fourteenth century. In China as well, official discourse on weddings did not acknowledge the significance of dowries, except to criticize extravagance. Sentiments attributed to Chu Hsi himself condemn "covetous and vulgar people [who] first ask about the value of the dowry when selecting a bride and the amount of the wedding present when marrying a daughter" (Ebrey 1991a:55).

tions of the Confucian wedding rite as practiced among *yangban*, formal presentations between the two households punctuated a gradual process of affinal alliance culminating in the transfer of a bride to her husband's kin. The entire wedding process might unfold over several years. After a careful negotiation of the wedding by the elders of both houses, the groom's family would send a formal request of matrimony and the groom's horoscope *(saju, sasŏng)* to the family of the bride. A favorable reply would be returned with an astrologer's determination of the auspicious dates and hours for the delivery of the betrothal gifts and for the rites which would be performed in the courtyard of the bride's home *(t'aegil)*. The betrothal was marked by the delivery of a box *(ham*, precursor to the gift box described in the next chapter) containing the marriage contract, lengths of cloth or colored threads, and various auspicious items betokening fertility *(napch'ae)*. When the groom appeared at the home of the bride, he presented a wooden goose as a pledge of fidelity *(chŏnallye)*, and the couple exchanged bows *(kyobaerye)* and cups of wine *(hapkŭllye)*.

As the last act of the marriage process, an event that might follow the ceremony in the bride's courtyard and the subsequent consummation of the marriage by months or even years, the bride, bearing gifts of wine, meat, and cloth, was inducted into the groom's home, where she bowed before the elders *(kugorye, kyŏn'gurye, p'yebaek)* and ancestors *(komyo)* of his house (Deuchler 1992:251–257; Lee Kwang-Kyu 1974:68–75; Pak Hyein 1991: 24–45). This sequence is rich in "exchanges" insofar as persons, documents, and goods pass between the two families. Actual presentations of *things*, of tangible and enduring material gifts sent by the groom's family and brought by the bride, seem to be no more significant than the documents and gestures of the rites in signifying a wedding.

It might be useful to consider here what "dowry" and "exchange" mean in a Korean and a broader East Asian context. In *Marriage and Inequality in Chinese Society*, Patricia Buckley Ebrey offers an illuminating contrast between Jack Goody's (Goody and Tambiah 1973) "dowry complex" (Ebrey's term), a feature of European and Indian societies, and Chinese practice. In Goody's scheme, the dowry represents a daughter's share of her family's property, transmitted to affines as a means of establishing a strong affinal alliance within a patriarchal system of significant class distinctions. In similarly patriarchal and class-based China, a full-blown dowry complex failed to develop; daughters had only weak claims to property, and both bridewealth (in the form of betrothal gifts) and dowry coexisted in Chinese practice. Ebrey argues that, by discouraging women's control of property, male family heads furthered the strength and solidarity of agnatic kin groups at the cost of strong affinal ties (Ebrey 1991b). In the same volume, Rubie Watson notes that although "throughout most of Chinese history women received dowry but in effect had no rights of inheritance," even a meager dowry was critical symbolic capital distinguishing a legitimate wife from a purchased concubine or serving woman. Succinctly stated, "wives are married not bought" (R. Watson 1991b:359).

The "uniqueness" of the Chinese case is belied by Korea, where, as we have seen, dowry and bridewealth (again in the form of betrothal gifts) similarly coexisted, and (from the seventeenth century on) daughters did not inherit.[32] The clothing and gifts of cloth, wine, and meats which brides brought to their in-laws' houses were at best only a tiny dowry, and dowry was not an overt preoccupation in the official discourse about weddings.

But did the presentation of these gifts, in and of themselves, signify a legitimate Korean wife, as Watson suggests for China? Ethnographic accounts of late Chosŏn and early-twentieth-century Korea do indicate a sharp distinction between weddings marked by ceremonious exchanges and those that were not. Some of Han Gyoung-hai's elderly informants describe the "wrapped-in" marriages practiced by poor families in early-twentieth-century Korea, in which "The bride didn't have to bring anything with her when she married, nothing, not even bedclothes. The groom's family prepares the bride's cloth and visits them and wraps her in that prepared cloth" (Han 1990:107).

Early accounts and informant memories suggest that the poor simply sent their daughters to the husband's house, perhaps with only a small bundle of clothing or a quilt and without rites or feasting in the courtyard of the bride's home.[33] The daughters of the very poor, who were sent out

---

32. Until the late sixteenth or early seventeenth century, sons and daughters inherited an equal share of the family estate. Daughter inheritance was bestowed not as dowry, but after the deaths of parents whom both daughters and sons honored as ancestors, a violation of Confucian practice whereby only male descendants performed the critical ritual link to the ancestors. "Dowry" would have made little sense in the uxorilocal society of early Chosŏn Korea. Deuchler notes, however, that as Chosŏn society came to accept the moral hegemony of Confucian practice, inheritance papers of the late sixteenth and early seventeenth centuries began to list daughters' property in the names of sons-in-law. The rationale for endowing women with property vanished once daughters came to be regarded as women who joined their husbands' families and served the ancestors of a husband's house (Deuchler 1977, 1992:56, 223).

33. See Han (1990), Lay (1913), Moose (1911:168–170), and Sorensen (n.d.).

at an early age to be raised in the households of future mothers-in-law (*minmyŏnŭri*), brought nothing. The "*min*" of the term "*minmyŏnŭri*" literally means "bald," "bare," "unadorned," or "void of trappings and appendages." It describes the little daughter-in-law's head, bare of a married woman's chignon, but the term seems also to imply that these unions were bare of goods and ceremony. "*Minmyŏnŭri*, what did they bring to the in-laws' house?" snapped a village gossip, critical of a *minmyŏnŭri* of yesteryear who now presumed to denigrate her own daughter-in-law's scanty dowry.

Explicit notions of ritual propriety gave distinction to a particular and clearly recognizable style of matrimony, but the ethnographic record also suggests that rites and feasting in the home of the bride were at least as distinctive a feature of status-enhancing weddings as was any exchange of material goods. Writing of a northern village in the 1930s, Han Chung-nim described how, if the bride's family were poor, the groom's family would send them money to subsidize their feast, a gesture which would give both families the "face" of a proper wedding. She noted, however, that a bride whose wedding had been so celebrated could anticipate poor relations with her husband's family, while her own family would be discredited as having "sold" their daughter (Han 1949:184).

The fundamental units of marriage exchange were thus, above all, units of "social capital" in Bourdieu's (1977:171, 180) sense: events which demonstrated an elite knowledge of ritual form and social propriety, a literate ability to pen documents in good calligraphy and determine auspicious hours in accord with a fluctuating but knowable cosmology, and an entitlement to reciprocal feasting among similarly *yangban* kin, affines, and associates. The fundamental worth of ceremonious goods was similarly symbolic rather than economic, insofar as their presence validated the status claims of both families and contributed to the legitimation of the marriage.

The orchestrators of these rites and exchanges would probably have been comfortable with Marcel Mauss's classic formulation of exchange as a contract between moral actors—families, lineages, or other social groups—and his insistence that "what they exchange is not exclusively goods and wealth, real and personal property, and things of economic value. They exchange rather courtesies, entertainments, ritual, military assistance, women, children, dances and feasts" (Mauss 1967:3). These same exemplars of Confucian ritual would have been far less comfortable with Arjun Appadurai's (1986) corrective to the long Maussean tradition whereby anthropologists have tended to focus upon the social form and function of exchange and have ignored the politics invested in specific objects of exchange. For Appadurai, what is political about exchange "is the constant tension between the existing frameworks (of price, bargaining, and so forth) and the tendency of commodities to breach these frameworks. This tension itself has its source in the fact that not all parties share the same *interests* in any specific regime of value, nor are the interests of any two parties in a given exchange identical" (Appadurai 1986:57).

Some contemporary Korean voices, those who invoke the folklore of the "three keys," would instantly recognize the wedding process as a transaction in commodities and statuses with but a thin and tattered veil of "custom" to mask its political intentions. Popular perceptions of upper-class Korean matchmaking are, of course, riddled with this assumption. What might seem to be a tale of lost innocence, the corruption of an older moral order in the face of rampant capitalism, could as easily be attributed to one commentator's romantic idealization of the past and another's cynical assessment of the present.

Ethnologists have conveyed their informants' impressions that before the 1970s, rural weddings were simple and dowries unelaborate (Sorensen 1981:210; Yoon Hyungsook 1989a:35, 1989b). When I asked about marriage goods in Enduring Pine Village, older women commonly mentioned the bride's own clothes and sometimes a storage chest and mirror stand. Even upper-middle-class urbanites insist that the lavish dowries so often derided in the press were unknown before the emergence of a full-blown consumer culture in the 1980s.

Other evidence suggests, however, that dowries have long been considered a burden. There is a fundamental logic to the perceived asymmetry of matrimonial exchanges in a patrilocal system where gifts made by the bride's side are carried away with their daughter while such tangible betrothal gifts as clothing and jewelry are returned to the groom's side with the bride. Proverbs reveal an abiding preoccupation with the cost of marrying off a daughter: "If you marry off just three daughters, then the house pillars will tumble down" *(ttal setman sijipponaemyŏn kidungbburiga ppajinda)*.[34] "When you've married off three daughters, then even a petty thief won't bother with you" *(ttal samhyŏngje sijipponaemyŏn komudodukto andoenda)* (Tieszen 1977:54). Even in the early Chosŏn period, moralists complained of the lavish goods used and exchanged in weddings (Deuchler 1992:245; Yi Kyut'ae 1987:156–157). For nearly a cen-

---

34. This proverb was cited in a Ministry of Social Welfare publication encouraging thrifty weddings.

tury, accounts of rural life have spoken of the perils of indebtedness over weddings, particularly for the bride's family, although the thrust of these complaints seems to be against feasting rather than exchanges of durable goods.[35]

A backward glance from contemporary Korea might suggest that dowries were burdensome in late traditional or early modern Korea because dowries could be deployed as instruments of political manipulation by socially ambitious commoners who sought elite status.[36] However tantalizing this possibility, there is no solid evidence for it. References to dowry goods in late-nineteenth-century accounts and twentieth-century ethnology indicate a great variability in regional customs, with respect both to the magnitude of gifts expected and to the relative obligations of the bride's side and groom's side in matrimonial exchanges. Writing of turn-of-the-century Korean life, Lay mentioned that among the "gentle-folk" in central Korea, in the provinces of Kyŏnggi and Ch'ungch'ŏng, the burden upon the bride's side to provide household goods and clothing was so great that "not unnaturally under the circumstances many daughters are said to be the ruin of a house." He contrasted these practices with marriage in the impoverished northwest, where families were more likely to sell their daughters as *minmyŏnŭri* (Lay 1913:14).

One still hears the generalization that in southwest Korea (the present-day provinces of North and South Chŏlla), the bride's side provides the bulk of the marriage goods, while in southeast Korea (the provinces of North and South Kyŏngsang), the burden is on the groom's side to provide most of the household goods, and the bride might bring only her own clothing and perhaps some bedding. Like all tidy generalizations, this one requires qualification. Ethnologists have identified intraregional variations (MCIBCPP 1977 "Chŏnnam":128, 1977 "Kyŏngnam":154) in addition to the obvious variations imposed by differences in wealth and social standing. In attempting to contrast a "then" and a "now," it makes more sense to shift our attention from unknowable and irrevocably relative quantities to the more readily apprehended nature of the goods them-

---

35. See Brunner (1928:116), Hulbert (1906:369), Knez (1959:70), and Lay (1913:13).

36. This theme occurs in Korean novels, but among social historians, the extent of class mobility in late traditional Korea is hotly debated. The early twentieth century seems to have been a period of great social maneuvering as unprecedented opportunities for wealth and advancement presented themselves (Eckert 1991: Ch. 1, Ch. 2).

selves as markers and communicators, as visible signs of those who made, bestowed, and received them (Douglas and Isherwood 1979:Ch. 3).

ABOUT CEREMONIOUS GOODS

Cloth and clothing, demonstrations of a skilled use of loom and needle, are the most commonly mentioned elements of dowry and other ceremonious exchanges recorded in Korean ethnography (see fig. 10). In the Chŏllas, where brides were expected to bring impressive dowries, "The expenses include[d] many valuable items such as clothes that have been made from material woven at home or bought years ago in anticipation of the wedding" (Pak and Gamble 1975:135, describing the 1950s or earlier). According to an early-twentieth-century account of marriage customs

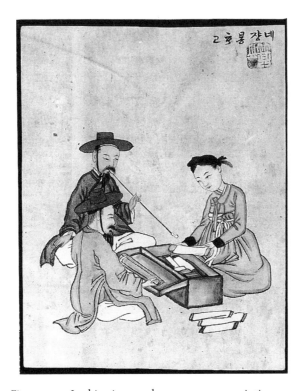

Figure 10.   In this nineteenth-century genre painting by Kisan, a woman fills the bride's gift box with lengths of cloth. Courtesy of the National Anthropological Archive, Smithsonian Institution, NAA MS-7355 (180:10).

among *yangban* in central Korea, the bride's family not only provided the bridegroom's wedding clothes, but "indeed so far does their duty in these matters extend that they must keep the bridegroom in raiment for years afterwards" (Lay 1913:14). In the Kyŏngsang Provinces, where brides were not expected to bring extensive dowry goods, they still carried small gifts of clothing to present to the groom's family on the occasion of their first meeting (Harvey 1979:215). Hand-sewn white cotton Korean socks were often distributed to all of the groom's extended kin (Lee Kwang-Kyu 1974:74).

Fragmentary reminiscences of custom suggest that many dowry goods were simultaneously demonstrations of the bride's skill with a needle. Women who were married more than three decades ago in rural Kyŏnggi Province described for me the custom of "clothes viewing" *(ot kugyŏng)*, when the garments brought by the new bride would be subjected to meticulous scrutiny by the women of her husband's family. According to one elderly seamstress, the quality of stitchery, as much as the quantity of wardrobe, was at issue. *Passage Rites Made Easy* recalls how, in a bygone era, the family of the groom would send his tailoring measurements to the family of the bride. Even before she had set eyes upon her future spouse, the bride would have stitched him a garment, and even before they had seen her, the groom and his family would have had proof of the new wife's skill as a seamstress (Ko 1982:117; MCIBCPP 1971 "Chŏn-buk":68). Younghill Kang recounts the wedding of his junior uncle in a northern village at the turn of the century. Upon arriving at the home of his bride, the groom "was given an entire new set of clothes, even stockings and underwear, all made by the bride's hands. . . . His friends gathered around him, and examined the sewing and congratulated him upon getting such a clever needle-woman for a wife" (Kang 1966:54). According to Miln, this first garment verified that the wife would, for the rest of her life, clothe her husband's family since "All the garments of a Korean family are made by the women of the family. The purchase of a ready-made garment . . . would be considered a disgrace to the family and a deeper disgrace to its women. Korean ladies sew as exquisitely as French nuns, and embroider as deftly as those Japanese men whose profession embroidery is" (Miln 1895:78, 81).

The betrothal gifts sent from the groom to the bride might also initiate a demonstration of needlework. Where the gift box contained several lengths of cloth, the bride would be expected to fashion her subsequent wardrobe before the wedding (Materi 1949:178). In P'yŏngan Province, in the northeast of Korea, the betrothal gifts, including a length of silk, would be sent to the bride on the day before the wedding, and from this silk she would stitch the long Korean skirt that she would wear at her wedding (Han 1949:184).

Beyond any commodity value, then, the bride's dowry goods and transformed betrothal gifts were extensions of her own worth as a wife, as a producer within the domestic economy who, in time of duress, might even support the household through the skill of her needle.[37] Where finely loomed cloth and expert needlework were produced by senior women in the bride's home rather than by the bride herself (Han 1949:184), their products testified to the skill, industry, and refinement of those who had raised the bride. Similarly, the ceremonial meats, sweets, and wine sent to the groom's family *(k'ŭnsang, sangsu)* witnessed the domestic tone of the bride's family, insofar as clean and careful preparations were taken as signs of a harmonious, well-managed household— moral qualities beyond literal "taste."[38]

The ready-made or professionally tailored clothing and the commercially processed, prepackaged gifts of ceremonious food given in contemporary weddings are all devoid of the social and moral nuances with which homemade gifts were imbued. They do evidence the financial ability and generosity of those who send them, and for some elite families, gifts evidence distinction in the choice of a well-known silk shop or a special purveyor of traditional rice cake. Only in the last few years have wedding halls begun to routinely cater the *p'yebaek* meat, severing the last link between ceremonious goods and domestic production, between the thing produced and the bride as a potential producer.

Worldwide, the products of capitalist production seldom carry the rich meanings once inscribed onto handicrafts, and the value of women as producers of handmade ritual goods is similarly effaced in the process of transformation (Schneider and Weiner 1989). The things given as ceremonious goods in Korea today are less signs of a bride's ability as a domestic producer and her family's moral worth and more nearly commodities with recognized market values. They furnish a new household in approximation of middle-class tastes and acknowledge to the groom's family his

37. For accounts of women's resourcefulness with a needle, see Bishop (1970:101–102), Gale (1898:232–233), and Jones (1896:229).

38. See descriptions of ritual food exchange in Chun (1984:51), Ko (1982:122), and MCIBCPP (1978 "Kyŏnggi":75).

potential value as a breadwinner. As wedding gifts, their transformation into pure commodities cannot be absolute. Ceremonious exchanges continue to signify family commitment and support for a socially recognized wedding, and, in Sukcha's world, they also testify to the productivity of unmarried women. The asymmetry of ceremonious goods in the contemporary Korean wedding replicates a motif introduced in Chapter 4: that as brides have ceased to be valued as domestic producers, marriage has come to be constructed as an investment in the worth of a groom.

CONCLUSION

Studies of the urban middle class by Pak Minja (1991) and of the urban poor by Pak Sukcha (1991) suggest that elaborations of dowry and ritual silk, and their attendant anxieties, rise with economic and educational levels. Among the upper middle class, ceremonious exchanges transmit distinction in Bourdieu's sense, "the values, virtues and competences that are the basis of legitimate membership in bourgeois dynasties" (1984:77), but in a more fluid social milieu than he describes for late-twentieth-century France. In Korea, new products and cultural revivals are manipulated to provide new legitimizations through a process rationalized as "traditional marriage custom," a broad-seeming concept that obscures the operation of class definitions and reinforcements.[39] Among the urban poor, where the cost of a simple wedding ceremony may be the most critical issue in becoming married, household goods are purchased gradually over the years of cohabitation, and extended kin do not receive ritual silk (Pak Sukcha 1991).

By contrast, Sukcha and most of the other Righteous Town brides accept the necessity of giving ritual silk as a requirement of a respectable wedding, but the elaboration of these gifts seems far less of an issue than among the upper middle class. When Yongsu's Mother realized she would have to give more ritual silk than she had originally estimated, her impulse was not to provide gifts of distinction so much as to find the most inexpensive means of creditably fulfilling her obligation. Ŏmŏni, following a practice I recorded for three other Righteous Town weddings, streamlined her efforts by sending Sukcha's ritual silk in the form of a large envelope of cash delivered to the groom's mother.[40] Instead of re-

39. I am indebted to Roger Janelli for this insight.
40. Yoon Hyungsook also notes the popularity, among residents of a village in this same region, of giving ritual silk in the form of cash (Yoon 1991:136).

ceiving a new Korean dress as a gift from her son-in-law, she received, in turn, a suitable fraction of the sum she had sent. She generously supplemented this money so that she and each of her daughters had a new Korean dress to wear in the wedding hall, and Kkach'i's husband, as the male most responsible for the wedding proceedings, appeared in a new winter overcoat.

Sending cash is a practical strategy insofar as the recipients of cash gifts may suit their own tastes and needs in wedding clothes, but it flies in the face of the wisdom dispensed by a purveyor of elegant wedding goods who stressed the importance of material things: "The mother-in-law should be able to look at a quilt and say, 'The first daughter-in-law brought that' or look at a folding screen and say, 'the second daughter-in-law brought that.' " The envelope of cash, or a Korean dress produced according to type by a marketplace tailor, cannot mean the same thing as a carefully selected folding screen, a mink coat, or a Korean costume delivered in the wrapper of an elegant silk shop. One is a requisite marker in a ritual process, significant primarily because the mark is made; the other carries additional messages about the bearer and the bearer's perception of the receiver, either by making a grand splash with mink or by evidencing a more refined eye. These concerns seem far removed from Sukcha's world.

If daughters' earnings enable rural and small-town families to approximate patterns of middle-class consumption, these rituals of status affirmation also assume their opposite: the inability of disadvantaged persons to participate in them. If my sister Sukcha and most of the other Righteous Town brides married well because they worked before marriage, family circumstances and meager wages forced Mrs. Sŏ, Mrs. Ch'oe, and many other women to postpone their weddings, and many other married couples to have no weddings at all. A sample focused on "brides" necessarily excludes those who lack the resources to wear for one day a borrowed lace dress and veil. Studies of the working poor in urban and peri-urban settings suggest the frequency of stories like Mrs. Ch'oe's, of women who cohabit with lovers and bear their children, always with the assumption that a wedding ceremony ought to be held. The communal *(haptong)* charity weddings intended to meet their needs are regarded as an embarrassing compromise with necessity (Pak Sukcha 1991:113–114), a cause for snickering in Enduring Pine Village. For all Sukcha's insistence upon a modest and practical wedding, for all the distance between her wedding and the status-conscious elaborations of the upper middle class, Sukcha's full dowry of household goods and ritual silk set her apart from the many

7
Betrothal Gifts
and "Bothersome Custom"

MY SISTER SUKCHA, 1991 WITH VIDEO CLIPS

Even before Sukcha returns from the beauty shop, Ŏmŏni raises the subject
of the gift box delivery, the occasion on which the betrothal gifts prepared
by the groom's family arrive at the home of the bride. Ŏmŏni turns toward
her future son-in-law and speaks in a low, urgent tone. "How would it be if
your friends bring the gift box into our house? Wouldn't that be nice? This
is our custom." Sukcha's intended mutters something noncommittal and
looks acutely uncomfortable. Even apart from the presence of an anthropologist and a videoteur, he has been placed in a difficult position. When the
groom's friends bring in the gift box *(ham)* containing the marriage contract
and betrothal gifts, they bargain and banter with the bride's family in the
hope of extorting from them a large "delivery fee" *(hamgap)*. To this end,
the bearers delay their final surrender of the gift box for as long as possible,
haggling with the bride's family every inch of the way as they shout their demands through the neighborhood alleyways. The money they receive from
the bride's family is usually spent on an evening's expansive and expensive
celebration, and the groom gains face by having won his friends a good time
at his future in-laws' expense. The bride's family thus offers reciprocity for
all the times the groom may have amused himself as a gift box bearer when
his close male friends got married. Sukcha's intended must thus not appear
too eager to accede to Ŏmŏni's request since everyone recognizes that he
will gain symbolic capital at Ŏmŏni's more literal expense. His friends may
already be anticipating a night of revelry, but good manners require that he
demur until Ŏmŏni overwhelms him with the certainty of her intention to
give a large delivery fee and fill the young men with food and drink on the
night before the wedding.

But Sukcha's intended is in a doubly uncomfortable position. By now
he must know Sukcha's mind regarding the gift box delivery, a custom she

considers both wasteful and unnecessary. I have been with the family for only an hour, and already I know that the gift box delivery is a point of contention between Sukcha and Ŏmŏni. I am not surprised that Ŏmŏni chooses to state her case before Sukcha's return. This being so, an otherwise polite hesitation on the part of Sukcha's fiancé might seem as though he were taking sides against his future mother-in-law in a family quarrel. Moreover, if Sukcha has her way, his friends will undoubtedly consider him henpecked.

When Sukcha returns from the beauty shop, she does not mince words. "Young people today can't be bothered with gift box deliveries. Young people today don't like to waste time and money on things like that." Her emphatic remarks are partly for my benefit, and again I marvel at her internalization of government slogans, but Ŏmŏni is nearly in tears. "The gift box delivery is part of the wedding. It's something you do when you get married. How else will the neighborhood know that this house is sending off a bride? If the gift box doesn't come in, then my friends will think that I didn't do well by my daughter when I married her off."

Ŏmŏni will prevail in the end, threatening to boycott the wedding if Sukcha refuses to have the gift box come in. Sukcha will also come to realize that it would be awkward for her husband if her household failed to meet his friends' expectations. There are limits to her independent-mindedness. Six months later, a newly pregnant Sukcha would have this to say about her capitulation:

> I was opposed to receiving the gift box, but when I thought about it, it might be fun. If I didn't do it, I might regret it.
> *What did your husband think?*
> He, well, it was a matter of face for him. His friends all insisted that you can't get married without a gift box delivery. They had to carry it in. At each and every one of their weddings, there had been a gift box delivery.
> *What about Ŏmŏni?*
> You know how that was. When I said I wouldn't receive the gift box, we fought about it. She said that everyone does it. If we don't, it will be so sad. If we don't, it will be so shameful. She said that I had to receive it, and in the end, I went along with it.

On Diana Lee's video of the gift box delivery, Sukcha faces the camera wearing a hot pink Korean dress appropriate for a bride.[1] A beautician has

---

1. Pink Korean dresses are also worn at engagement parties, and some brides wear them for the *p'yebaek,* but this fashion seems to have receded in favor of the

added switches to her short, permanented hair in a glamorous and complicated approximation of a traditional style. Her face is thick with beauty parlor makeup. "I just want it to be over," she tells the camera. "I just want the wedding day to get here." She describes the hours she spent in the beauty parlor in procedures that will all be repeated tomorrow before she appears in the wedding hall. She tells the camera that the gift box will be filled with clothing she has already selected, that she will not be disappointed when the gift box is opened.

The house is full of relatives. Sukcha's best friend, herself recently married, arrives to offer moral support. The groom appears in festive Korean dress. Again he is bashful. He stands awkwardly in front of the camera with Sukcha, who seems to be thoroughly enjoying herself. She relates that these days some bridegrooms have light makeup applied to their faces just before the wedding. "My bridegroom isn't going to do that," she says, full of giggles, while her bridegroom looks as if he would like nothing so much as to sink into the floor and escape the camera's gaze.

The long hours of winter evening pass with no sign of the gift box bearers. Diana and her crew pose hesitant questions about marriage customs. Ŏmŏni and her kinswomen compliment the Americans on their spoken Korean and say the usual things about Korean being the most difficult language in the world.

Sukcha receives a telephone call from the delinquent young men. They are stalling in a beer hall in the neighborhood. Sukcha asks the location, but they will not tell her. She urges them to hurry up. Since there is only one likely drinking spot nearby, Minja, the youngest sister, and the nieces and nephews head out with Diana and her crew. Kkach'i's teenage son strides up to the beer hall door and flings it wide in a manner reminiscent of a saloon showdown in a Hollywood western movie. Diana trains her camera on the groom's friends, who wave and giggle, already feeling no pain.

The video follows the young men in their zig-zagging progress as they carry the gift box through the winter streets. Lighting their path with two

---

revival of a "traditional" green or yellow jacket and red or hot pink skirt. On a video of an upper-middle-class *ham* delivery, the bride wore a distinctive blue and yellow Korean dress. Her mother, who was showing me the video, explained that the dress was cut in a special style worn only by unmarried women. In addition to demonstrating the family's refined knowledge of and respect for Korean customs, the dress was an object of conspicuous consumption insofar as it would be worn only on this occasion, the last night of maidenhood. On the other hand, pink dresses in a standard style, like the one Sukcha wore, can be worn by young matrons for any special occasion.

Figure 11.   In this nineteenth-century genre painting
by Kisan, a gift box bearer is accompanied by two men
with lanterns, all in formal attire. This portrayal is a
long way from the events described for Sukcha's gift
box delivery in the winter of 1991. Courtesy of the
National Anthropological Archive, Smithsonian Institution, NAA MS-7355 (180:11).

red and blue silk lanterns (cf. fig. 11),[2] the bearers sing snatches of Korean
pop music with raucous voices, breaking off to bellow "Gift box for sale! Gift
box for sale!" at any innocent passerby or cruising taxicab. Because it is almost Christmas, they sing a chorus of "Rudolph the Red-nosed Reindeer."
Between the cold and the alcohol, many noses are red.

2. The joined strips of red and blue fabric on the lanterns symbolize the union
of male and female. Wedding lanterns are sold by purveyors of shaman supplies
and other ritual goods (*manmulsa*).

Sukcha's middle-aged male cousin *(sach'on)*, a substitute for her deceased father, stands firm in front of the house holding a sheaf of white envelopes filled with cash, the money he will use to lead in the gift box by spreading envelopes on the ground at wide intervals and urging the bearers to march forward and claim their due. They, of course, will stall and haggle, demanding more envelopes at shorter intervals and trays of drinks and snacks. The cousin is tall and thin and has a weathered face, and again I am reminded of western movie motifs, of a lanky sheriff facing off in a showdown on Main Street.

Even after Sukcha's cousin has set all of his envelopes in the bearers' path, they still demand more money. In the end, they will receive 400,000 *wŏn* (approximately $500 U.S.), 100,000 *wŏn* more than the negotiated fee, and Ŏmŏni will call their behavior "disgusting and tiresome" *(chigyŏpta)*. Ŏmŏni and Sukcha will both recall the negotiations as excruciatingly slow. By custom, the bride must remain inside the house and out of sight until the gift box comes in. Sukcha will later confess to a burning impatience and admit that she had contemplated rushing outside to see what was taking so long. Under no such constraint, Ŏmŏni bustles out to give the bearers a scolding and plead with them to come inside and eat. One of the bearers playfully grabs her two arms and moves her out of the way. Another repeatedly injects his face into the camera frame, leering, grinning, and waving.

Eventually, as everyone always knew it must, the gift box comes in and rests on top of a great steamer of rice cake *(pongch'iddŏk)* under the main roof beam where the house tutelary (Sŏngju) resides.[3] The tray that holds the rice cake and the gift box has to be rearranged to allow space in the small rented room for Ŏmŏni to kneel and exact a full kow-tow from all the bearers as they face each other across the offerings. Ŏmŏni draws out the contents of the gift box: a Korean dress in heavy orange satin, a Western dress, a winter coat, jewelry, including a diamond ring, and a handbag. "There was supposed to be another Korean dress," Ŏmŏni mutters. "They wouldn't have been able to fit it in the suitcase," her practical third daughter reassures her.

The gifts are passed from hand to hand, inspected and admired by the visiting kin. Plates of elaborate dishes from the family restaurant are served up

---

3. The rice cake is probably intended as an offering which reports the forthcoming marriage to Sŏngju, the house tutelary, although none of the accounts that I have read and none of my conversations about the gift box delivery made this association explicit. One woman told me that while other festive rice cake is shared out to the neighborhood and sent home with guests, the rice cake on which the gift box is received *(pongch'iddŏk)* must be consumed within the home so as not to dissipate the good fortune brought in with the gift box.

to the bearers and relations; the food ranges from batter-fried shrimp to plates of "Western salad" smeared with mayonnaise. More liquor is poured. Everyone sings, tapping time against the tables with their chopsticks. Despite the cramped conditions inside Ŏmŏni's two rented rooms, some even manage to dance. Ŏmŏni dances. She will remember this evening with great joy and tell me more than once how even when she was washing the dishes, the young men called her out three times and made her sing. Even now, the evening is not over. The bride's friends, the groom's friends, and the couple themselves go out to celebrate and spend the delivery fee. Because it is so close to Christmas and the season for year-end parties, the popular night club in the main hotel in Righteous Town is packed with revellers, and the party has to seek out another bar. The bride does not return home until after midnight on what is now her wedding day.

<hr />

For Ŏmŏni, the gift box delivery has the sentimental appeal of "custom"; her experience with Sukcha's gift box is a pleasant memory despite the "disgusting and tiresome" behavior of the bearers. For Sukcha, at least initially, it is a bothersome and expensive practice, best dispensed with. Between Ŏmŏni's position and Sukcha's falls a great deal of discussion and argument among Koreans concerning whether receiving a gift box with full ceremony is a matter of merit or of dissipation. The practice is contentious not only in the innate haggling between gift box bearers and representatives of the bride's family, but in Korean society at large, where the gift box fee draws heated commentary—in the media, as a target of reformist campaigns, and in such intimate settings as Ŏmŏni's household. In part, the gift box delivery is faulted because it is a "new custom"; it lacks the authority of tradition and is subsequently implicated in more general critiques of the rampant mammonism *(paegŭmjuŭi)* of contemporary life (e.g., *Yŏng Reidi*, October 1984:154). As in the case of inflated gifts of ritual silk discussed in Chapter 6, we might seek both symbolic precedents and the reasons why producers of popular culture have chosen to reconfigure these same elements in a particular way at a particular historic pass. Simultaneously, we might wonder why Ŏmŏni was so fervid in her defense of a custom that was clearly to her own economic disadvantage. A discussion of the rise and popular perceptions of gift box deliveries will lead us to a more general consideration of debates on the morality of matrimonial practices and how women in particular have been implicated in this critique.

DELIVERING A GIFT BOX

Delivering the gift box has been described as an "improvisational roadside drama in which there is cheerful bantering between the gift-box bearers who determinedly pursue their targeted sum and members of the bride's family, who stand equally steadfast in their resolve to receive the gift box for the bare minimum of cash-filled envelopes" (*Yŏng Reidi*, October 1984:146). The groom is caught at cross-purposes appropriate to his transitional status between bachelor and son-in-law. He has the delicate task of presenting his friends' predetermined fee to the bride's father before the event, of championing his friends' desires without offending his future father-in-law. One poor groom confessed to me that when the bride's father refused to meet the requested figure, the embarrassed young man hid himself and never returned to his waiting friends.

One among the groom's friends, ideally but infrequently a married man whose first child was a son, plays the "horse," bearing the cloth-wrapped box on his shoulders. (Because this is a mute part, a few foreign male scholars have found themselves in this role.) Though the "horse" be a silent beast of burden, not so the horse groom *(mabu)*, selected for his verbal skills, wit, and tenacity; he will lead the banter and bargaining with the men who defend the interests of the bride's family. The groom's side contends that the horse requires "feed" in the form of cash and liquid refreshment, that the horse is weary and will not advance without the incentive of envelopes of money spread under his "hooves."

The young men of the bride's family attempt to lure the groom's side into the house with cash, with promises of the splendid repast that has been prepared for them, and, in desperation, with threat of force. Sometimes women of the bride's family emerge to scold the young men for their procrastination, a tactic that Ŏmŏni attempted without much effect on the night Sukcha's gift box was delivered. When I observed a gift box delivery at an upper-middle-class home in Seoul, one of the bride's friends told me that this particular delivery was not so interesting because the bride's aunts were not bursting out of the house to take the young men to task. She assured me that the transaction at her own wedding had been far more exciting.

The groom's friends have time on their side; by delaying and complaining in good strong voice, they let all the neighbors know that the bride's family is reluctant to meet their fee, and they otherwise embarrass the bride's family by their noisy behavior in the dead of night. Even once inside the house, when the gift box has been ceremoniously received by the bride's father (or mother) and set on a steamer of rice cake under the main house beam, an obstinate bearer may yet withhold the key to the locked chest and claim an additional fee. After Oksuk's wedding, Yongsu's Mother complained that, in the past, "you could just lead the bearers in with a packet of money, but now, if they don't think it's thick enough, they'll go all around the village shouting, 'Gift box for sale, gift box for sale!' " In "My Daughter's Wedding Expenses," Kim Yugyŏng's informant vents her exasperation over the gift box bearers' unreasonable demands:

> Two days before the wedding, the gift box arrived. Thinking of our son-in-law's "face" we prepared a splendid feast for the six gift-box bearers, liquor, and the ritual rice cake *(pongch'iddŏk)* on which the gift box was to be received. But the food grew cold and had to be reheated and grew cold again before the gift-box bearers so much as thought of entering the house. Even when the sum of 150,000 *wŏn* [at the time, $188 U.S.], which we had firmly settled in advance, had all been disbursed in 10,000 *wŏn* notes, the bearers were still ten meters from the house and would not budge. They asked for another 100,000 *wŏn*. "The elders are waiting, let's all go in and eat," we said. "The horse hasn't had enough feed. He has no strength. He can't walk," they said and stalled for thirty minutes more. Only after we had laid out another fifty-thousand *wŏn* did the gift box come in (Kim 1984:164).

Worse is reported in the women's magazine *Yŏng Reidi*, where a young woman tells how the bearers had kept everyone out on a cold night until an hour before dawn. She laments that whenever she hears mention of a gift box delivery, she thinks of "cold and hunger" and regrets that a pretty custom has been so transformed by the materialism of the present day (*Yŏng Reidi*, October 1984:155). Another bride succumbed to the same impulses which had tempted Sukcha and took matters into her own hands. As she reported in *Yŏng Reidi*, she hitched up the skirt of her pink Korean dress, rolled up her sleeves, and ran outside in a fit of anger to accost the young man responsible for the delay. It then became the hapless gift box bearer's task to reconcile the angry bride and the humiliated groom in time for the wedding the next day (*Yŏng Reidi*, October 1984:150). In her popular novel on modern matrimony, *Staggering Afternoon*, Pak Wansŏ describes how, on the morning of her wedding, a young woman's image of her soon-to-be husband is colored by her distasteful memory of the gift box delivery:

> [Uhŭi] remembered receiving the gift box as if it had been some awful dream and even the dress she had worn then was as disgusting to her as goblin's gall.

They had begun bawling, "Gift box for sale! Gift box for sale!" from even beyond the alleyway and brought out the entire neighborhood with their cries. For every step forward, they insisted upon taking two steps back. These drunken rowdies, these brigands who demanded large bills for each small advance, were Minsu's friends. It made her see Minsu in an entirely new light.

But wasn't it a bit late in the day to be reconsidering Minsu? Yesterday, they had even received the marriage contract in the gift box and the wedding would take place in just a few hours.

It couldn't be helped. Tonight sometime she'd have to bring it up. Yes, bring it up, demand an explanation, take him to task, just as she had learned at home from watching her mother browbeat her father. Uhŭi felt her confidence rise. She would be an even better nag than her mother (Pak Wansŏ 1985, vol. 2:33).

While nearly everyone I spoke with complained that it had taken too long for their gift box to come in, I heard nothing to compare with these published accounts. During the most procrastinatory delivery in my own survey, the friends of the groom demanded an extra 50,000 *wŏn* and, being thwarted, carried the gift box back to the groom's village. There his mother gave them 30,000 *wŏn*, told them they should be ashamed of themselves, and sent them back to the bride's house. People had heard, secondhand, of bearers who held the gift box until the wedding day, causing some anxiety since the bride was expected to greet her parents-in-law wearing a Korean dress delivered in the gift box. Most, however, claimed that their gift boxes came in after, at the very most, two and a half hours of excruciating bargaining and that the bearers usually accepted the predetermined fee.

Similarly, while I observed some halfhearted pushing and shoving during one gift box delivery where the bride's family interests were being defended by her young cousins, I never saw blood and heard no firsthand reports of gore comparable to those reported in the popular press (see fig. 12). One man of letters lamented in print that "with persons who are quick tempered and lacking in cultural refinement, there are even instances of violence in which the blood flows" (Cho P'ungyŏn 1983:33). *Yŏng Reidi* reports a groom who championed his future wife's family and "made his appearance on his wedding day with an honorably acquired bandage on his face" (*Yŏng Reidi*, October 1984:146). Another report spoke of a fire ignited by one of the bearers' lanterns during a scuffle between the friends of the groom and the brothers of the bride (*Yŏng Reidi*, October 1984:151).

Passage Rites Made Easy offers advice under the heading, "If you absolutely must send the gift box." The groom's side is encouraged to

Figure 12. Battling for the gift box. Seoul, 1983. Photograph by Homer Williams.

send no more than five bearers to avoid "the mischief that arises from mob psychology," while the bride's side should "try to receive [the gift box] with a joyful heart," noting also that "this requires an understanding frame of mind. The groom's friends who deliver the gift box are young, and may easily go too far with their jests. If you can't take their jokes in good humor, then there can easily be a row, or even a fight" (Ko 1982:104, 106). "People say" that betrothals have been broken off in the wake of violence over delivering the gift box (Cho P'ungyŏn 1983:33; Lee Kwang-Kyu 1983:1274). Again, I note that in all my admittedly limited sample, no one reported firsthand or even secondhand instances of violence, much less broken engagements, but only some predictable grumbling about the ever-inflating fees and the bearers' procrastination.

The establishment of a son-in-law and the bringing in of a bride, the exchange of negotiated gifts between the two families, the very process of matrimony, imply a "their side/our side" dialectic that is most explicitly acknowledged in the drama of the gift box delivery. The bearers might sing of losing sleep for wanting to carry off a maiden from the neighborhood, and the young men of the bride's side threaten, "If you don't give us the gift box, then we won't give you the bride." The delivery of a gift box, as a passage within the larger passage rite of matrimony, seems to have engendered its own folklore, its own ominous potential for ritual dangers of great consequence when things go awry, when procedures signifying transition from one state to another cannot be brought to a satisfactory conclusion (Douglas 1966:96, following van Gennep 1960; Geertz 1973:142–169).

The groom's friends are expected to use the delivery fee to carouse. "They use the money for drinking, of course," one matron scoffed at my innocent question. "Yes, drinking and other things," an American veteran of gift box deliveries scoffed at another manifestation of innocence. In some circles, the custom holds that the money must all be spent in one evening. Gift box bearers told me they used some of the money to cover expenses such as the taxi used to transport the gift box to the bride's neighborhood, and in many of the Righteous Town weddings, leftover delivery money was used to have a final drink with the bridal couple before the honeymoon. In several weddings, the groom's friends bought the couple a housewarming gift and brought it to the first party *(chiptŭri)* in their new home.[4]

Sometimes the tables are turned on the wedding day when friends of the bride "sell" her bouquet to the gift box bearers for the "flower fee" *(kkotkap)*, a small share of the gift box fee (see fig. 13). This is also used for fun and for the purchase of another wedding gift. The popular columnist Yi Kyut'ae opines with tongue in cheek, "it is just possible that the custom has evolved out of the struggle for women's rights" (Yi 1987: 148–149). With prior consent, I witnessed the elaborate transaction over the fee for Pak Yŏnghŭi's flowers from an adjoining table in a bakery. The bearers restated the case they had made at the bride's house, how they had exhausted themselves by carrying the gift box such a great distance, hired a taxi, worn their feet out, how they really were entitled to the lion's share of cash. But in paying the women, they adopted the tactics of the bride's family, gradually and grudgingly doling out a slow succession of white envelopes, some of them empty. The women, for their part,

---

4. *Passage Rites Made Easy* advises against squandering the money on drink and suggests, "If one deducts transportation and such expenses and then with the remaining money selects a wedding present, this is a friendly gesture, in my opinion both meaningful and satisfying" (Ko 1982:105).

Figure 13.   Bargaining over the bride's flowers in a Righteous Town bakery, early 1980s. The woman holds one of the envelopes of cash doled out by the men. The bouquet is on the table. Photograph by Homer Williams.

praised the quality of each leaf and flower in the bouquet and attempted to set a price on each one. The exchange was playful, almost flirtatious, and in looking at my photographs of this same encounter, one bride's sister told me, "Things are supposed to work out for the man and the woman who bargain over the flowers. Just look at those two." However this may be, when I reported the results to Kim Eun-Shil, who had picked up wedding hall gossip concerning the large delivery fee that the men had extracted, she was indignant that the men had apparently lied, denying their windfall, and that the women had therefore settled for a modest flower fee. (I felt guilty at having been called upon to witness the rightness of the transaction.)[5]

Although some brides' families may make provisions for the flower fee when they settle the bearers' price, the practice is new and by no means universal. When I asked about it among a cluster of bride's kin during an

5. If the groom's friends fail to purchase the flowers, then the groom is expected to pay the fee. One of the grooms in my survey, whose family did not send bearers with a gift box because it was the bride's second marriage, told me he had bought the flowers so that his friends would have some money with which to celebrate. The couple joined them for a scenic drive and celebratory drink.

interview in a village near Righteous Town, one of the groom's sisters explained to the older women that this was done in Seoul now, that she had recently heard about it on the radio. In a reverse flow of information, one of my Korean research assistants from Seoul first learned of the remunerative possibilities of selling the bride's bouquet while accompanying me on interviews in Righteous Town. When I last saw her, she reported with great pride that, at a recent wedding, she had successfully extracted a flower fee from the groom's friends and had thereby won for the women's side an evening in a hotel discotheque. Such are the unanticipated advantages of fieldwork.

Everyone knows that the flower fee is an innovation, but some of the brides and grooms I spoke with assumed, from the narrow historical horizons of youth, that the groom's friends had accompanied the gift box and demanded a delivery fee since dynastic times. Members of their parents' generation, however, easily recognize that friends of the groom began to deliver the gift box only in the late 1940s. The advent of this new custom, like so many other changes in social life, is associated with that major watershed of "present" and "past" in historical reminiscences, "around the time of the Korean War" *(yugio sabyŏnttae)*. One commentator goes so far as to link squabbles over the delivery fee to the rising climate of violence in the struggles between left and right from 1945 to the outbreak of open warfare in 1950, an extremely negative dialectical association (Cho P'ungyŏn 1983:33). For critics, this lack of historical depth denies the legitimacy of "tradition" and links delivery fees and flower fees to those aspects of contemporary life considered distasteful, increasingly more distasteful, the rising standards of conspicuous consumption and the irrepressible enthusiasms of youth. Participants in the journal *Yŏng Reidi's* symposium issue on gift box deliveries deplore the "extortionate demands" and general rowdiness of the bearers which, they contend, have destroyed the proper solemnity of the occasion, baring the rampant materialism of the modern age (*Yŏng Reidi*, October 1984:146, 148, 152, 155).

The appearance of a new demand, the "flower fee" for the bride's bouquet, is further confirmation of degenerate customs. "In time gone by, it was of no consequence whether or not the flower fee was given, so why, of all things, should we take up such an inappropriate practice?" (*Yŏng Reidi*, October 1984:147). "This harmful practice whereby the groom's friends extract an extortionate and wasteful fee and even a feast is a rootless custom that has arisen in recent times. Moreover this evil custom is the ill wind that has blown in the evil custom of giving a flower fee" (Yi Kyut'ae 1987:149). Yet in contrast to other "new customs," like the ceremony performed in the commercial wedding hall, the delivery fee is not considered a "Western" innovation. Its roots are authentically Korean. In probing for them, we might better understand both the tenacious appeal of this particular practice and the capacity of producers of popular culture for refashioning older material to suit the contemporary moment.

PRECEDENTS AND ANTECEDENTS

The act of sending a gift box *(ham)* containing the groom's family's betrothal gifts is integral to Korean Confucian marriage procedures. Antique wooden *ham*, made of light paulownia wood and decorated with iron or brass fittings, are standard items on the Seoul antique market. Those who can afford display buy modern reproductions made of exquisitely carpentered wood or lacquered and inlaid with mother-of-pearl. The box becomes a mark of distinction indicating the family's respect for Korean traditions, in contrast to the cheap but practical nylon suitcases most people now use for gift box deliveries. Like all exchanges associated with the old rite of matrimony, the gift box was sent with due ceremony to ensure the most fortunate consequences for the forthcoming marriage. In normative accounts of Korean marriage customs set in a vague folkloric past, the gift box was delivered quietly, in an auspicious hour, on a lucky day, by a family servant or hired porter—ideally, a "lucky person" *(tabokhan saram)* who enjoyed a harmonious marriage and whose first child had been a son or, in addition to these attributes, by someone whose children had all survived and whose house had never caught fire.

At the bride's house, a similarly lucky person, a woman this time, would receive the gift box and bear it off to the bride's room, proclaiming, "Here's a lot of good fortune coming in *[Pok manhi wannae]*." As in many gift box deliveries today, a member of the bride's family would reach into the gift box without looking and draw out one of the two parcels of wrapped silk placed on the top—blue wrapped in red, implying that the bride's first child would be a boy, or a disappointing red wrapped in blue, foretelling the birth of a girl. These accounts also mention that, for his effort, the gift box carrier would receive a treat of wine or food and possibly some travel money.[6] The journalist Cho P'ungyŏn conjures the image of a "lucky servant, embracing a kettle of rice wine, [who] eats as if to burst" (Cho 1983:33). Recalling the minuscule tips once given the

6. See Lee Kwang-Kyu (1974:71, 1984) and MCIBCPP (1977 "Chŏnnam":130, 1977 "Kyŏngnam":145–146, 1978 "Kyŏnggi":72).

bearer, he muses, "When I married [around 1940] our servant bragged that he had received five *wŏn* for delivering the gift box. Five *chŏn* bought a bowl of noodles so five *wŏn* would cover the cost of a hundred bowls of noodles. But these days, [the gift box fee] is more like 70,000 or 80,000 *wŏn* [$95 to $100 U.S.]. This is normal" (Cho 1983:33). By the late 1980s, one would even hear of $1,000 delivery fees among the upper middle class, and Ŏmŏni, of more modest means, would give half this in 1991.

Observing village life in South Kyŏngsang Province nearly forty years ago, Knez reported what may have been the harbinger of the contemporary imperative to feast and satisfy the groom's friends: The gift box "is carried by a servant, or possibly a hired pack board (A-frame) carrier, who is accompanied by one, usually more, representatives of the family of the bridegroom. The family of the bride is expected to entertain the group exceptionally well and is therefore evaluated accordingly by the family of the bridegroom as to wealth and cultural refinement" (Knez 1959:70).

Although critics of the contemporary practice tend to romanticize the good old days and the absence of sordid bantering over cash, Korean folklorists' gleanings suggest a sense of playful competition even in that bygone era of decorous gift box delivery. In South Kyŏngsang Province, it was noted that since the bearer received some money, he could "be a pest and act in a teasing manner" (MCIBCPP 1977 "Kyŏngnam":147). Writing of Seoul customs in the late 1950s, Chai relates how "The carrier of the wedding chest usually has his face painted black to play the role of a clown and to elicit laughter from the people, thus making the confrontation of the families a merry occasion" (Chai 1962:94). In rural Kyŏnggi Province, the bearer would obstinately fold his arms so that the box could not be lowered from his shoulders. It would be the task of a servant girl of the bride's house to persuade him to loosen his arms, sometimes by smearing his face with soot as an antidote to stoicism (MCIBCPP 1978 "Kyŏnggi":73).[7] The smearing of the bearer's face with soot seems to have been widely practiced as part of the playful antagonism surrounding a gift box delivery. In another Kyŏnggi community in the late 1940s, Osgood observed, "One amusing feature of the presentation occurs in the traditional play of a young boy of the bride's family who waits surreptitiously to rub charcoal on the face of the bridegroom's relative when he delivers the

---

7. The soot is a purifying agent used in several ritual contexts including the initial segment of a shaman's *kut* (Kendall 1985a). Rutt observed an uproarious wedding wherein the groom was greeted with a smearing of soot on his arrival at the bride's house (Rutt 1964:156–157).

lacquer box" (Osgood 1951:107). Dredge witnessed more recent instances of soot smearing in the 1970s in a proper *yangban* community farther south (cited in Dix 1987:105).

Bargaining and banter often fuel Korean passage rites where changes in status are marked by the spatial transmission of persons or objects. Instances drawn from a full lexicon of Korean passage rites more nearly replicate the haggling which takes place in gift box deliveries today. In the Korean funeral, as recorded by ethnologists, bier carriers would routinely stop in their tracks and demand wine or cash before continuing while the mourners pretended a reluctance to pay, a reluctance to usher the dead from their midst (Janelli and Janelli 1982:70). According to Dredge, "bearers take the opportunity of the funeral to extort extra rewards for their efforts at a time when the bereaved can least afford to deny them. Each bridge or stream along the route to the grave is an opportunity to balk and demand cigarettes or money or wine" (Dredge 1987:88). Similarly, the bearers of the bridal sedan chair might stall for cash and wine or threaten to shake the chair and nauseate the bride (Kang 1966:57).[8] On Chin Island, it is the family of the groom who must pay those who bear the nuptial pallet and quilt to the groom's home. "The bed carriers demand the price of the bed from the groom's family, arguing that they had a hard time carrying the heavy beds so great a distance" (Chun 1984:53).

Those who once carried the funeral biers and bridal sedan chairs of the *yangban* elite, like those who once delivered the gift box, were slaves or tenants who gave customary service as part of their obligation to the landlord. In a community comprised of *yangban* and tenants who had once been their slaves, Kim T'aek-kyu describes how the stalling bier bearers would not only demand food and drink but also conspicuous marks of respect such as a bow from the dead man's son (Kim 1964:66). Insofar as the sponsoring family had no choice but to acquiesce to the menials' demands, Korean passage rites could be interpreted as providing a rare ludic opportunity for ritualized redress (cf. Gluckman 1954).[9]

8. Although I have thus far found only one printed reference to the misbehavior of the sedan chair bearers, I had a rare opportunity to observe these antics at a rural wedding held in the early 1970s. Unfortunately, I do not know, in any instance, which side the bearers represented and which side paid their fee.

9. Ritualized expressions of status antagonism are found in other contexts as well. Griffin Dix (1987:117) describes the complex of rituals and practices marking the transition to the New Year in a Korean village as a time when "those of low status, females, and the young have unusual liberty and power." Korean folk theater invariably includes a comic performance in which the *yangban* are bested by their servants in a battle of wits (Lee Du-hyun 1969).

One might similarly interpret the behavior of the servant who refused to let down his arms and release the gift box or the servant who was a "pest" about his travel money. Yet it would be a mistake to assume that bantering during passage rites was simply "about" ritualized rebellion. After the liberation, when former tenants issued their ultimate protest by refusing to provide customary service, voluntary coffin-carrying associations, formed among status equals, perpetuated the stalling and demands as an essential element of the ritual (Dredge 1987). The theme of class antagonism need not be causal so much as useful and appropriate to the ritual statement being made. Class antagonism, to whatever degree it might have once been found in all of these rituals, underscored the polarities of passage implicit in the comedy of extortion. One stalls, one bargains, and one pays because passages are supposed to be difficult, and bargaining marks the dearness of ritual goods, daughters, and dead kin.

This theme appears again in the *chinogi kut,* the shaman ritual that eases souls out of hell and into paradise. A long cloth "bridge" symbolizes the road to paradise, but it also leads away from the household and the world of the living. The soul, in the person of the shaman, tears through the cloth bridge but stops in its tracks, voices its unwillingness to proceed, returns to the house to weep over assorted kin and friends, resumes the journey, and halts again, inevitably coaxed through the entire length of cloth with fresh allotments of "travel money" *(nobi).* As in the antics of the bier carriers, the passage evokes ambivalence at its own progress. One longs for the dead; one must distance the dead (Kendall 1985a:Ch. 7, 1985c). In the *chinogi kut,* the agent of passage is the shaman who, like the gift box bearers, is always susceptible to charges of exploitation and greed, and like the gift box bearers, she often sets her fee in advance (a detail everyone necessarily pretends away for drama's sake). Both shamans and gift box bearers might try to squeeze extra pay from their patrons, but shamans have more incentive to honor the set fee, insofar as they are looking for return business and wider networks of clients. The young men who carry the gift box suffer no such constraints, and, as we have seen repeatedly, they are not above trying to extort more cash.

In Korean passage rites, then, the transition of persons, objects, or souls seems often to be marked by an idiomatic show of extortionate demands and obstinate resistance and realized in a slow, sometimes exasperating, often humorous bargaining and bantering game. In each case, those who pay assume a contradictory role. By meeting the bearers' demands, they move the action along, promoting processes which are ritually desirable—the dead must be distanced and daughters married off—but which also engender a sense of loss. A slow, contentious passage is perhaps an appropriate metaphor and dramatic realization of the emotional ambivalence associated with these transformations.

Servants, who do not share the interests of their masters, and shamans, who are free to utter what the spirits will, are ideal interlocutors for these encounters, but why the friends of the groom? Has an idiom of class conflict been transformed into one of generational conflict to become, in the final selling of the flowers, a battle of the sexes?

Older accounts reveal other instances wherein the groom's friends used him to extort concessions from the bride's family. Cho P'ungyŏn, reminiscing over his own wedding in 1940s Seoul, recalls that the friends of the groom might "take him by force to a restaurant and, with the groom as security, eat their fill. Without the groom there is no wedding night, so it was customary for the bride's family to ask the cost and extricate the groom. This was a transformation of the old custom of groom hazing *(sillang tarugi)* [wherein young men, usually of the bride's side, would hang the groom from a beam and beat him until he agreed to ransom himself with food and drink]" (Cho 1983:33). However innovative this custom seemed to Cho's friends, the business of extorting a feast from the bride's parents was not unknown, even at the turn of the century. Attending a wedding sometime before 1891, Ross wrote of a bridegroom whose fellow scholars "now suddenly dash on him in a body, and carry him off in spite of all striving and remonstrance on his part. They hold him a prisoner till his father-in-law redeems him with a handsome bribe, on which they hand him over, and depart to make merry with their plunder" (Ross 1891:314).

The groom's discomfort recalls other forms of hazing which young Korean men traditionally endured in the process of becoming husbands and affines. Beatings and literary jousts are most often cited. As with the gift box delivery, folklore injects an element of ritual danger into these proceedings: "It is said that long ago grooms were beaten so vigorously that some of them died." The set-upon groom was either expected to ransom himself with a treat to the young men of the bride's family, or the bride's senior kin would rescue him.[10] In sum, past practices suggest that youths have long felt a sense of entitlement to wedding spoils, either as close associates of the groom or as kinsmen of the bride who is being

10. See Chung (1975:261), Han (1949:62, 188), Han (1972:104), Lay (1913:13–14), Lee Kwang-Kyu (1974:74), MCIBCPP (1978 "Kyŏnggi":77, 1977 "Chŏnnam":130, 1977 "Kyŏngnam":150), and Rutt (1964:158–159).

relinquished to another kin group. They gained this end by discomfiting the groom and sometimes by requiring the bride's family to succor their new son-in-law, a dynamic which foreshadows contemporary gift box deliveries.

Older customs provide precedents for the symbolic appropriateness of haggling, the impetuous participation of youths, and the bride's family's attentiveness to a son-in-law's interests. This trip down memory lane does not yet explain why these elements should have come together in the late twentieth century in the particular configuration of the gift box delivery. Why should the bargaining over the gift box, of all possible Korean marriage exchanges, become the focus of a play of extortion? Why should the bride's family be required to pay the *groom's* friends with inflationary generosity? Why, when the *bride's* friends demand their share of the action, is the flower fee often calculated as an addition to the sum that the *bride's* family provides, rather than simply extracted from the groom's friends' delivery fee?

ASYMMETRICAL ACKNOWLEDGEMENTS

Of all the exchanges associated with contemporary Korean matrimony, only the major gift from the groom's family is bargained over and commands a "delivery fee." The more expensive dowry and ritual silk sent by the bride's family arrives without ritual comment. One could argue that the sending of betrothal gifts is the only rite which still retains its original form as a transfer of ceremonious goods from house to house, while gifts sent by the bride's side have never been so clearly associated with specific rites. The gift box was always sent in advance of the groom, while dowry goods and ritual silk once accompanied the bride on her wedding journey. The symbolic import of their transmission would have been overshadowed by the very literal incorporation of the bride into her husband's home. But this is "just so" logic. Why was "sending silk" retained and elaborated rather than, say, "setting the day," the transfer of a ceremonious document from the bride's side to the groom's side? Why do Seoulites not follow the custom of Chin Island and bargain over the delivery fee for dowry goods? Why do grooms not bargain their way into the bride's house across barriers of ribbons and chains as in some local variants of Chinese weddings?

In Seoul and its environs, gifts from the bride's side are assumed while gifts from the groom's side are privileged. This was not always the case. Writing at the turn of the century, Lay noted that when the wedding gifts arrived in a lacquer box, "if the offering be of meager description, it is sometimes slightingly rejected" (Lay 1913:15). In contemporary practice, the bride's parents, by their generosity and hospitality, demonstrate not only their appreciation of the marriage goods sent by the groom's family, but also their gratitude for the groom himself. In an older Korea, the bride's family's generosity carried a different meaning. Both the ritual hazing of the groom by the bride's kin and ceremonial pranks requiring his "rescue" by his new in-laws affirmed affinal ties in a society where, in centuries past, grooms had been initiated into uxorilocal residence, and many grooms might yet have anticipated months or even years of residence under the affinal roof (Deuchler 1977, 1992; Lee Kwang-Kyu 1974, 1977).

That Korean weddings have traditionally acknowledged the groom's incorporation into the bride's family (in addition to her incorporation into his) provides one more contrast with the marriage customs of a similarly patrilocal China. When, in the not-so-distant past, weddings were held in the bride's family courtyard, a variety of ritual acts marked the groom's passage from his home to hers: a pelting with cinders, rice grains, or red beans; a smearing with charcoal; the firing of a pop gun; a final stride over burning straw—acts intended to purify the groom of baleful influences carried from outside and to bring auspicious forces into the house.[11] These meanings have shifted in contemporary practice; uxorilocal traditions having slipped from cultural memory even as the wedding ceremony has been displaced from the bride's family home to neutral public space. Like unequal matrimonial exchanges, paying the gift box bearers now implies a high regard for the groom at the expense—both literal and figurative—of the bride and her family.

The gift box holds two portents for the bride's future. The first is symbolic, the piece of silk that will reveal, by its color, the gender of her firstborn child. The second is economic; the gifts of cloth, clothing, and jewelry the groom's family bestows upon the bride index the material condition of the family into which she will wed.[12] Gifts of jewelry, the

11. See Chai (1962:94), Han Sang-bok (1972:104), Lay (1913:7), Lee Kwang-Kyu (1974:74, 1983:1275), MCIBCPP (1978 "Kyŏnggi":73), and Rutt and Kim (1974:156–157).

12. Basic notions of betrothal gifts seem to have changed little from the past, although the content of the gift box satisfies contemporary tastes. While there was considerable variation in the number of betrothal gifts given in the past, cloth, clothing, and jewelry (rings and hairpins) seem to have been common elements,

most expensive gifts given by the groom's side, function as "treasure," static prestige goods which will not generate more wealth but can be used as insurance against a family emergency, like the gold jewelry that bedecks Chinese brides (Watson 1984) or the elaborate embroidered linens in Sicilian dowries (Schneider 1980). I interviewed older women in Enduring Pine Village who had surrendered their wedding rings and hairpins[13] to feed their families during the Korean War, and I know of one young wife who pawned her wedding jewelry to settle a husband's debt. The battered wife who had been mendaciously wed to a drug addict was finally motivated to seek divorce when her husband tore her wedding ring from her finger and made off with it to feed his habit. She now felt that she had nothing left to lose.

In the genre of tales of matrimonial deceit, of families who appear at the first meeting in borrowed furs and jewels and driving borrowed automobiles, I heard tell of ritual silks borrowed and then reclaimed after the wedding—a possibility which shocked the teller's Korean listeners as much as the anthropologist.[14] The "face" of several parties is at stake in the contents of the gift box: the groom's family for their ability to provide, the bride as a measure of her being esteemed, and the bride's parents as an indication of the match they have made for their daughter. As we saw when Sukcha's gift box was delivered, all of the contents are lifted out and carefully examined by all of the bride's assembled kin. One bride's father, chuckling, told me to be sure to photograph his family's examination of the betrothal gifts. Novelist Pak Wansŏ describes the humiliation of a bride whose gift box did not meet her family's expectations:

> It wasn't enough that they had covered [the bearers'] every step with cash as if they were receiving some great treasure and coaxing it in with all the requisite coyness. With all the family ready to swoon away in anticipation, they saw what the gift box contained. . . . Uhŭi gnashed her teeth when she thought of the insult she had received last night.

---

as they are today (Bergman 1938:51–52; Han 1949:184; Lay 1913; MCIBCPP 1977 "Chŏnnam":130, 1977 "Kyŏngnam":144–145; Moose 1911:164–165).

13. When all married women bound their hair in a chignon at the nape of the neck, a heavy metal hairpin was a standard item of adornment, sometimes presented in silver or gold as bridewealth.

14. Writing of Korean life in the 1930s, Bergman (1938:51–52) made a similar observation: "If the bridegroom's parents are poor, it may happen that a number of these things [the betrothal gifts] are borrowed by them, and the unhappy bride has to return them when she has moved to her new home."

Was it Chohŭi who had managed to speak first or had it been their maternal aunt? The ritual silk (ch'aedan) that came out of the gift box was not pure silk but only cheap synthetic.

In a twinkling of an eye, there were whispers here and whispers there, "It may be fake, it may be. Could the ritual silk be fake?"

As for the family, they each took their turn at fingering the synthetic while the country relatives, in each and every corner, pursed their lips and echoed, "They say it's fake. Could the ritual silk be fake?" (Pak Wansŏ 1985, vol. 2:34).

As an indication of the bride's future material well-being, the contents of the gift box are necessarily linked to the prospects of the man she is marrying. Paying and feasting the gift box bearers is most explicitly something one does on the groom's behalf. Kim Yugyŏng's informant explained, "Thinking of our son-in-law's 'face' we prepared a splendid feast" (Kim 1984:164). Similar concerns prompted Sukcha to yield her erstwhile principles and participate in a gift box delivery. Another bride complained in the pages of Yŏng Reidi that insofar as hers was a love marriage, she had expected that her family could dispense with the expense and bother of a gift box delivery. The groom, however, "was the second to marry among his group of ten classmates and, being more-or-less their spokesperson, he thought it would be dishonorable to dispense with . . . [the gift box delivery]. He was most apprehensive of trouble that might arise later" (Yŏng Reidi, October 1984:151). I heard of cases where, fearing the complaints of neighbors in high-rise apartment buildings, some urban families provided the groom's friends with a generous fee and a restaurant party while dispensing with the theatrics of the delivery. In a neighborhood where a recent gift box delivery had alerted a thief that jewelry and fine new clothing had entered the house, the next family to marry off a daughter reassured the groom that a healthy delivery fee would be given but urged him to have his friends bring the gift box in quietly, without argument, stalling, or procrastination.

Such adjustments confound my assertion that haggling effects the ritual work of transformation, that haggling is, in some sense, emotionally satisfying and therefore important to the process of a wedding. While the dynamics of a gift box delivery may indeed fall within the logic of Korean ritual practice, as I have suggested, these abbreviated contemporary examples suggest that the symbolic satisfactions of performance are now seen by some participants as being far less critical than the bare necessity of feting the groom's friends to honor the groom.

AS A "NOISY AND BOTHERSOME NEW CUSTOM"

Some years back, the magazine *Yŏng Reidi* devoted a special issue to the gift box delivery, which it characterized as a "noisy and bothersome new custom," denouncing both the greed and the rowdy behavior of the young men who make the delivery (*Yŏng Reidi*, October 1984:145–156):

> "The day the gift box comes in" ought to leave a happy memory with both the bride's side and the groom's side. Instead, it has become an occasion for a frantic struggle in which one side inevitably loses. The romantic image of bearers lighting the way to the bride's house with red and blue lanterns is nowhere to be seen. Rather, a new custom has come into being with the gift box and the gift-box fee as its ulterior motive. We have attempted to illuminate this squabble over the gift box that inevitably gets out of hand at the time of a wedding (*Yŏng Reidi*, October 1984:145).

Defenders see in these same procedures a "particularly Korean sense of humor": the bride's family serves up a feast in the hope of drawing the bearers into the house while the bearers stall, say their feet hurt, say they haven't been given enough travel money, and carry on in this vein. "In our country," contends one veteran of many gift box deliveries, "most insults are signs of affection." The obstreperous friends are merely showing their affection for the soon-to-be married groom (*Yŏng Reidi*, October 1984:153). Others argue that it is a compliment to the groom to "sell" his gift box dear, a wish for good luck and a firstborn son, or a magical means of preventing bickering after the wedding (*Yŏng Reidi*, October 1984:147). The Family Ritual Code (*kajŏng ŭirye chunch'ik*), in effect until the late 1980s, expressly forbade the practice of sending gift box bearers (*hamjaebi*), "thus prohibiting the harmful practice whereby friends of the groom act surly and extort money in the bride's neighborhood" (Kim et al. 1983:342–343; Pogŏnsahoebu n.d.:15–16, 41). *The Great Compendium of Family Ritual (Kajŏng ŭirye taebaekkwa)* illustrates this principle with a brawny cartoon personification of "The Family Ritual Code" resolutely barring three mischievous bearers from the path to the bride's house (Kim et al. 1983:343) (fig. 14). Even so, I suspect that most Righteous Town families remained innocent of the prohibition.[15]

15. Those prohibitions affecting the conduct of wedding ceremonies, rather than related activities, were probably the most effectively enforced since the wedding halls themselves were held accountable and made it their business to prominently display relevant sections of the Family Ritual Code (as described in Chapters 2 and 3).

Figure 14.   The Family Ritual Code obstructs the gift box
bearers' path to the bride's house (Kim et al. 1983).

In 1987, the practice of bargaining over the gift box was a target of
the Korean Mothers' Club's "Moderate Wedding and Dowry Movement"
(Hollye honsu chŏlche undong) and the "Let's Have Right and Proper
Weddings!" *(Parŭn kyŏrhonŭl hapsida!)* campaign of the Seoul YWCA.
Such public-spirited and highly placed concern over the gift box delivery,
and more generally over "right and proper weddings" (as discussed in
Chapter 3), reminds us that, in Korea, issues of ritual and custom are also
moral issues and that, as such, they become matters of social policy. Even
so, the author of a contemporary government-sponsored survey of urban
wedding expenses was chagrined to report that "insofar as most respondents said that they gave a fee to the gift-box bearers we have still not been
able to shake the specter of waste embodied in this enduring practice"
(Chŏch'uk Ch'ujin Chungang Wiwŏn Hoe 1985:44). Fully 69.7 percent of
the respondents indicated they had paid the groom's friends for delivering
the gift box (Chŏch'uk Ch'ujin Chungang Wiwŏn Hoe:25). My own far
smaller and consequently far more volatile sample of eighteen weddings
for 1985 yielded a reassuringly similar figure of two-thirds (66 percent).[16]

16. My sample of ten weddings for the summer of 1983 was far lower; only
four brides' families received the gift box. Since the hot, wet summer is not a
prime marrying season, my summer sample was skewed by a large number of
marriages after cohabitation and remarriages. If we take the 1983 and 1985 sam-
ples together for a total of twenty-eight weddings, slightly more than half of all
the Righteous Town brides had a gift box delivered.

Like wearing fresh new "ritual silk" in the wedding hall, receiving a gift box marks a proper wedding. Recall the logic of Ŏmŏni's stated opposition: "How else will the neighborhood know that this house is sending off a bride? If the gift box doesn't come in, then my friends will think that I didn't do well by my daughter when I married her off."

A gift box is most likely to be delivered in an arranged marriage where delicate negotiations necessarily imply considerations of face. No gift box was sent in four of the matchmade weddings in my survey, but these marriages were, in other ways, exceptional. Two were remarriages; the brides had already been sent off once, and a noisy delivery would only have drawn attention to their unfortunate histories. In the third, an impoverished bride was brought from a great distance to marry a mysterious groom, the son of a prosperous rural family. When Kim Eun-Shil and I arrived for our interview, we were told that the bride we had seen in the wedding hall had "gone home." We were discouraged from interviewing or even meeting the groom, who hid in his room and turned out the light while his mother gave us an otherwise cooperative interview with wonderful details of her own wedding, including a gift box delivery. We suspected the groom was either handicapped or retarded (and the bride appropriately disadvantaged). Eun-Shil remembered that the groom had turned away to avoid speaking with us in the wedding hall. The fourth bride had been reluctant to marry an older bridegroom and to move in with his mother. She felt the matchmaker had applied undue pressure to achieve the match. This was the only classically miserable bride of all those whom I met in wedding halls. Her father was dead, and she and her mother were supported by a married brother. I suspect that these circumstances both forced her hand and deprived her of optional festivities. Moreover, the groom was more than a decade older than the bride, old to be marrying and perhaps less invested in the demands of an exuberant peer culture.

If matchmade weddings are more likely to include gift box deliveries, cohabiting couples who must scrape together the funds for meager weddings do not bother with them.[17] The bride's family may be very poor, she may be estranged from them, or, as in the case of Mrs. Sŏ, they may not exist at all. Symbolically, as in a remarriage, the cohabiting bride is not leaving her own home. One exception to this principle was Mrs. Yun, the pretty tearoom cashier. Once reconciled to her wayward daughter, the

17. These expectations are also borne out in Pak Sukcha's (1991) study of the urban poor.

mother had insisted that the bride, already the mother of a precocious child, spend the night before her wedding in the natal home and that a gift box be delivered. "My mother is so old-fashioned," said Mrs. Yun. Apart from the cohabiting couples, there were three other love marriages where the groom's side claimed that, at their insistence, there had been no dramatic gift box delivery, although appropriate betrothal gifts had been sent without fanfare. Those who did not send gift box bearers called the procedure "complicated" *(pokchaphada)* or "bothersome" *(kwi-ch'ant'a)*, but there were also extenuating circumstances. One groom was a student in a military academy and could get leave only for the day of the wedding. His father was a village chief and may have had his own incentives for avoiding an officially unattractive practice. One bride's family was extremely poor. In only one marriage could I find no obvious reason for dispensing with a gift box delivery other than the family's insistence that it was a bothersome practice.

People do talk when no gift box is delivered. When two daughters of the Sŏng family in Enduring Pine Village were married after their mother's death, an overbearing sister-in-law refused to receive gift boxes on their behalf, saying that the custom was burdensome and unnecessary. This, along with other tyrannies imposed by the sister-in-law, were grist for the village gossip mill.[18] In 1985, as the wedding of their sister-in-law's own daughter approached, the married daughters were heard to mutter, "We'll just see if a gift box comes in for her child. We'll just see what she does for her own daughter."

WOMAN THE CONSUMER?

The image of Ŏmŏni, willing to spend her hard-earned savings out of concern for the opinions of others, would seem to replicate a stereotype put forth by critics of matrimonial extravagance. Women who are active in campaigns to reform marriage practices routinely complained that mothers accelerate inflated spending out of concern for face—not only with respect to their new in-laws, but from a desire to strut in elegant

---

18. The relationship between a husband's sister *(sinu)* and a brother's wife *(ork'e)* is often stressful. The sister is in a position to torment and criticize the newcomer, while as the sister-in-law gains stature in the family, she may advance the interests of her own children over those of her husband's unmarried siblings. Women like Hangil's Mother, whose marriages were arranged after their mothers' deaths, complain bitterly that the sister-in-law, in her desire to see them wed, made undesirable matches and doomed them to lives of misery.

ritual silk and show their friends and relations how well they have done by a child's marriage. This is the ready and pervasive image of woman the consumer. When I discussed the issue of dowry inflation with the staff of a well-appointed shop specializing in dowry goods, the proprietor described at great length how he assists his customers in making rational expenditures, prioritizing purchases against an intended sum. He then added that sometimes greedy daughters urge their mothers to spend beyond their means. He was gently but firmly interrupted by his female assistant, who said, "In my experience, it isn't the daughters anymore. These days, it's the mothers who want to spend more and the daughters who tell them to spend less," a replication of the dynamic between Sukcha and Ŏmŏni in their argument over the gift box delivery.

The most frequently portrayed antagonists, however, are not mothers and daughters but rather husbands and wives. I saw this in the weeks before Kkach'i's wedding when her father grumbled drunkenly at the cost of marrying off a daughter and at the wife, Ŏmŏni, who had only produced daughters. (To my eyes, his protestations but thinly masked his sorrow at marrying off a favorite child.) I have heard of husbands' complaints in numerous other intimate accounts of weddings, while the husband's consternation over the wife's supposed profligate spending is a staple of literary reconstructions of weddings.[19] In the novel *Staggering Afternoon*, the wife is a grotesque caricature who indulges in an orgy of spending well beyond her husband's modest means. In the essay "My Daughter's Wedding Expenses," the well-intentioned wife is caught between her husband's objections and the matchmaker's incessant demands.

However pervasive, the stereotype of mothers as irresponsible consumers is not totally convincing and ultimately obscures the work of women in weddings. When ritual consumption becomes an object of criticism, the abuser is always some other mother. When I discussed the rising cost of dowries with Kkach'i, she saw "women's influence" (*ch'imabaram*, literally "skirt impulses") as the cause, but restricted her criticism to an imagined upper middle class in the capital city. She would never think of her own mother in this light. Ŏmŏni herself would probably be incredulous at any overarching model equating her desire for a gift box delivery with

19. These minidramas counter others in which it is the husband who would honor social relations by spending freely in entertaining his friends and the frugal wife who withholds his pocket money. But here again men hold the moral high ground insofar as they are seen as valuing human relations over economic self-interest.

portrayals of upper-class extravagance as seen on Korean television. She would hasten to affirm that Sukcha had a modest wedding. And let us not forget Ŏmŏni's joyful singing on the night the gift box arrived, her satisfaction at having finally received Sukcha's betrothal gifts, her sense of relief at having accomplished something. The event had meaning for her, and she accomplished more than mere display in satisfying the expectations of son-in-law, affines, daughter, and kin.

The image of woman the consumer is shallow insofar as it ignores the complex web of relationships and concerns within which middle-class Korean women purchase and allocate goods and orchestrate ceremonies.[20] Hanna Papanek's notion of "family status production work" offers a useful summation of how allegedly "leisured" women invest considerable time, energy, and intellect in activities designed to maintain and advance a family's status, activities so time-consuming and so critical to upwardly mobile families that they may legitimately be called "work." What Papanek calls "the politics of status maintenance" includes the formal and informal gift exchanges between families which accompany ceremonies and the recognition that "Women often work hard at making marriage arrangements for children carefully groomed to meet status-appropriate offers" (Papanek 1979:776). In Korea, while the results of these efforts may be valued and their enactment often viewed as a social, if not a moral, necessity, the work of matchmaking and effecting ceremonious exchanges is vested with an aura of profound ambivalence. This ambivalence emerges from the very core of Korean gender ideology.

At its most extreme, Korean gender typing nearly inverts the Victorian ideal of the lady on the pedestal whose purity of character is preserved in isolation from mundane matters of livelihood. Pak Chi-wŏn's eighteenth-century *Tale of Yangban (Yangbanjŏn)* presents the comic stereotype of a shrewishly pragmatic wife in counterpoint to a principled but improvident *yangban* husband (Peter Lee 1981:222–225), a caricature of the wife's role as manager of household affairs and the Confucian gentleman's high-minded preoccupation with propriety. In the much transformed world of the new middle-class Korean family, housewives are intensely involved

---

20. See Cho Hyoung (1975), Kim Myung-hye (1992), and Moon (1990).

in family economic planning, dealings in real estate, and all manner of investment (Cho Uhn and Koo 1983; Kim Myung-hye 1992), undertakings more likely to compromise the dignity of a middle-class Korean man (Moon 1990). Anthropologist Moon Okpyo invokes traditional precedent for her observation that

> In some cases, especially in the families of government officials or scholar[s] . . , the ideology seems to direct the division of labor within the household in such a way that the husbands care for more noble business while the wives are supposed to look after the more mundane business of "earning money." This of course does not necessarily mean that men are less interested in raising the family's economic standing, but simply reflects the idea . . . that it is unseemly for respectable gentlemen to be engaged in such business (Moon 1990:36).

Similarly, female matchmakers and female shamans excel in domains of activity which demand an excruciating risk of face *(ch'emyŏn)* in the necessity of saying disagreeable things and ever having one's motives questioned.

Korean women make matches, make marriages, make money, make rituals for the spirits; and all of these activities fall under the shadow of disapprobation: money lending and real estate dealings are sordid and avaricious, religious activities are superstitious and sometimes disreputable, celebrations and ceremonious exchanges have the potential to become an unwholesome extravagance, a source of intrafamilial strife, and a target of reformist campaigns. As predictable as a husband's complaints about wedding expenses is a husband's stated opposition to shaman rituals; in both instances, his words are almost a ritualistic necessity, but seldom effective (Kendall 1985a). Things happen as they are supposed to happen, but with an institutionalized chorus of argument against extremes, a chorus that in effect validates the generosity of a mother's intentions while preserving the father's purity of purpose. Proper weddings benefit families while, insofar as women's activities make weddings proper, excesses can be safely attributed to the assumed character flaws of women. The burdens of matrimony are thus not seen as a women's issue so much as a problem caused by women. Even so, Korean feminist voices, including members of the Alternative Culture Group *(Ttohanaŭi Munhwa)* whose writings are cited throughout this volume, have begun to challenge the structural and economic underpinnings of an ideology which regards the bride as both a vulnerable newcomer in her husband's family and an unproductive consumer.

CONCLUSION

Among other things, this examination of the gift box delivery as an un-abashedly invented tradition reminds us that our studies of Korean ritual in the late twentieth century are situated in the sort of place where forces set in motion by ritual events entitle a group of young women to an evening in a discotheque. Symbolic elements, the shreds and patches of old "custom," are reconfigured to fit a new moment in time. Paying a gift box fee for the sake of the groom's "face" and in gratitude to his family evoke, once again, themes that thread through this work. Proper families have proper weddings, and the ritual exchanges required of a proper wedding celebrate the groom's prospects at a symbolic and material cost to the bride and her family. The moralistic critique of gift box deliveries, with resonances in Sukcha's opposition to the practice and Ŏmŏni's enthusiasm for it, caused us to consider how women's pivotal role in the wedding process is subject to an ambivalent regard; women do the things which risk face and are blamed when, in the name of family honor, social practice would seem to stretch the boundaries of propriety. Gender dichotomies play against a major contradiction in Korean ritual life. The rites, as Confucians understand them, are vehicles of morality and affirmations of personal virtue; good people do them well. A thin line divides notions of doing the rites properly from doing them extravagantly, demonstrations of virtue from exhibitions of conspicuous consumption. Women bridge this contradiction by making weddings which garner praise or blame, depending upon the context of argument.

Conclusion

LATE SPRING 1992, MY SISTER SUKCHA

We sit in the rented room furnished with her dowry goods and decorated with wedding photographs. It is my first visit to her new home, and I have brought an early watermelon as a gift. Sukcha's face is chalk white from the nausea of a difficult first pregnancy. She has been lying down, too uncomfortable to move, but she says that she wants to talk and sits up slowly. Ŏmŏni mutters at how Sukcha, in her illness, has left the household tasks to her husband, how Sukcha and her married friends still meet for coffee when they ought to be serving their mothers-in-law like responsible married women. They would not have gotten away with this behavior in the past, she reminds Sukcha. Mothers-in-law would even decide when a bride could sleep with her husband. I know very well that Ŏmŏni has never "served a mother-in-law." The woman who might have been her mother-in-law had run away when Ŏmŏni, at seventeen, began her married life as the sole source of domestic labor for a household of three men. Hunger and hard work were the fundamental hardships she remembers.

Whatever her own experience, mother-in-law mythology looms large in Ŏmŏni's consciousness these days. Of her four married daughters, Sukcha, as the wife of a firstborn son from a local family, is the only one who lives in close proximity to a mother-in-law. The three oldest daughters married men who had migrated to Righteous Town from villages far to the south: a soldier turned taxi driver, a vendor, and a short-order cook. The three daughters' households revolve around Ŏmŏni's household like planets around the sun. The daughters and their husbands even spend the Mid-Autumn Festival and the lunar New Year with Ŏmŏni, occasions when much of the Korean population travels a great distance to visit senior kin and honor the ancestors. But Sukcha has broken the pattern and married very good groom material into the bargain. Ŏmŏni is anxious lest her strong-willed younger daugh-

ter be found lacking as a wife. Ŏmŏni questions the wisdom of Sukcha's
current living arrangement, of the mother-in-law's agreement to let the couple live by themselves in town until her own unmarried children leave
home.

I place my sleeping child on Sukcha's quilt and mention the Chinese custom of encouraging male children to romp on the nuptial bed. The practice is
unknown in Korea (where beds are "Western" furniture), but its logic is
transparent. "Stay there! Stay there!" Sukcha tells my son with theatrical urgency. He, with the arbitrariness of a three-year-old, rouses himself and wan-
ders to a far corner of the room. I ask Sukcha if she feels up to talking about
her wedding. She does, and as she speaks, a rosy tinge appears on her pale
cheeks. Sukcha tells me how on the night before her wedding, she left her celebrating friends early and returned home at twelve-thirty in the morning. I
tease that this hardly seems "early." She tells me that she was able to rouse
herself on her wedding day and go through the entire ceremony without feeling the least bit tired. Once it was over, though, she collapsed into utter ex-
haustion.

How did you feel on your wedding day?
Until I put on the wedding dress, I didn't feel anything in particular. I thought, 'Hey, am I really getting married? Is this happening to
me?' That's all. I had to keep telling myself, "Today is my wedding
day."

I had so many things to do, everything in such a rush, so many details to fret about. They made me up in the beauty parlor, and then in
the dressing room, they put on the wedding dress. Just then, bang! I
was so overwhelmed with joy that I burst into tears. "Wow! Now I'm
getting married!" That was when I really felt it.

Some brides say that during their weddings, they are so over-
whelmed with emotion that they don't even know what's going on
around them.
It was like that with me. Just before the wedding, you know, I was
sitting in the bride's waiting room with my friends. It was just for a
short while, but I thought about so many things, about my dead father
and how I'd cried when I put on the wedding dress. It all passed in an
instant, and they were saying, "Now the bride enters the hall." I had
no idea what was happening. When I look at the video, I don't feel as
though I actually experienced it. I wanted to do it all over again. It
went by too quickly.

You can't even remember the churye's *speech?*
Of course I know that. He's a national assemblyman. Everyone
tries to get him, but he's a busy person with no time to spare.
Through connections in my husband's office, he agreed to be our
churye. In his speech, he told us that in our country, the primary prin-

ciple is filial piety, that you must render filial piety to your parents. You must raise your children well. In addition, the couple must love each other deeply. They must believe in each other, trust each other, and understand each other. That's what he said.

That does sound like a churye's *speech. . . . Do you remember how much money you received in the* p'yebaek?

I don't know how it happened. Perhaps I didn't have my wits about me because I was so tired, but the money went into my bridegroom's wallet! When I thought about it later, aw gee! It was as though I hadn't received any money for bowing. But it worked out all right in the end, since it was money we used on our honeymoon.

Have your attitudes changed since you got married?

Of course. Before I got married, life was so easy and comfortable. If I wanted to do something, well then I could just do it. If I wanted to go out and have fun, I would, and I could even stay out until all hours. Now, before I do anything, I have to consider so many things. Is there housework to do? Is there some task that I should be doing for my husband? [She says this without the least note of regret in her voice. She sounds downright smug in her newfound maturity.]

And then there's money. I used to think that 1,000 *wŏn* was a laughable sum, but now that I'm keeping house, even 1,000 *wŏn* is important. In the past, when I would meet my friends for coffee, I'd be the one to say, "Sure, I'll treat." Nowadays when I meet them, I begrudge spending even the smallest amount of money. I've changed, just like that.

———◆▪◆▪◆———

She had changed, just like that. The young woman who had been fuming and grumbling over the ordeal of matchmaking was, less than one year later, a pregnant and contented young wife. At the time of this writing, she is the mother of a toddler—a boy, to her family's delight. Simultaneously, with subsequent readings of her wedding story, Sukcha's own life moves on to new chapters.

Having begun this work with a memory from my own first encounter with Korea, I have been reminded throughout its construction of the relentless passage of time. I recall, like any sentimental wedding guest, how when I first knew Sukcha she was a gawky child in a shapeless black middle-school uniform. Time passages of short and long duration have been an unstated motif of this work as Sukcha approached her marriage, as her family moved from the country house, where the pregnant Kkach'i was frugally married, to the restaurant in town that would finance Sukcha's modestly middle-class wedding. I began this work with the reminiscence of a Peace Corps volunteer who became an anthropologist, and I travelled between brief field trips and even briefer visits during the course of its construction. Fashions changed, demonstrations filled the streets, the Chun regime came to an end, "democracy" became the watchword of the day. Women reminisced about the weddings of thirty and forty years ago, and ethnographies published even a decade ago became history. My own fieldnotes became historical data. As more general background to this work, the Korean nation passed through the twentieth century, constructing its own images of "tradition," "modernity," and "nation," implicating weddings and women in transmuting valuations of "old" and "new."

Because of my own personal and professional circumstances, I organized this project as a series of short field trips over several years, years of rapid and sometimes tumultuous transition in Korea. I was forced by raw experience, more than by any postmodern critique, to construct an ethnographic present whose outlines are blurred by potential motion, like the configurations of mountains, water, and clouds in a Chinese (or Korean) ink painting.

The (south) "Korea" presented in the preceding chapters is intended to be unambiguously coeval with a Western experience of late twentieth-century life: developed, dynamic, media-hyped, and contentious (cf. Fabian 1983). At the same time, the numerous missionaries, travellers, folklorists, and ethnologists who saw fit to record Korean weddings over more than a century of assumed transformation have given me a sense of history, but also the contradictory and the perverse temptation to regard life in Korea "before the turn of the century," "before the Korean War," or "before the 1960s" as a frozen baseline "tradition," much as I once thought cultural authenticity could be found in the countryside. These demarcations of time and space are strong in local discourse as well as in the localizing strategies of written ethnographies (cf. Fardon 1990).

Old weddings and new weddings, arranged marriage and love marriage, countryside and city, tradition and modernity, anthropology and folklore, the West and the rest—the signs seduce us with the promise that logic and order may be imposed upon the messier stuff of experience, but the signs themselves take on shifting colorations of value, even as the signified are in perpetual motion.

Dichotomies of space and time are prominent within a Korean intellectual tradition which has sought to record, codify, and analyze national "traditions" (*chŏnt'ong*) and "customs" (*p'ungsok*). They are part and parcel of how many people in Korea think about weddings and, through weddings, the experience of social change. Recall the assertion of the early 1970s, echoed again during my fieldwork more than a decade later, that the old wedding rite should be sought deep in the countryside. Things known to be new and events transacted in places other than villages force a different awareness upon the ethnographer, but with the exhilaration of seeing Korea from a fresh vantage point, we also risk overlooking what an older ethnography and an even older tradition of folklore studies might teach us.

While critics justifiably contend that the reification of a chronological "tradition" and "modernity" denies the process of history, nostalgic studies of folk custom may yet help us to see the hand of the past moving in the present and give us a measure of the manner in which the present differs from the past. Yes, one wishes much of this material was more clearly labeled as aged memory or current practice, ubiquitous or specialized, the product of a particular social class. Even so, recorded "customs" come to us as the tenderly preserved fragments from a time capsule, a partial and imperfect sense, but sometimes our only sense of how ordinary people did things in Korea fifty, seventy-five, or a hundred years ago. My discussions of the first meeting, the argument over the gift box fee, inflated obligations in dowries and ritual silk, and the construction of the new-style ceremony—invented traditions tailored from the fabric of contemporary life—would not have made sense without a considerable body of Korean folklore and ethnography, a literature once all but exclusively devoted to the description of Korean "traditions" before the word came to be so routinely and gingerly placed in quotation marks.

WEDDINGS, GENDER, AND CHANGE

Roger Janelli recently observed that his long involvement with Korea since 1968 has partly inscribed him "with the often-expressed perception of South Koreans that the United States is a place where little changes" (Janelli with Yim 1993:3). If change is the expectation and experience of contemporary Korean life, if economic and demographic statistics bear witness to this fact, the human consequences of late-twentieth-century Korean history are still but little understood, although a spate of new ethnographies has begun to address this lacuna.

I have found in my own work that weddings provide an excellent lens upon a changing present precisely because they will not submit to any fixed ethnographic description of a "Korean wedding." Indeed, weddings are contested ground. Government injunctions to frugality war with a slick wedding industry, and feminist critiques war with commonsensical notions of Korean "tradition." Arguments about matchmaking and matrimonial exchanges are waged in many households. Discussions in the preceding chapters embraced questions of what it means to be modern, to be Korean, to be desirable "bride and groom material," to become middle class. Weddings are likely flashpoints for these concerns, in part because weddings are integral to the construction of adult identities, in part because many Koreans consider rituals to be vehicles of morality. In the 1970s, the Park regime saw ritual reform as a rational economy of time and money, a spur to development. In the next decade, a successor government would support attempts to revive the old Confucian wedding rite, arguing that the superficiality of the Western-influenced new-style wedding contributed to a moral climate of extravagance and social discontent.

As we have seen, the roots of the new-style wedding are to be found in early-twentieth-century Korean confrontations with "modernity," in colonial period intellectuals' disillusionment with the past, and in the reconfiguration of work, marriage, and family among an emergent colonial elite. The arranged meeting was also a product of this moment, a compromise that bridged the abiding significance of family interests and the extrafamilial identities, and Western-influenced expectations, of men educated to participate in a new professional, bureaucratic, and entrepreneurial class. The new-style wedding and the arranged meeting have flowered to near ubiquity in recent decades as the Korean nation moved to town, grown children found livelihoods independent of family enterprises, and commercial services replaced village communal feasts. The spatial and symbolic content of the new wedding asserted the primacy of public space over domestic space, the vernacular over the classical language of Confucian texts, and explicitly Western styles over antique dress. It celebrated conjugality with romantic music and imagery. At the same time, it retained elements which affirmed the role of ritual in perpetuating morality, the primacy of virtuous male elders, and the subordination of women.

Critiques of the new wedding as being too "Western" emerged at a moment when Korea claimed great pride in national accomplishment and when disillusionment with America, the Western Other, could be heard from both left and right. It was a moment for celebrating a distinctive Korean past, but definitions of that past were contested. Many young Koreans rejected or modified the revived Confucian wedding rite so as to celebrate the music and vitality of the culture of the masses. Protest songs and traditional Korean music could be heard in the wedding halls. Feminists critiqued the androcentric premises of both the old wedding and the new wedding.

Following Clifford (who follows Bakhtin), weddings are cultural practices insofar as " 'culture' is, concretely, an open-ended, creative dialogue of subcultures, of insiders and outsiders, of diverse factions" (Clifford 1988:46). As Ong suggests, the "riot of social meanings" revealed in such a dialogue brings forth unresolved issues of gender, and through gender, unresolved tensions between tradition and modernity (Ong 1988:88). Discussions about weddings in Korea—and through weddings, "the status of women"—are premised upon the assumption of change, both past and potential, but the contended construction of both ritual and gender is easily elided in facile comparisons of a fixed and reified past and present. Any discussion of contemporary courtship and matchmaking practices prompts a favorable comparison with bygone days when elders chose a child's mate and couples met for the first time on their wedding day. Even so, modern matchmaking carries the fundamentally unequal premise that, insofar as a groom's career prospects define a future life-style, men choose and women are to be chosen. This premise is underscored by a vast industry in media and commodities intended to address a woman's need to be desirable and contended, at least in small ways, in some intimate personal histories of courtship.

The elaboration of asymmetrical matrimonial exchanges in dowries and gifts of ritual silk to the groom's kin, as well as the appearance of a "new custom" of paying the groom's friends when they deliver betrothal gifts, compound the notion that grooms are valued over brides. The large dowries of contemporary weddings most often furnish a bride's new household, independent of her mother-in-law and the extended family enterprise of a rural household. At the same time, extensive dowries affirm perceptions of the capitalist household as a realm of consumption counterpoised to the productive realm of male work. Ideology has not caught up with a demographic trend that sees more married women working, but even here, limited career paths and severe wage discrimination constrict a married woman's earning capacity. An urban wife's role as the manager of consumption has many resonances with that of the preindustrial farm wife, but positive images of a frugal and productive wife putting loom and needle to good use have been overshadowed by more sordid portrayals of women engaged in financial schemes and all manner of extravagance. Women are criticized for the excesses of contemporary weddings, for unrealistic ambitions brought into play in matchmaking, and for the conspicuous consumption associated with gifts and ceremony.

I have argued that blame is a function of both structure and ideology. Women make weddings to maximize a child's prospects and maintain a family's reputation, the proper expectation of a wife and mother, but "women," both individually and as a collective category, bear the burden of an irreconcilable contradiction between performing the wedding rites properly and making sufficient display to perform them well.

A category "women" obscures distinctions of class which surface and sink in discussions of weddings. The families of modest means whom I interviewed assumed that general procedures for a "Korean wedding" could be discussed and understood, but they were uncomfortable with the notion that I should derive my foreigner's understanding from the weddings of *their* children. More affluent families, they felt, would give me a better picture of a right and proper Korean wedding. Weddings are widely recognized as occasions for affirming or advancing a family's status claims or for acknowledging, at least tacitly, that one lacks the social and economic resources to make any claim at all. Although the stakes in performing a proper Korean wedding have been rising at dizzying rates, the prospect of work before marriage has enabled some (but by no means all) working daughters to approximate the marriages of the middle class. The Righteous Town brides, grooms, and their families described their weddings as fulfilling the bare essentials of propriety, in contrast to the weddings of the upper middle class, where remarkable displays are marks of distinction and grist for the gossip mill. These contrasts are blurred in a common vocabulary of wedding customs and intensified in perceptions derived from media portrayals of upper-middle-class life-styles.

The ubiquitous possibility of matchmaking, and the common association of "matchmade marriages" with "tradition," obscure the manner in which different social classes construct matrimony. Like Sukcha, many women might find themselves enmeshed in maternal matchmaking strategies as their thirtieth birthdays approach. Mothers in more affluent households, however, begin seeking a daughter's spouse as soon as she graduates from college. These women are frank in their assumptions that there are real material and social stakes in a daughter's wedding, that the daughter of a wealthy and socially prominent family could easily be exploited by the wrong man, or that their own sheltered children are too naive to take sole responsibility for their future lives. Others opine that it takes a neutral third party, a matchmaker, to engage in face-risking negotiations between socially prominent families. These women are in marked contrast to the rural mother who, when I asked whether her daughter had told her about her boyfriend, laughed: "Why should she have told us? We would have just gotten all hot and bothered about it." If the new urban elites of the early twentieth century were the first to demand marriage based upon choice, it is the children of rural households and recent urban migrants who today have the least to lose by entering into consensual unions.

If styles of weddings are to be taken as indicators of "class," then class itself is a highly variable proposition amidst the changing circumstances of families. The very different weddings of Sukcha and her sister Kkach'i are products of time and circumstance, of family strategy and individual agency. That the family was able to scrape together the resources for Kkach'i's wedding set her apart from the many working-class brides, like Mrs. Ch'oe and Mrs. Sǒ, who were legally married but felt the lack of a wedding as a social and moral deficit. Many years after Kkach'i married, her sister Sukcha's wedding—with its extensive dowry, ritual silks (gifted in cash), and stylish wedding hall—evidenced her family's new claim to middle-class status among families who had crested the precarious move from country to town. Sukcha also enjoyed the benefits of a younger daughter, both by coming of age in the years of prosperity made possible by Kkach'i's family enterprise and by being absolved of the necessity to contribute her earnings to a household of school-age children.

If weddings en*gender* a "creative dialogue," in Clifford's terms, or in Ong's, "a riot," then women are very much in the fray. Feminist writers who denounce a pernicious confluence of patriarchal traditions and capitalist commoditization and women activists who spearhead campaigns for "wholesome weddings" are positioned to address a public audience. Many other discussions occur in more intimate settings. Matchmakers, mothers, and brides, by their expressed desires and explicitly stated strategies, by their complaints and frustrations, by their sometimes contradictory actions, and by the arguments provoked among them, perpetuate a tension of possibilities in the business of getting married.

AFTERWARD, AFTERWORD, LATE AUTUMN 1992

She has a full, round pregnant belly now and looks radiant. Everyone is so relieved. The sisters are excited about the forthcoming Korean elections. For the first time in their lifetimes, the nation will elect a civilian president. They tell me the latest family gossip. Minja, the youngest

Bibliography

Abelmann, Nancy. 1990. The Practice and Politics of History: A South Korean Tenant Farmers Movement. Ph.D. dissertation, University of California, Berkeley.

Abu-Lughod, Lila. 1990. The Romance of Resistance: Tracing Transformations of Power Through Bedouin Women. *American Ethnologist* 17(1):41–55.

———. 1991. Writing Against Culture. In *Recapturing Anthropology: Working in the Present,* ed. R. G. Fox, 137–162. Santa Fe: School of American Research Press.

———. 1993. Writing Women's Worlds: Bedouin Stories. Berkeley: University of California Press.

Agricultural Census. 1960. Seoul: Republic of Korea, Ministry of Agriculture and Forestry.

Amsden, Alice H. 1989. *Asia's Next Giant: South Korea and Late Industrialization.* New York: Oxford University Press.

An Chŏngnam. 1991. Hyŏndae kyŏrhon ŭiryeŭi ŭimi [The meaning of modern marriage rituals]. In *Chabonjuŭi sijanggyŏngjewa honin* [The capitalist market economy and marriage], Yi Hyojae et al., 177–198. Seoul: Tosŏch'ulp'an, Tto hanaŭi munhwa.

Anagnost, Ann. 1994. The Politics of Ritual Displacement. In *Asian Visions of Authority: Religion and the Modern States of East and Southeast Asia,* ed. C. F. Keyes, L. Kendall, and H. Hardacre, 221–254. Honolulu: University of Hawaii Press.

Andrews, Roy C. 1919. Exploring Unknown Corners of the "Hermit Kingdom." *National Geographic* 36(1):24–48.

Appadurai, Arjun, ed. 1986. *The Social Life of Things: Commodities in Cultural Perspective.* Cambridge, England: Cambridge University Press.

Arrigo, Linda Gail. 1984. Taiwan Electronics Workers. In *Lives: Chinese Working Women,* ed. M. Sheridan and J. W. Salaff, 123–145. Bloomington: Indiana University Press.

Atkinson, Jane. 1989. *The Art and Politics of Wana Shamanship.* Berkeley: University of California Press.

Austin, J. I. 1962. *How To Do Things with Words* (The William James Lectures delivered at Harvard University in 1955). Cambridge, Massachusetts: Harvard University Press.

Ayscough, Florence. 1937. *Chinese Women Yesterday and Today.* Boston: Houghton Mifflin.

Bailey, Beth L. 1988. *From Front Porch to Back Seat: Courtship in Twentieth-Century America.* Baltimore: Johns Hopkins University Press.

Baker, Don. n.d. The Resurrection of Rural Tradition in Modern Urban Korea: The Case of Songp'a Sandae Nori. Unpublished ms.

Barth, Fredrik. 1989. The Analysis of Culture in Complex Societies. *Ethnos* 3–4:120–142.

Baudrillard, Jean. 1987. Modernity. *Canadian Journal of Political and Social Theory* 11(3):63–72.

Bauman, Richard. 1986. *Story, Performance, and Event: Contexts of Oral Narrative.* Cambridge, England: Cambridge University Press.

———, and Patricia Sawin. 1990. The Politics of Participation in Folklife Festivals. In *Exhibiting Cultures: The Poetics and Politics of Museum Display,* ed. I. Karp and S. Lavine, 288–314. Washington, D.C.: Smithsonian Institution Press.

Behar, Ruth. 1993. *Translated Woman: Crossing the Border with Esperanza's Story.* Boston: Beacon Press.

Bell, Catherine. 1989. Religion and Chinese Culture: Toward an Assessment of "Popular Religion." *History of Religions* 29(1):35–57.

Bergman, Sten. 1938 [1935]. *In Korean Wilds and Villages,* trans. F. Whyte. London: John Gifford.

Bernstein, Gail Lee. 1991. Introduction. In *Recreating Japanese Women, 1600–1945,* ed. Gail Lee Bernstein, 1–14. Berkeley: University of California Press.

Biernatzki, William Eugene. 1967. Varieties of Korean Lineage Structure. Ph.D. dissertation, St. Louis University.

Bishop, Isabella Bird. 1970 [1898]. *Korea and Her Neighbors.* Seoul: Yonsei University Press.

Boddy, Janice. 1989. *Wombs and Alien Spirits: Women, Men, and the Zar Cult in Northern Sudan.* Madison: University of Wisconsin Press.

Bourdieu, Pierre. 1977. *Outline of a Theory of Practice.* Cambridge, England: Cambridge University Press.

———. 1984. *Distinction: A Social Critique of the Judgement of Taste.* Cambridge, Massachusetts: Harvard University Press.

Brandt, Anthony. 1978. A Short Natural History of Nostalgia. *Atlantic Monthly* 242 (December):58–63.

Brandt, Vincent S. R. 1971. *A Korean Village Between Farm and Sea.* Cambridge, Massachusetts: Harvard University Press.

Brown, Karen McCarthy. 1991. *Mama Lola: A Vodou Priestess in Brooklyn.* Berkeley: University of California Press.

Brunner, Edmund de Schweinitz. 1928. Rural Korea: A Preliminary Survey of Economic, Social, and Religious Conditions; Inquiries Regarding the Christian Church in Rural China; Rural India and the Christian Church. In *The Christian Mission in Relation to Rural Problems.* Jerusalem Meeting of the International Missionary Council, March 24–April 8, vol. 6, 84–177. New York: International Missionary Council.

Caplan, L. 1984. Bridegroom Price in Urban India: Class, Caste and "Dowry Evil" Among Christians in Madras. *Man* 19(2):216–233.

Census of Korea. 1949. *Advanced Report of the First General Census, Korea 1949.* Seoul: Ministry of Public Information, Bureau of Statistics.

————. 1959. *Report of the Simplified General Population Census, Republic of Korea. 1955.* Seoul: Ministry of Home Affairs, Bureau of Statistics.

————. 1968–1969. *1966 Population Census Report of Korea.* Seoul: Bureau of Statistics, Economic Planning Board.

Chai, Alice Y. 1962. Kinship and Mate Selection in Korea. Ph.D. dissertation, Ohio State University.

Chang-Michell, Pilwha. 1984. *Women and Work, a Case Study of a Small Town in Republic of Korea: A Report Presented to UNICEF, Seoul, Korea.* Seoul: UNICEF.

Chen, Jack. 1973. *A Year in Upper Felicity: Life in a Chinese Village During the Cultural Revolution.* New York: Macmillan.

Cho Haejoang (Cho Hyejŏng). 1988. *Han'gugŭi yŏsŏnggwa namsŏng* [Korean women and men]. Seoul: Munhaggwa chisŏngsa.

————. 1991. Kyŏrhon, sarang, kurigo sŏng [Marriage, love and also sex]. *Tto hanaŭi munhwa* 7:23–44.

Cho Hyoung. 1975. The Kin Network of the Urban Middle Class Family in Korea. *Korea Journal* (June):22–33.

————. 1986. Labor Force Participation of Women in Korea. In *Challenges for Women: Women's Studies in Korea,* ed. Chung Sei-wha, trans. Shin Chang-hyun et al., 150–172. Seoul: Korean Women's Institute Series, Ewha Womans University Press.

————. 1987. The Position of Women in the Korean Work Force. In *Korean Women in Transition: At Home and Abroad,* ed. E. Y. Yu and E. H. Phillips, 85–102. Los Angeles: Center for Korean-American and Korean Studies, California State University.

Cho Kihong, et al. 1983. *Yeron* [Treatise on propriety]. Seoul: Sŏngsin Women's University Press.

Cho Oakla. 1979. Social Stratification in a Korean Peasant Village. Ph.D. dissertation, State University of New York at Stony Brook.

————. 1987a. Women in Transition: The Low Income Family. In *Korean Women in Transition: At Home and Abroad,* ed. E. Y. Yu and E. H. Phillips, 71–83. Los Angeles: Center for Korean-American and Korean Studies, California State University.

————. 1987b. Social Resilience: In the Korean Context. *Korea Journal* (October):28–34.

————. 1992. Doing a Fieldwork as a Native Anthropologist. Paper presented to the 91st meeting of the American Anthropological Association, San Francisco, California, December 2–6.

Cho P'ungyŏn. 1983. Honingwa kyŏrhon [Matrimony and weddings]. *Chŏnt'ong munhwa* (June):30–35.

Cho Uhn (Moon Cho Uhn) and Hagen Koo. 1983. Economic Development and Women's Work in a Newly Industrializing Country: The Case of Korea. *Development and Change* 14:515–531.

Ch'oe Kilsŏng. 1974. Misin t'ap'a e taehan ilgoch'al [A study on the destruction of superstition]. *Han'guk Minsokhak* [Korean Folklore] 12:39–54.

Ch'oe Sang-su. 1982. *Kajŏng mansa pogam* [Comprehensive household compendium]. Seoul: Sangnok Ch'ulp'an Sa.

Chŏch'uk Ch'ujin Chungang Wiwŏn Hoe [Central Committee for the Promotion of Thrift]. 1985. *Honin piyong chich'ule kwanhan silt'ae mit ŭisik chosa* [Investigation of facts and awareness of marriage expenses]. Seoul: CCCWH.

Choi Chungmoo. 1987. The Competence of Korean Shamans as Performers of Folklore. Ph.D. dissertation, University of Indiana.

———. 1989. The Artistry and Ritual Aesthetics of Urban Korean Shamans. *Journal of Ritual Studies* 3(2):235–249.

———. 1991. Nami, Ch'ae, and Oksun: Superstar Shamans in Korea. In *Shamans of the 20th Century*, ed. Ruth-Inge Heinze, 51–61. New York: Irvington.

Choi In-Hak. 1987. Non-academic Factors in the Development of Korean and Japanese Folklore Scholarship. Paper presented to the annual meeting of the American Anthropological Association, Chicago, Illinois, November.

Chow, Rey. 1991. *Woman and Chinese Modernity: The Politics of Reading Between West and East.* In *Theory and History of Literature,* vol. 75. Minnesota: University of Minnesota Press.

Chun Kyung-soo. 1984. *Reciprocity and Korean Society: An Ethnography of Hasami.* Seoul: Seoul National University Press.

Chung Cha-Whan. 1975. Social Units of a Korean Village. M.A. thesis, University of Hawaii.

———. 1977. Change and Continuity in an Urbanizing Society: Family and Kinship in Urban Korea. Ph.D. dissertation, University of Hawaii.

Clark, Charles Allen. 1919. Marriage Questions in Chosen. *Korea Mission Field* 15 (August):159–163.

Clark, Donald N. 1986. *Christianity in Modern Korea.* Asian Agenda Report, no. 5. New York: University Press of America for the Asia Society.

———. 1991. Bitter Friendship: Understanding Anti-Americanism in South Korea. In *Korea Briefing, 1991,* ed. D. N. Clark, 147–167. Boulder: Westview Press.

———, ed. 1988. *The Kwangju Uprising: Shadows Over the Regime in South Korea.* Boulder: Westview Press.

Clifford, James. 1983. On Ethnographic Authority. *Representations* 1(2):118–146.

———. 1988. *The Predicament of Culture: Twentieth-Century Ethnography, Literature, and Art.* Cambridge, Massachusetts: Harvard University Press.

———. 1990. Notes on (Field)notes. In *Fieldnotes: The Makings of Anthropology,* ed. Roger Sanjek, 47–70. Ithaca, New York: Cornell University Press.

———, and George Marcus, eds. 1986. *Writing Culture: The Poetics and Politics of Ethnography.* Berkeley: University of California Press.

Cohen, Myron. 1976. *House United, House Divided: The Chinese Family in Taiwan.* New York: Columbia University Press.

———. 1991. Being Chinese: The Peripheralization of Traditional Identity. *Daedalus* 120(2):113–134.

Comaroff, Jean. 1985. *Body of Power, Spirit of Resistance: The Culture and History of a South African People.* Chicago: University of Chicago Press.

———. 1994. Defying Disenchantment: Reflections on Ritual, Power, and History. In *Asian Visions of Authority*, ed. C. F. Keyes, L. Kendall, and H. Hardacre, 301–314. Honolulu: University of Hawaii Press.

Comaroff, John. 1980. Introduction. In *The Meaning of Marriage Payments*, ed. J. L. Comaroff. New York: Academic Press.

———, and Jean Comaroff. 1992. *Ethnography and the Historical Imagination*. Boulder: Westview Press.

Croll, Elisabeth. 1981. *The Politics of Marriage in Contemporary China*. Cambridge, England: Cambridge University Press.

Cumings, Bruce. 1981. *The Origins of the Korean War: Liberation and the Emergence of Separate Regimes*. Princeton, New Jersey: Princeton University Press.

Dallet, Charles. 1954 [1874]. *Traditional Korea*. New Haven, Connecticut: Human Relations Area Files.

Deuchler, Martina. 1977. The Tradition: Women During the Yi Dynasty. In *Virtues in Conflict: Tradition and the Korean Woman Today*, ed. S. Mattielli, 1–49. Seoul: Royal Asiatic Society.

———. 1980. Neo-Confucianism: The Impulse for Social Action in Early Yi Korea. *Journal of Korean Studies* 2:71–112.

———. 1987. Neo-Confucianism in Action: Agnation and Ancestor Worship in Early Yi Korea. In *Religion and Ritual in Korean Society*, ed. L. Kendall and G. Dix, 26–55. Berkeley: Institute of East Asian Studies, University of California.

———. 1992. *The Confucian Transformation of Korea: A Study of Society and Ideology*. Cambridge, Massachusetts: Council on East Asian Studies, Harvard University.

Dirks, Nicholas B. 1990. History as a Sign of the Modern. *Public Culture* 2(2):25–32.

Dix, M. Griffin. 1977. "The East Asian Country of Propriety": Confucianism in a Korean Village. Ph.D. dissertation, University of California, San Diego.

———. 1979. How To Do Things with Ritual: The Logic of Ancestor Worship and Other Offerings in Rural Korea. In *Studies on Korea in Transition*, ed. D. R. McCann, J. Middleton, and E. J. Shultz, 57–88. Occasional Papers, no. 9. Honolulu: Center for Korean Studies, University of Hawaii.

———. 1987. The New Year's Ritual and Village Social Structure. In *Religion and Ritual in Korean Society*, ed. L. Kendall and G. Dix. Berkeley: East Asian Institute, University of California.

Douglas, Mary. 1966. *Purity and Danger: An Analysis of Concepts of Pollution and Taboo*. London: Routledge and Kegan Paul.

———, and Baron Isherwood. 1979. *The World of Goods*. New York: Basic Books.

Dredge, C. Paul. 1987. Korean Funerals: Rituals as Process. In *Religion and Ritual in Korean Society*, ed. L. Kendall and G. Dix, 71–92. Berkeley: East Asian Institute, University of California.

Duncan, John. 1988. The Decline of Traditional Confucian Social Values in the Face of Korea's Economic Development. Paper presented to the Conference on Religion and Contemporary Society in Korea, Berkeley, November 12.

Ebrey, Patricia Buckley. 1991a. *Chu Hsi's Family Rituals*. Princeton, New Jersey: Princeton University Press.

————. 1991b. Introduction. In *Marriage and Inequality in Chinese Society*, ed. R. S. Watson and P. B. Ebrey, 1–24. Berkeley: University of California Press.

————, and James L. Watson, eds. 1986. *Kinship Organization in Late Imperial China 1000–1940*. Berkeley: University of California Press.

Eckert, Carter J. 1991. *Offspring of Empire: The Koch'ang Kims and the Colonial Origins of Korean Capitalism 1876–1945*. Seattle: University of Washington Press.

————, Ki-baik Lee, Young Ick Lew, Michael Robinson, and Edward W. Wagner. 1990. *Korea Old and New: A History*. Cambridge, Massachusetts: Korea Institute, Harvard University.

Edwards, Walter. 1989. *Modern Japan Through Its Weddings: Gender, Person, and Society in Ritual Portrayal*. Stanford, California: Stanford University Press.

Eikemeier, Dieter. 1980. *Documents from Changjwa-ri: A Further Approach to the Analysis of Korean Villages*. Wiesbaden, Germany: Otto Harrassowitz.

Elson, Diane, and Ruth Pearson. 1981. The Subordination of Women and the Internationalization of Factory Production. In *Of Marriage and the Market: Women's Subordination in International Perspective*, ed. K. Young, C. Wolkowitz, and R. McCullagh, pp. 145–166. London: CSE Books.

Emerson, Tony, with Bradley Martin. 1991. Too Rich, Too Soon. *Newsweek*, November 11, 12–17.

Erwin, Cordelia. 1918. Transition: A Korean Christian Wedding. *The Korea Mission Field* 14(4):73–76.

Ewha Womans University, Committee for the Compilation of the History of Korean Women (EWUCCHKW). 1972. *Han'guk Yŏsŏngsa* [History of Korean women]. Seoul: Ewha Womans University Press.

Fabian, Johannes. 1983. *Time and the Other: How Anthropology Makes Its Object*. New York: Columbia University Press.

Fang, Chaoying. 1969. *The Asami Library: A Descriptive Catalogue*. Berkeley: University of California Press.

Fardon, Richard, ed. 1990. *Localizing Strategies: Regional Traditions of Ethnographic Writing*. Edinburgh and Washington: Scottish Academic Press and Smithsonian Institution Press.

Foucault, Michel. 1980 [1978]. *The History of Sexuality*, vol. 1: *An Introduction*. New York: Vintage Books.

Frolic, B. Michael. 1980. *Mao's People: Sixteen Portraits of Life in Revolutionary China*. Cambridge, Massachusetts: Harvard University Press.

Gale, James S. 1898. *Korean Sketches*. New York: Flemming H. Revell.

Geertz, Clifford. 1973. *The Interpretation of Cultures*. New York: Basic Books.

Gluckman, Max. 1954. *Rituals of Rebellion in South-East Africa* (The Frazer Lecture, 1952). Manchester, England: Manchester University Press.

Goody, Jack, and S. J. Tambiah. 1973. *Bridewealth and Dowry*. Cambridge, England: Cambridge University Press.

Griffis, William Elliot. 1911. *Corea, the Hermit Nation*. New York: A.M.S.

Guillemoz, Alexandre. 1983. *Les algues, les anciens, les deux: La vie et la religion d'un village de pêcheurs-agricultueurs Coréens*. Paris: Le Léopard d'Or.

Haggard, Stephan, Byung-kook Kim, and Chung-in Moon. 1991. The Transition to Export-led Growth in South Korea: 1954–1966. *Journal of Asian Studies* 50(4):850–869.

Hall, Stuart. 1981. Notes on Deconstructing "the Popular." In *People's History and Socialist Theory*, ed. R. Samuel, 227–240. London: Routledge and Kegan Paul.

Hamabata, Matthews Masayuki. 1990. *Crested Kimono: Power and Love in the Japanese Business Family*. Ithaca, New York: Cornell University Press.

Han Chungnim Choi. 1949. Social Organization of Upper Han Hamlet in Korea. Ph.D. dissertation, University of Michigan.

Han Gyoung-hai. 1990. Social Change, Parental Strategy, and the Timing of Marriage of Korean Men. Ph.D. dissertation, Pennsylvania State University.

Han Sang-bok. 1972. Socio-economic Organization and Change in Korean Fishing Villages: A Comparative Study of Three Fishing Communities. Ph.D. dissertation, Michigan State University.

———. 1977. *Korean Fishermen: Ecological Adaptation in Three Communities*. Seoul: Seoul National University Press.

Handler, Richard, and Jocelyn Linnekin. 1984. Tradition, Genuine or Spurious. *Journal of American Folklore* 97(385):273–290.

Haraven, Tamara K. 1982. *Family Time and Industrial Time: The Relationship Between the Family and Work in a New England Industrial Community*. Cambridge, England: Cambridge University Press.

Hardacre, Helen. 1989. *Shinto and the State, 1868–1988*. Princeton, New Jersey: Princeton University Press.

Harrell, Stevan, and Sara A. Dickey. 1985. Dowry Systems in Complex Societies. *Ethnology* 24(2):105–120.

Hart, Dennis Michael. 1991. From Tradition to Consumption: The Rise of a Materialist Culture in South Korea. Ph.D. dissertation, University of Washington.

Harvey, Youngsook Kim. 1979. *Six Korean Women: The Socialization of Shamans*. St. Paul, Minnesota: West.

———. 1983. Minmyŏnŭri: The Daughter-in-law Who Comes of Age in her Mother-in-law's Household. In *Korean Women: A View from the Inner Room*, ed. L. Kendall and M. Peterson, 45–61. New Haven, Connecticut: East Rock Press.

———. 1987. The Shaman and Deaconess: Sisters in Different Guises. In *Religion and Ritual in Korean Society*, ed. L. Kendall and G. Dix, 149–170. Berkeley: Institute for East Asian Studies, University of California.

Hendry, Joy. 1981. *Marriage in Changing Japan*. New York: St. Martin's Press.

Hobsbawm, Eric, and Terence Ranger, eds. 1983. *The Invention of Tradition*. Cambridge, England: Cambridge University Press.

Hulbert, Homer B. 1906. *The Passing of Korea*. New York: Doubleday, Page.

Hung Chang-tai. 1985. *Going to the People: Chinese Intellectuals and Folk Literature 1918–1937*. Cambridge, Massachusetts: Council on East Asian Studies, Harvard University.

Iyer, Pico. 1988 [1989]. *Video Night in Kathmandu and Other Reports from the Not-So-Far-East*. New York: Vintage.

Janelli, Roger L. 1975. Anthropology, Folklore, and Korean Ancestor Worship. *Korea Journal* 15(6):34–43.

———. 1986. The Origins of Korean Folklore Scholarship. *Journal of American Folklore* 99(391):24–49.

———, and Dawnhee Yim Janelli. 1982. *Ancestor Worship and Korean Society.* Stanford, California: Stanford University Press.

———, with Dawnhee Yim. 1993. *Making Capitalism: Cultural Metaphors, Political Advantage, and Material Incentives in a South Korean Conglomerate.* Stanford, California: Stanford University Press.

Jones, George Heber. 1896. The Status of Women in Korea. *Korea Repository* 3:223–229.

Kang, Younghill. 1966 [1959]. *The Grass Roof.* New York: Follett. Also New York: W.W. Norton, 1975 [1931].

Kapferer, Bruce. 1983. *A Celebration of Demons: Exorcism and the Aesthetics of Healing in Sri Lanka.* Bloomington: Indiana University Press.

Kawashima, Fujiya. 1980. The Local Gentry Association in Mid-Yi Dynasty Korea: A Preliminary Study of the Ch'angnyŏng Hyangan, 1600–1839. *Journal of Korean Studies* 2:113–138.

———. 1992. *The Andong Hyangan in the Mid-Chosŏn Dynasty, 1589–1647.* Unpublished paper presented to the Conference on Confucianism and Late Chosŏn Korea, University of California, Los Angeles, January 7.

Kelley, John D., and Martha Kaplan. 1990. History, Structure, and Ritual. *Annual Review of Anthropology* 19:119–150.

Kelly, Joan. 1984. Did Women Have a Renaissance? In *Women, History and Theory: The Essays of Joan Kelly,* 19–50. Chicago: University of Chicago Press.

Kendall, Laurel. 1977. Caught Between Ancestors and Spirits: A Korean *Mansin's* Healing *Kut. Korea Journal* 17(8):8–23.

———. 1985a. *Shamans, Housewives, and Other Restless Spirits: Women in Korean Ritual Life.* Honolulu: University of Hawaii Press.

———. 1985b. Ritual Silks and Kowtow Money: The Bride as Daughter-in-law in Korean Wedding Rituals. *Ethnology* 24(4):253–267.

———. 1985c. Death and Taxes: A Korean Approach to Hell. *Transactions of the Korea Branch of the Royal Asiatic Society* 60:1–14.

———. 1988. *The Life and Hard Times of a Korean Shaman: Of Tales and the Telling of Tales.* Honolulu: University of Hawaii Press.

———, and Mark Peterson. 1983. Introduction. In *Korean Women: View from the Inner Room,* ed. L. Kendall and M. Peterson, 5–21. New Haven, Connecticut: East Rock Press.

Keyes, Charles F., Helen Hardacre, and Laurel Kendall. 1994. Introduction. In *Asian Visions of Authority: Religion and the Modern Nation States of East and Southeast Asia,* ed. C. F. Keyes, L. Kendall, and H. Hardacre, 1–16. Honolulu: University of Hawaii Press.

Kim Ch'anho. 1991. Kyŏrhon, kŭ tathimgwa yŏllim [Marriage, openings and closings]. *Tto hanaŭi munhwa* [Alternative culture] 7:56–70.

Kim Choong Soon. 1974. The *Yŏn'jul-hon* or Chain-String Form of Marriage Arrangement in Korea. *Journal of Marriage and the Family* 36(August):575–579.

———. 1992. *The Culture of Korean Industry: An Ethnography of Poongsan Corporation.* Tucson: University of Arizona Press.

Kim Dongno. 1990. The Transformation of Familism in Modern Korean Society: From Cooperation to Competition. *International Sociology* 5(4):409–425.

Kim Eun Mee. 1991. The Industrial Organization and Growth of the Korean *Chaebol:* Integrating Development and Organizational Theories. In *Business Networks and Economic Development in East and Southeast Asia*, ed. Gary Hamilton, 272–299. Hong Kong: University of Hong Kong Press.

Kim Eun-Shil. 1993. The Making of the Modern Female Gender: The Politics of Gender in Reproductive Practices in Korea. Ph.D. dissertation, University of California, San Francisco and Berkeley.

Kim Hyontay. 1957. *Folklore and Customs of Korea*. Seoul: Korea Information Service.

Kim Kwang-ok. 1988. A Study on the Political Manipulation of Elite Culture. Paper presented to the 5th International Conference on Korean Studies, Academy of Korean Studies, June 30–July 3.

———. 1994. Rituals of Resistance: The Manipulation of Shamanism in Contemporary Korea. In *Asian Visions of Authority*, ed. C. Keyes, L. Kendall, and H. Hardacre, 195–220. Honolulu: University of Hawaii Press.

Kim Kwangon, Yi Kwanggyu, Yi Hyŏnsun, and Ha Hyogil, eds. 1983. Kŏnjŏnhan kajŏng ŭirye chunch'ik [The wholesome family ritual code]. In *Kajŏng ŭirye taebaekkwa* [Great compendium of family ritual], 338–354. Seoul: Hando Munhwasa.

Kim Myung-hye. 1992. Late Industrialization and Women's Work in Urban South Korea: An Ethnographic Study of Upper-Middle-Class Families. *City and Society* 6(2):156–173.

Kim Seong-Nae. 1989a. Chronicle of Violence, Ritual of Mourning: Cheju Shamanism in Korea. Ph.D. dissertation, University of Washington.

———. 1989b. Lamentations of the Dead: The Historical Imagery of Violence on Cheju Island, South Korea. *Journal of Ritual Studies* 3(2):251–285.

Kim Seung-Kuk. 1987. Class Formation and Labor Process in Korea: With Special Reference to Working Class Consciousness. In *Dependency Issues in Korean Development: Comparative Perspectives*, ed. K. Kim, 398–415. Seoul: Seoul National University Press.

Kim Seung-Kyung. 1990. Capitalism, Patriarchy, and Autonomy: Women Factory Workers in the Korean Economic Miracle. Ph.D. dissertation, City University of New York.

Kim Sŏngbae. 1983. Naŭi sinhon sijŏl [My newlywed season]. *Chŏnt'ong munhwa* [Traditional culture] 6:52–57.

Kim Taik-kyoo (Kim T'aekkyu). 1964. *Tongjok puragŭi saenghwal kujon yŏn'gu* [A study of the structure of social life in a lineage village]. Seoul: Ch'onggu.

Kim Tuhŏn. 1969 [1948]. *Han'guk kajok chedo yŏn'gu* [A study of the Korean family system]. Seoul: Ulyu.

Kim Yugyŏng. 1984. Naeddalŭi honin piyong [My daughter's wedding expenses]. *Saemigip'ŭnmul* [Water from a deep spring] 2:161–165.

Kim Yun (Kim Yŏn). 1966. The Population of Korea 1910–1945. Ph.D. dissertation, Australian National University.

Kim Yung-Chung, ed. and trans. 1977. *Women of Korea: A History from Ancient*

Times to 1945. Ewha Womans University, Committee for the Compilation of the History of Korean Women. Seoul: Ewha Womans University Press.

Knez, Eugene. 1959. Sam Jong Dong: A South Korean Village. Ph.D. dissertation, Syracuse University.

Ko Chonggi. 1982. *Algiswiun kwanhonsangje* [Passage rites made easy]. Seoul: Huri Ch'ulp'ansa.

Koh Taiwon. 1959. *The Bitter Fruit of Kom-pawi.* New York: Holt, Rinehart, and Winston.

Kondo, Dorinne K. 1990. *Crafting Selves: Power, Gender and Discourses of Identity in a Japanese Workplace.* Chicago: University of Chicago Press.

Koo Hagen. 1987. Dependency Issue, Class Inequality, and Social Conflict in Korean Development. In *Dependency Issues in Korean Development: Comparative Perspectives,* ed. K. Kim, 375–397. Seoul: Seoul National University Press.

———. 1990. From Farm to Factory: Proletarianization in Korea. *American Sociological Review* 55(October):669–681.

Koo Hagen, and Kim Eun Mee. 1992. The Developmental State and Capital Accumulation in South Korea. In *States and Development in the Pacific Rim,* ed. R. P. Appelbaum and J. Henderson, 121–149. Thousand Oaks, California: Sage.

Kopytoff, Igor. 1986. The Cultural Biography of Things: Commoditization as Process. In *The Social Life of Things: Commodities in Cultural Perspective,* ed. Arjun Appadurai, 64–94. Cambridge, England: Cambridge University Press.

Korea Statistical Yearbook. 1981, 1990. Seoul: Republic of Korea, Economic Planning Board, Bureau of Statistics.

Korean Women's Development Institute [Han'guk Yŏsŏng Kyebalwŏn]. 1985. *Yŏsŏng paeksŏ* [White paper on women]. Seoul: Han'guk Yŏsŏng Kyebalwŏn.

Kung, Lydia. 1983. *Factory Women in Taiwan.* Ann Arbor, Michigan: UMI Research Press.

Kwon Tai Hwan. 1977. *Demography of Korea: Population Change and Its Components 1925–1966.* Seoul: Seoul National University Press.

Laderman, Carol. 1991. *Taming the Wind of Desire: Psychology, Medicine, and Aesthetics in Malay Shamanistic Performance.* Berkeley: University of California Press.

Landis, E. B. 1898. The Capping Ceremony of Korea. *Journal of the Anthropological Institute of Great Britain and Ireland* 27:525–531.

Lasch, Christopher. 1984. The Politics of Nostalgia: Losing History in the Mists of Ideology. *Harper's* (December):65–70.

Lay, Arthur H. 1913. Marriage Customs of Korea. *Transactions of the Korea Branch of the Royal Asiatic Society* 3(4):1–15.

Lebra, Takie Sugiyama. 1984. *Japanese Women: Constraint and Fulfillment.* Honolulu: University of Hawaii Press.

Lee Du-hyun (Yi Tuhyŏn). 1969. *Han'guk kamyŏn'guk* [Korean mask-dance drama]. Seoul: Ministry of Culture and Information, Bureau of Cultural Properties Preservation.

Lee Hyo-jae (Lee Hyo-chae, Yi Hyojae). 1971. Life in Urban Korea. Special issue of *Transactions of the Korea Branch of the Royal Asiatic Society* 46.

———. 1977. Protestant Missionary Work and Enlightenment of Korean Women. *Korea Journal* 17(11):33–50.

————. 1983 [1976]. *Kajŏkkwa sahoe* [Family and society], rev. ed. Seoul: Kyŏng-munsa.

————. 1986. Yŏsŏnggwa yŏksa [Women and history]. In *Hyŏndae Han'guk yŏ-sŏng'non* [Essays on modern Korean women], Yi T'aeyŏng et al., 258–268. Seoul: Samminsillon.

————, et al. 1991. *Chabonjuŭi sijanggyŏngjewa honin* [The capitalist market economy and marriage]. Seoul: Tosŏch'ulp'an, Tto hanaŭi munhwa.

Lee Kwang-Kyu (Yi Kwanggyu). 1974. Kwanhonsangje [Weddings, funerals, and ancestor worship]. In *Han'guk minsokhak kaesŏl* [Introduction to Korean ethnology], ed. T. Yi., K. Yi, and C. Chang, 59–87. Seoul: Minjung Sŏgwan.

————. 1975. *Han'guk kajogŭi kujo punsŏk* [Analysis of Korean family structure]. Seoul: Ilchisa.

————. 1977. *Han'guk kajogŭi sajŏk yŏn'gu* [Historical study of the Korean family]. Seoul: Ilchisa.

————. 1983. Kwanhonsangje [Weddings, funerals, and ancestor worship]. In *Seoul yukpaeg'nyŏnsa* [A 600 year history of Seoul] 5:1272–1283.

————. 1984. Koch'u, mokhwassi, sot'ŭl nohnŭnge kongt'ongjŏk [Usual to include peppers, cotton seed, and charcoal]. *Yŏng Reidi* [Young lady] 10:154–155.

Lee Man-gap (Yi Man'gap). 1960. *Han'guk nongch'onŭi sahoe kujo* [The social structure of Korean villages]. Seoul: Han'guk Yŏn'gu Tosŏgwan.

Lee, Peter, ed. 1981. *Anthology of Korean Literature from Early Times to the Nineteenth Century*. Honolulu: University of Hawaii Press.

Lee Tai-Young (Yi T'aeyŏng). 1981. *What Can I Do?* Seoul: Korea Legal Aid Center for Family Relations.

Linke, Uli. 1990. Folklore, Anthropology, and the Government of Social Life. *Comparative Studies of Society and History* 32(1):117–148.

Lodge, David. 1984. *Small World: An Academic Romance*. New York: Warner Books.

Luong, Hy V. 1992. *Revolution in the Village: Tradition and Transformation in North Vietnam, 1925–1988*. Honolulu: University of Hawaii Press.

Lystra, Karen. 1989. *Searching the Heart: Women, Men, and Romantic Love in Nineteenth-Century America*. New York: Oxford University Press.

Mace, David, and Vera Mace. 1959. *Marriage: East and West*. Garden City, New York: Dolphin Books.

Malarney, Shawn Kingsley. 1993. Ritual and Revolution in Viet Nam. Ph.D. dissertation, University of Michigan.

Mani, Lata. 1987. Contentious Traditions: The Debate on SATI in Colonial India. *Cultural Critique* 11(Fall):119–156.

Marcus, George E., and Dick Cushman. 1982. Ethnographies as Texts. *Annual Review of Anthropology* 11:25–69.

Marcus, George E., and Michael M. J. Fischer. 1986. *Anthropology as Cultural Critique: An Experimental Moment in the Human Sciences*. Chicago: University of Chicago Press.

Materi, Irma Tennani. 1949. *Irma and the Hermit: My Life in Korea*. New York: W.W. Norton.

Mauss, Marcel. 1967 [1925]. *The Gift*. New York: W.W. Norton.

McCullough, William H. 1967. Japanese Marriage Institutions in the Late Heian Period. *Harvard Journal of Asiatic Studies* 27:102–167.

McKnight, David. 1990. The Australian Aborigines in Anthropology. In *Localizing Strategies: Regional Traditions of Ethnographic Writing*, ed. R. Fardon, 42–70. Edinburgh and Washington, D.C.: Scottish Academic Press and Smithsonian Institution Press.

Miln, Louise. 1895. *Quaint Korea*. New York: Scribner.

Ministry of Culture and Information, Bureau of Cultural Properties Preservation (MCIBCPP). 1969–1978. *Han'guk minsin chonghap chosa pogosŏ* [Report of the comprehensive investigation of Korean folk beliefs], cum. vols. Seoul: Munhwaje Kwalliguk, Munhwa Kongbobu.

Mohanty, Chandra. 1988. Under Western Eyes: Feminist Scholarship and Colonial Discourses. *Feminist Review* 30:61–88.

Moon Okpyo. 1990. Urban Middle Class Wives in Contemporary Korea: Their Roles, Responsibilities and Dilemma. *Korea Journal* 30(11):30–43.

Moon Uhn Cho (Cho Uhn). 1982. Married Women and Urban Employment in Korea: Class Differentiation in Income-Opportunities. Ph.D. dissertation, University of Hawaii.

Moore, Sally Falk. 1987. Explaining the Present: Theoretical Dilemmas in Processual Ethnography. *American Ethnologist* 14:727–736.

Moose, Robert J. 1911. *Village Life in Korea*. Nashville: Methodist Church.

Moskowitz, Karl. 1982. Korean Development and Korean Studies—A Review Article. *Journal of Asian Studies* 42(1):63–90.

Myrdal, Jan. 1965. *Report from a Chinese Village*. New York: New American Library.

———, and Gun Kessle. 1970. *China: The Revolution Continued*. New York: Pantheon.

Naemubu (Ministry of the Interior). 1986. *Uriŭi chŏnt'ong hollye* [Our traditional wedding rite]. Seoul: Saemaŭl Kihoekkwan [New Village Planning Commission].

Naquin, Susan. 1988. Funerals in North China: Uniformity and Variation. In *Death Ritual in Late Imperial and Modern China*, ed. James L. Watson and Evelyn Rawski, 37–70. Berkeley: University of California Press.

Narayan, Kirin. 1993. How Native Is a "Native" Anthropologist? *American Anthropologist* 95(3):671–686.

Ŏ Yŏng-jin. 1983. *Wedding Day*, trans. Song Yolu. Seoul: Si-sa-yong-o-sa for Korean National Commission for UNESCO.

Ong, Aihwa. 1987. *Spirits of Resistance and Capitalist Discipline: Factory Women in Malaysia*. Albany: State University of New York Press.

———. 1988. Colonialism and Modernity: Feminist Re-presentations of Women in Non-Western Societies. *Inscriptions* 3(4):79–93.

———. 1990. State Versus Islam: Malay Families, Women's Bodies, and the Body Politic in Malaysia. *American Ethnologist* 17(2):258–276.

Ortner, Sherry B. 1984. Theory in Anthropology Since the Sixties. *Comparative Studies in Society and History* 26:126–166.

Osgood, Cornelius. 1951. *The Koreans and Their Culture*. New York: Ronald Press.

Pae Pyŏnghyu. 1984. Chaebŏlgaŭi hugyeja, sawi myŏnŭri [Monopolist families' heirs, son-in-law, daughter-in-law]. *Yŏng Reidi* [Young lady] 8(August):124–129.

Pahk Induk. 1954. *September Monkey*. New York: Harper and Brothers.

Pak Hyein. 1991. Han'guk chŏnt'onghollyeŭi yŏnsokkwa tanjŏl [Korea's traditional wedding ceremonies' continuities and ruptures]. In *Chabonjuŭi sijanggyŏngjewa honin* [The capitalist market economy and marriage], ed. Yi Hyojae et al., 17–73. Seoul: Tosŏch'ulp'an, Tto hanaŭi munhwa.

Pak Hyeran. 1991. Nangmanjŏk sarangesŏ "aein namp'yŏn" ŭro [From romantic love to "husband lover"]. *Tto hanaŭi munhwa* [Alternative culture] 7:163–176.

Pak Ki-hyuk, and Sidney D. Gamble. 1975. *The Changing Korean Village*. Seoul: Shin-hung.

Pak Minja. 1991. Tosi chunggan'gyech'ungŭi honingŏraegwanhaenge kwanhanyŏngu [A study on the customary marriage transactions of the urban middle class]. In *Chabonjuŭi sijanggyŏngjewa honin* [The capitalist market economy and marriage], ed. Yi Hyojae et al., 147–175. Seoul: Tosŏch'ulp'an, Tto hanaŭi munhwa.

Pak Sukcha. 1991. Tosi chŏsutŭkch'ungŭi honinyangt'ae [The marriage mode of the urban poor]. In *Chabonjuŭi sijanggyŏngjewa honin* [The capitalist market economy and marriage], ed. Yi Hyojae et al., 75–116. Seoul: Tosŏch'ulp'an, Tto hanaŭi munhwa.

Pak Wansŏ. 1985 [1977]. *Hwich'ŏnggŏrinŭn ohu* [Staggering afternoon], 2 vols. Seoul: Ch'angjak kwa Pip'yŏng Sa.

Palais, James B. 1975. *Politics and Policy in Traditional Korea*. Harvard East Asian Series no. 82. Cambridge, Massachusetts: Harvard University Press.

Papanek, Hanna. 1979. Family Status Production: The "Work" and "Non-Work" of Women. *Signs* 4(4):775–781.

Park, Chai Bin. 1962. A Review of Korean Population Statistics. *Monthly Statistics of Korea* 1(2):26–45.

Peacock, James L. 1968. *Rites of Modernization: Symbolic and Social Aspects of Indonesian Proletarian Drama*. Chicago: University of Chicago Press.

Peterson, Mark. 1983. Women Without Sons: A Measure of Social Change in Yi Dynasty Korea. In *Korean Women: View from the Inner Room*, ed. L. Kendall and M. Peterson, 33–44. New Haven, Connecticut: East Rock Press.

Pogŏnsahoebu (Bureau of Social Welfare). n.d. *Kŏnjŏnhan kajŏngŭirye* [Wholesome family rituals]. Seoul: Pogŏnsahoebu.

Potter, Sulamith Heins, and Jack M. Potter. 1990. *China's Peasants: The Anthropology of a Revolution*. Cambridge, England: Cambridge University Press.

Pratt, Mary Louise. 1986. Fieldwork in Common Places. In *Writing Culture*, ed. J. Clifford and G. Marcus, 27–50. Berkeley: University of California Press.

Rawski, Evelyn S. 1988. A Historian's Approach to Death Ritual. In *Death Ritual in Late Imperial and Modern China*, ed. James L. Watson and Evelyn Rawski, 20–34. Berkeley: University of California Press.

Republic of Korea, Economic Planning Board, National Bureau of Statistics (ROK, EPB, NBS). 1982 (December). *1980 Population and Housing Census Report*, vol. 1, complete enumeration; 12–13, whole country. Seoul: Economic Planning Board, National Bureau of Statistics.

Research Center for Asian Women, Sookmyung Women's University (RCAW-SWU). 1986. *Women of the Yi Dynasty*. Studies on Korean Women, series 1. Seoul: Sookmyung Women's University.

Robinson, Michael E. 1988. *Cultural Nationalism in Colonial Korea, 1920–25*. Seattle: University of Washington Press.

————. 1991. Perceptions of Confucianism in Twentieth-Century Korea. In *The East Asian Region: Confucian Heritage and Its Modern Adaptation*, ed. G. Rozman, 204–225. Princeton, New Jersey: Princeton University Press.

Rofel, Lisa. 1992. Rethinking Modernity: Space and Factory Discipline in China. *Cultural Anthropology* 7(1):93–114.

Rosaldo, Renato. 1989. *Culture and Truth: The Remaking of Social Analysis*. Boston: Beacon Press.

Ross, John. 1891. *History of Corea: Ancient and Modern*. London: Elliot Stock.

Roy, Manisha. 1972. *Bengali Women*. Chicago: University of Chicago Press.

Rutt, Richard. 1964. *Korean Works and Days: Notes from the Diary of a Country Priest*. Seoul: Royal Asiatic Society.

————, and Kim Chong-Un, trans. 1974. *Virtuous Women: Three Classic Korean Novels*. Seoul: Royal Asiatic Society, Korea Branch, for UNESCO.

Salaff, Janet W. 1981. *Working Daughters of Hong Kong: Filial Piety or Power in the Family?* Cambridge, England: Cambridge University Press.

Sanjek, Roger. 1990. On Ethnographic Validity. In *Fieldnotes: The Makings of Anthropology*, ed. R. Sanjek, 385–418. Ithaca, New York: Cornell University Press.

————. 1991. The Ethnographic Present. *Man* (n.s.) 26:609–628.

Sant Cassia, Paul. 1992. *The Making of the Modern Greek Family: Marriage and Exchange in Nineteenth-Century Athens*. Cambridge, England: Cambridge University Press.

Saunderson, H. S. 1894. Notes on Corea and Its People. *Journal of the Anthropological Society of Great Britain and Ireland* 24:299–316.

Savage-Landor, Henry. 1895. *Korea or Cho-sen: The Land of the Morning Calm*. London: William Heineman.

Schein, Louisa. 1993. Popular Culture and the Production of Difference: The Miao and China. Ph.D. dissertation, University of California, Berkeley.

Scheper-Hughes, Nancy, and Margaret Lock. 1987. The Mindful Body: A Prolegomenon to Future Work in Medical Anthropology. *Medical Anthropology Quarterly* 1(1):6–41.

Schieffelin, Edward L. 1976. *The Sorrow of the Lonely and the Burning of the Dancers*. New York: St. Martin's Press.

Schlegel, Alice, and Rohn Eloul. 1988. Marriage Transactions: Labor, Property, Status. *American Anthropologist* 90:291–309.

Schneider, Jane. 1980. Trousseau as Treasure: Some Contradictions of Late Nineteenth Century Change in Sicily. In *Beyond the Myths of Culture*, ed. C. Ross, 323–356. New York: Academic Press.

————, and Annette B. Weiner. 1989. Introduction. In *Cloth and the Human*

Experience, ed. Annette B. Weiner and Jane Schneider, 1–29. Washington, D.C.: Smithsonian Institution Press.

Scott, Joan W., and Louise A. Tilly. 1975. Women's Work and the Family in Nineteenth-Century Europe. *Comparative Studies in Society and History* 17:36–64.

Scranton, Mrs. M. F. 1898. Grace's Wedding. *Korean Repository* 5:295–297.

Shils, Edward. 1981. *Tradition.* Chicago: University of Chicago Press.

Sievers, Sharon. 1981. Feminist Criticism in Japanese Politics in the 1880's. *Signs* 6(4):602–616.

Sorensen, Clark Wesley. 1981. Household, Family, and Economy in a Korean Mountain Village. Ph.D. dissertation, University of Washington.

———. 1984. Farm Labor and Family Cycle in Traditional Korea and Japan. *Journal of Anthropological Research* 40(2):306–323.

———. 1986a. Migration, the Family, and the Care of the Aged in Rural Korea: An Investigation of a Village in the Yŏngsŏ Region of Kangwŏn Province 1918–1983. *Journal of Cross-cultural Gerontology* 1:139–161.

———. 1986b. Concubines, Wives, and the Struggle for Succession in Rural Korea. Paper presented at the 85th annual meeting of the American Anthropological Association, Philadelphia, December 5.

———. 1988. *Over the Mountains Are Mountains: Korean Peasant Households and Their Adaptations to Rapid Industrialization.* Seattle: University of Washington Press.

Spencer, Robert F. 1988. *Yŏgong: Factory Girl.* Seoul: Royal Asiatic Society, Korea Branch.

Spivak, Gayatri Chakravorty. 1988. Can the Subaltern Speak? In *Marxism and the Interpretation of Culture,* ed. C. Nelson and N. Grossberg, 271–313. Urbana: University of Illinois Press.

Stockard, Janice E. 1989. *Daughters of the Canton Delta: Marriage Patterns and Economic Strategies in South China.* Stanford, California: Stanford University Press.

Stone, Lawrence. 1979. *The Family, Sex and Marriage in England 1500–1800.* New York: Harper and Row.

Sun Soon-Hwa. 1991. Women, Religion, and Power: A Comparative Study of Korean Shamans and Women Ministers. Ph.D. dissertation, Drew University, Madison, New Jersey.

Tambiah, S. J. 1973. Dowry and Bridewealth, the Property Rights of Women in South Asia. In *Bridewealth and Dowry,* ed. J. Goody and S. J. Tambiah, 59–160. Cambridge, England: Cambridge University Press.

———. 1977. The Cosmological and Performative Significance of a Thai Cult of Healing and Meditation. *Culture, Medicine, and Psychiatry* 1:97–132.

———. 1979. A Performative Approach to Ritual. Radcliffe-Brown Lecture in Social Anthropology. *Proceedings of the British Academy* 65:113–169.

Thane, Pat, Geoffrey Crossick, and Roderick Floud, eds. 1984. *The Power of the Past: Essays for Eric Hobsbawm.* Cambridge, England: Cambridge University Press.

Thomas, James Philip. 1993. Contested from Within and Without: Squatters, the

State, the *Minjung* Movement, and the Limits of Resistance in a Seoul Shanty Town. Ph.D. dissertation, University of Rochester.

Tieszen, Helen Rose. 1977. Korean Proverbs About Women. In *Virtues in Conflict: Tradition and the Korean Woman Today*, ed. Sandra Mattielli, 49–66. Seoul: Royal Asiatic Society.

Tipps, Dean C. 1973. Modernization Theory and the Comparative Study of Societies: A Critical Perspective. *Comparative Studies in Society and History* 15:199–226.

Trawick, Margaret. 1990. *Notes on Love in a Tamil Family*. Berkeley: University of California Press.

Trinh T. Minh-ha. 1989. *Woman, Native, Other*. Bloomington: Indiana University Press.

Turner, Bryan S. 1984. *The Body and Society: Explorations in Social Theory*. New York: Basil Blackwell.

Turner, Victor. 1967. *The Forest of Symbols: Aspects of Ndembu Ritual*. Ithaca, New York: Cornell University Press.

———. 1968. *The Drums of Affliction: A Study of Religious Processes Among the Ndembu of Zambia*. Ithaca, New York: Cornell University Press.

van Gennep, Arnold. 1960 [1908]. *The Rites of Passage*. Chicago: University of Chicago Press.

Visweswaran, Kamala. 1988. Defining Feminist Ethnography. *Inscriptions* 3(4):24–44.

Vitebsky, Piers. 1993. *Dialogues with the Dead: The Discussion of Mortality Among the Sora of Eastern India*. Cambridge, England: Cambridge University Press.

Wagner, Edward W. 1972. The Korean Chokpo as a Historical Source. In *Studies in Asian Genealogy*, ed. Spencer J. Palmer. Provo, Utah: Brigham Young University Press.

———. 1974. The Ladder of Success in Yi Dynasty Korea. In *Occasional Papers on Korea*, no. 1, rev. ed., series ed. James B. Palais. New York: Joint Committee on Korean Studies of the American Council of Learned Societies and the Social Science Research Council.

———. 1983. Two Early Genealogies and Women's Status in Early Yi Dynasty Korea. In *Korean Women: View from the Inner Room*, ed. L. Kendall and M. Peterson, 23–32. New Haven, Connecticut: East Rock Press.

Watson, James L. 1988a. The Structure of Chinese Funerary Rites: Elementary Forms, Ritual Sequence, and the Primacy of Performance. In *Death Ritual in Late Imperial and Modern China*, ed. James L. Watson and Evelyn Rawski, 3–19. Berkeley: University of California Press.

———. 1988b. Funeral Specialists in Cantonese Society: Pollution, Performance, and Social Hierarchy. In *Death Ritual in Late Imperial and Modern China*, ed. James L. Watson and Evelyn Rawski, 109–134. Berkeley: University of California Press.

Watson, Rubie S. 1984. Women's Property in Republican China: Rights and Practice. *Republican China* 10(1a):1–12.

———. 1991a. Wives, Concubines, and Maids: Servitude and Kinship in the Hong Kong Region, 1900–1940. In *Marriage and Inequality in Chinese Society*, ed.

Rubie S. Watson and Patricia Buckley Ebrey, 231–255. Berkeley: University of California Press.

———. 1991b. Afterword: Marriage and Gender Inequality. In *Marriage and Inequality in Chinese Society,* ed. Rubie S. Watson and Patricia Buckley Ebrey, 347–368. Berkeley: University of California Press.

———, and Patricia Buckley Ebrey, eds. 1991. *Marriage and Inequality in Chinese Society.* Berkeley: University of California Press.

Werblowsky, R. J. Zwi. 1976. *Beyond Tradition and Modernity: Changing Religions in a Changing World.* London: Athlone Press.

Wharton, Edith. 1987 [1920]. *The Age of Innocence.* New York: Macmillan.

White, Theodore H., and Annalee Jacoby. 1946. *Thunder Out of China.* New York: Wm. Sloane Assoc.

Williams, Homer Farrand. 1982. Rationalization and Impoverishment: Trends Affecting the Korean Peasant Under Japanese Colonial Rule, 1918–1942. M.A. thesis, University of Hawaii.

Williams, Raymond. 1973. *The Country and the City.* New York: Oxford University Press.

———. 1977. *Marxism and Literature.* Oxford, England: Oxford University Press.

Wilson, Brian. 1983. The Korean Shaman: Image and Reality. In *Korean Women: View from the Inner Room,* ed. L. Kendall and M. Peterson, 113–128. New Haven, Connecticut: East Rock Press.

Winn, R. A. 1921. The New Wife, a New Woman. *Korea Mission Field* 17(January):21.

Wolf, Diane L. 1990. Daughters, Decisions and Domination: An Empirical and Conceptual Critique of Household Strategies. *Development and Change* 21:43–74.

———. 1992. *Factory Daughters: Gender, Household Dynamics, and Rural Industrialization in Java.* Berkeley: University of California Press.

Wolf, Margery. 1975. Women and Suicide in China. In *Women in Chinese Society,* ed. M. Wolf and R. Witke, 111–141. Stanford, California: Stanford University Press.

———. 1985. *Revolution Postponed: Women in Contemporary China.* Stanford, California: Stanford University Press.

———. 1992. *A Thrice-told Tale: Feminism, Postmodernism, and Ethnographic Responsibility.* Stanford, California: Stanford University Press.

Yanagisako, Sylvia Junko. 1985. *Transforming the Past: Tradition and Kinship Among Japanese Americans.* Stanford, California: Stanford University Press.

Yanagita, Kunio. 1970 [1945]. *About Our Ancestors.* Tokyo: Ministry of Education.

Yi Eunhee Kim. 1993. From Gentry to the Middle Class: The Transformation of Family, Community, and Gender in Korea. Ph.D. dissertation, University of Chicago.

Yi Kyŏngnam. 1983. Han'gugŭi honbŏl [Korea's marriage cliques]. *Chubu saenghwal* [Housewives' lives] 4(April):251–267.

Yi Kyut'ae. 1987. *Nunmulŭi Han'gukhak* [Tearful Korean studies], vol. 1. Seoul: Kirinwŏn.

Yi Ujŏng. 1986. Yŏsŏng nodongjadŭlgwa minjuhwaundong [Women workers and the Democracy Movement]. In *Hyŏndae Han'guk yŏsŏngnon* [Essays on modern Korean women], Yi Taeyŏng et al., 90–112. Seoul: Samminsa.

Yim Dawnhee (Im Tonhŭi, Dawnhee Yim Janelli). 1986. Potlatchwa Han'gug'-nongch'on maŭlesŏŭi kajŏngŭirye [The potlatch and family rituals in Korean rural villages]. *Han'guk minsokhak* [Korean folklore] (9):273–294.

Yoon Hyungsook (Yun Hyŏngsuk). 1989a. Kinship, Gender, and Personhood in a Korean Village. Ph.D. dissertation, University of Michigan.

―――. 1989b. Rethinking Traditional Marriage in Korea. *Korea Journal* 29(12):17–27.

―――. 1991. Sŏulgŭn'gyonongch'onŭi kyŏngjewa kyŏrhon [The economics and matrimony of a village on the periphery of Seoul]. In *Chabonjuŭi sijanggyŏngjewa honin* [The capitalist market economy and marriage], ed. Yi Hyojae et al., 117–145. Seoul: Tosŏch'ulp'an, Tto hanaŭi munhwa.

Index

Abelmann, Nancy, 14n
Abu-Lughod, Lila, 19n, 20, 21, 23
Adulthood initiation, 7, 8–9, 50n
Agricultural Cooperatives, Federation of, 5
Alternative Culture Group (*Ttohanaŭi Munhwa*), 116, 117, 219
American Museum of Natural History, 71
American Other. *See* United States
Anagnost, Ann, 70–71n, 82n
Ancestor veneration (*che*), 50n, 59, 68–69
An Chŏngnam, 9n, 169–170
Andong region, 99
Andrews, Roy Chapman, 7, 103n
Announcer (*sahoe*): of new-style wedding steps, 31, 32–33, 34, 35, 37, 41
Anthropology: current sites for, 13; by foreign ethnographer, 22–23; intimate perspective of, 20; of non-Western other, 10–11; as reflexive, 18; rural focus of, 11–12; and trope of alienation, 21; of women by women, 23–24
Appadurai, Arjun, 182–183
Arranged meetings (*massŏn*): bride's role in, 103–104, 105, 106, 109, 139; commercial aspect of, 107–108; countryside's acceptance of, 106–107; etiquette for, 105, 112–114; prevalence of, 87–88; as reciprocal evaluation, 109; as traditional-progressive compromise,

89–90, 100–102, 226; women's magazines on, 88, 89–90, 104–105, 107–108, 112–114. *See also* Matchmakers
Attire. *See* Dress
Austin, J. I., 35

Bachelors. *See* Rural bachelors
Bae, Mrs. (pseud.). *See* Female wedding attendant
Bailey, Beth, 88, 117
Baker, Donald, 78
Banishment: love marriages and, 96–97, 106n
Bargaining: over bride's bouquet, 31, 42–43, 201–202; over gift box delivery, 31, 197–199, 206, 212, 214; ritual significance of, 206–209, 212
Barth, Frederick, 18
Bauman, Richard, 12n
Bergman, Sten, 211n
Betrothal gifts. *See* Gift box
Birthday celebrations, 50n, 68–69
Bishop, Isabella Bird, 12n
Boddy, Janice, 19n
Book of Rites, 60n
Bouquet. *See* Wedding bouquet
Bourdieu, Pierre, 19–20, 182, 188
Bows: asymmetrical, 34, 44; contestation over, 80; money for, 48, 49; reciprocal, 45–46, 66
Box of gifts (*ham*). *See* Gift box
Brandt, Anthony, 72
Brandt, Vincent, 96–97

Compositor:	Maple-Vail Manufacturing Group
Text:	10/13 Aldus
Display:	Aldus
Printer:	Maple-Vail Manufacturing Group
Binder:	Maple-Vail Manufacturing Group